Since

collab

The

Chris

lectur

to 'st

the c

Also by Lynn Picknett and Clive Prince

THE TEMPLAR REVELATION

THE STARGATE CONSPIRACY

THE SION REVELATION

By Lynn Picknett, Clive Prince and Stephen Prior
(with Robert Brydon)

DOUBLE STANDARDS:
THE RUDOLF HESS COVER-UP

WAR OF THE WINDSORS

FRIENDLY FIRE: THE SECRET WAR
BETWEEN THE ALLIES

By Lynn Picknett

MARY MAGDALENE: CHRISTIANITY'S
HIDDEN GODDESS

THE SECRET HISTORY OF LUCIFER

TURIN SHROUD

HOW LEONARDO DA VINCI
FOOLED HISTORY

LYNN PICKNETT and CLIVE PRINCE

TIME WARNER
BOOKS

TIME WARNER BOOKS

First published in Great Britain as a hardback
in 1994 by Bloomsbury Publishing Ltd
under the title *Turin Shroud: In Whose Image?*
Paperbacked in 2000 by Corgi
This revised edition published in April 2006
by Time Warner Books

A CIP catalogue record for this book is
available from the British Library.

ISBN 0 7515 3862 0

Typeset in Bembo by M Rules
Printed and bound in Great Britain by
Clays Ltd, St Ives plc

Time Warner Books
An imprint of
Time Warner Book Group UK
Brettenham House
Lancaster Place
London WC2E 7EN

www.twbg.co.uk

'Miserable mortals, open your eyes'

Leonardo da Vinci (1452–1519)

To Keith
who helped Leonardo make history

Contents

Illustrations

Acknowledgements

Over the past fifteen years, a great many people have contributed to this story by sharing research and information, giving us support and encouragement or helping to promote our work. We are immensely grateful to the following:

Keith Prince, for all his hard work, inspiration and commitment, especially his genius with camera obscuras. We literally couldn't have done it without him.

Craig Oakley, for his unswerving loyalty, highly honed sense of the absurd, and frequently unorthodox ideas.

'Giovanni' (whoever he really is), whose extraordinary information set us off on an astonishing journey of discovery.

Our friend and colleague, the much-missed Stephen Prior, who was always so supportive.

Lavinia Trevor, our agent, for succeeding in securing a third life for this book. And her colleague Elizabeth Cochrane.

Joanne Dickinson at Time Warner for seizing the opportunity to relaunch this book, and Sheena-Margot Lavelle, Viv Redman and Linda Silverman for all their hard work.

Andy Haveland-Robinson, for his long and arduous hours in front of a computer for *Turin Shroud*, particularly for the computer analysis of the 'severed head' anomaly.

Abigail Nevill, whose comment on Shroudman — 'Why is his head too small, and why is it on wrong?' — was such a blinding revelation and changed so much. Out of the mouths of babes . . .

Amanda Nevill, former Chief Executive of the National

Museum of Photography, Film and Television, Bradford, for her spirited support and advice from the very earliest days, and for her original intuition that led to the exhibition of the Shroud replica, both at the Royal Photographic Society, Bath, and later in Bradford. (And for being Abigail's mum.)

Janis Britland and her team at the National Museum of Photography, Film and Television, for featuring our work so prominently in a major exhibition, and for finally exhibiting the replica of the Shroud in its rightful home.

Ysenda Maxtone Graham for the London *Evening Standard* article that first got us noticed, and which led directly to the birth of this book. Thanks, too, to A. N. Wilson for his part in making this happen.

Michael Austin, Past President of the Royal Photographic Society, for his generous advice and encouragement.

Ian Dickinson, who – although disagreeing with our hypothesis – has always been happy to share information and support us against smear campaigns, prejudice and corruption, even though he also became a target.

Professor Nicholas Allen, for the long discussion about his major achievement in replicating the Shroud image and for being so open and cordial about the areas of research we share.

Caroline Rye, whose entrancing exhibition *Turin Machine* gave us a completely new insight into the artistry behind the Shroud, and also Jennifer and Christopher Rye for a wonderful night out in Bristol.

Bill Homer, H. Rodney Sharp, Professor of Art History, University of Delaware, and his wife Christine, for their advice on Leonardo the artist, and their encouragement.

Lillian Schwartz of Bell Laboratories and her husband Jack, for sharing their work with us on Leonardo as the *Mona Lisa*, and for a pleasant evening at Chelsea Harbour.

The team on David Paradine Productions' BBC *Everyman* programme: Trevor Poots; Nikki Stockley; Jo Kessel; Amanda George;

Giulia Maura; Tony Bragg; Patrick Quirke – and Leonardo the Sparks. And of course, Sir David Frost for making the idea a reality.

Susan Gray and Dolores Cassano at Stefilm for the National Geographic *Leonardo – The Man Behind the Shroud* documentary.

Clive Bull, Michael van Straten, Karen Krizanovich, Sean Bulger and Russell Grant for all the air time they have given us, and for making our radio appearances such fun. And John Sugar at BBC World Service for the invitation that may have really started something (albeit unintentionally)!

Vida Adamoli, for energetically translating a key Italian article – and incidentally entertaining Gascogne's other diners hugely.

Mary Aver, who saw it coming.

Jane Lyle, for providing facilities for our experiments and being such fun.

We would like to thank the following for providing us with the opportunity to address their gatherings:

The late Robert Cowley, and Veronica Cowley at RILKO; the late Ralph Noyes at the Society for Physical Research; Professor Archie Roy at the Scottish SPR; Andrew Collins at the Questing Conference; Lionel Beer at TEMS; Steve Wilson at Talking Stick; Commander Bill Bellars at the Ghost Club; Rob Stephenson at London Earth Mysteries Circle, and all the organisers of the *Fortean Times* UnConvention.

We would also like to thank the following people for their help, support and encouragement in a great many different ways:

David Bell; Mark Bennett; Debbie Benstead and Yvan Cartwright; Ashley Brown; Robert Brydon; Jim Burge; the late Manfred Cassirer; Alison Cochran; Jim Cochrane; Ian Dougan; Charles and Annette Fowkes; Kate Glass; Tim Haigh; Moira Hardcastle; Barry Johnstone; Michèle Kaczynski; Sarah Litvinoff; Robert Lomas; Loren McLaughlin; Gareth Medway; Sally 'Morgana' Morgan; Helen Moss; Mark Naples; Joe Nickell; Steve and Jacqueline Pear; Graham Phillips; Nick Pope; Lily and David Prince; Sue Prince; Francesca Prior; Tony Pritchett;

Dr Carl Sargent; Mary Saxe-Falstein; the late Frank Smyth; Sheila and Eric Taylor; Penny Thornton; Peter Tilbury; Mike Wallington; the late Alan Wills; and Caroline Wise.

The staff at the Westminster Reference Library and the British Library Reading Rooms for their tireless help in chasing the elusive and the esoteric.

And finally . . .

We owe an incalculable debt to Leonardo da Vinci, the fruits of whose dark humour and tormented genius can still provide the twenty-first century with a few surprises – not to mention several shocks.

Introduction

Irony and Inspiration

The exquisite, perfect irony would have appealed to Leonardo da Vinci. It certainly appealed to us . . . When the Catholic nun Sister Mary Michael demonstrated against the filming of *The Da Vinci Code* – based on Dan Brown's phenomenal bestseller – at Lincoln Cathedral in August 2005, declaring during her twelve-hour prayer vigil that it was 'against the essence of what we [Christians] believe'[1], she was clutching a photograph of the face of the man on the Shroud of Turin. The irony is that if we are right, and of course we believe we are, then the image she held so fervently to her bosom was not that of her beloved Jesus Christ at all, but actually the image of the old trouble-maker himself – Leonardo da Vinci. Sister Mary Michael's holy talisman is – as we hope to demonstrate in this book – nothing less than the image of the ultimate freethinkers' hero, and now the inspiration for the most-read book of the early twenty-first century, the very one that Sister Mary Michael was demonstrating against. (In fact, new and exciting evidence that Leonardo *is* the man on the Shroud is presented for the first time in this revised and updated edition.) Even in the twenty-first century, da Vinci clearly has a lot to teach us.

There is another, similar irony in the presentation of full-sized reproductions of the front and back images of the Shroud in a side chapel of the important church of Saint-Sulpice in Paris, facing the Chapel of Angels with its enigmatic paintings by Eugène Delacroix (which also, it has been suggested, contain coded messages). Not only is the church a major location in *The Da Vinci Code*, but of course the Shroud is, we claim, a major hoax by da Vinci, one with its very own code for courageous seekers to unlock.

The controversy surrounding both Dan Brown's original book and the movie has ensured that the side of da Vinci that is conspicuous by its absence from school textbooks and worthy art-history tomes is now receiving unprecedented attention. Da Vinci (or 'Leonardo' as he should be known) the heretic, the game-player and gleeful, irrepressible encoder now emerges into the limelight half a millennium after his death, entrancing count-less millions with what may be termed his 'sleight of mind' – just as he delighted and bewildered his peers with demonstrations of his conjuror's abilities of sleight of hand. His whole mindset was geared to causing misdirection – and even perhaps a form of psy-chological mayhem.

Since the first edition of *Turin Shroud* came out in 1994, it is no exaggeration to say that our lives have changed immeasurably – mostly very much for the better – because of this book and the strangely fascinating world into which it led us. Not only did we become a proven writing team, but we travelled extensively, sometimes with film crews and sometimes with new friends. But although we have since written several other books on widely differing mysteries – including three with our late friend Stephen Prior, and Robert Brydon – we are particularly pleased to have had the opportunity to update this, our first joint book, and to present a wealth of new material that will hopefully fill in any gaps and inspire new debate.

Since 1994, our two paperback editions have given us the chance to catch up with new developments in Shroud research – fresh claims, intriguing ideas and, of course, all the many reactions to our hypothesis. And since the first edition, after a gap of twenty years the Shroud itself has been displayed not once but twice – although this nearly did not happen, as a dramatic fire a few months before the first of the recent expositions, in 1998, threatened to destroy the relic completely. To many, the very presence of the sacred cloth was intensely reassuring, not only after the fire, but also after the carbon dating results of 13 October 1988 that revealed it to be a fake. Somehow, to the pilgrims, seeing its familiar haunting outline on the cloth was still almost like touching God himself, a tangible, physical manifestation of their faith. Seeing it seemed to give a lie to the bleak pronouncement of science, and hope lived again.

However, blind faith alone cannot wipe out the shock of the carbon dating results. They happened – and we of all people have cause to remember them with something approaching gratitude, for although we had both been greatly intrigued by the Turin Shroud for some time, they finally galvanised us into active research on the topic. But we did not join the many scientists and professional 'Skeptics' who were queuing up to sneer at the imaged cloth, now derided openly as a fake, with more than a little of 'we told you so'. To us, now that this strange and astonishing image had been shown to be man-made, it was if anything *more*, rather than less, fascinating. If, as we soon came to see for ourselves, it was indeed man-made, then who was the genius who had created it? And how on earth had he achieved the near impossible, somehow making an image that continued to baffle the best minds of the late twentieth and early twenty-first centuries?

Strange as it may seem, it did not prove too difficult to answer both those questions (although we did receive some help along the way). Pointed in the direction of none other than Leonardo da Vinci by a man who claimed to belong to the same secret organisation as that Maestro, at first we were sceptical. But after a great deal of intensive research – not to mention many frustrating dead ends – we discovered that our informant had been correct. The world's most famous fake turned out to be the world's least known Leonardo! Yet the 'Holy Shroud' is not a painting, nor a brass rubbing, nor anything else one might readily ascribe to a Renaissance artist, no matter how prolifically endowed with genius. So what is it?

Taking as a major clue the strange *photographic* characteristics of the Shroud which are shared by no other works of art, we were faced with an astonishing possibility. Had Leonardo da Vinci, working 500 years ago, actually created the world's first photograph? Just confronting such a thought was intimidating – but, of course, very exciting. Supposing we were right? Supposing, moreover, that we could *prove* it is a photograph . . . So we decided to try to replicate all the characteristics of the Turin Shroud, using chemicals and equipment that would have been available to Leonardo. Embarking, at least at first, with more enthusiasm than skill – and enlisting the help of Keith Prince, without whom we would never have got past first base – *we did it!* At the time we had no idea that far away in South Africa Professor Nicholas Allen was doing pretty much the same thing – although with considerably more generous resources – but given our ad hoc experiments and completely amateur standing, we were very pleased with our results. And although we may not have been the first people to succeed in reproducing a Shroud-like image on cloth using a basic photographic process, we *were* the first to replicate *all* the characteristics of the Shroud.

However, Shroud research never ceases, and we are pleased to say that our own has taken a new quantum leap forward – with almost perfect timing. Just as this revised edition was going into publication, we were visited by a true bombshell. Although the details are given in the new Epilogue, suffice it to say here that fate handed us the first concrete evidence to link Leonardo with the Turin Shroud. And incredibly, that evidence had been staring us in the face for a decade.

The other major changes to this book arose out of our subsequent research into more esoteric areas such as the interlinked network of heretical secret societies including the Knights Templar and certain forms of occult Freemasonry, and the origins of their apparently sacrilegious beliefs. This research has clarified, modified and – in some cases – corrected our original conclusions. Looking back, we now realise that writing this book was only an introduction into a much wider and more revelatory world, which we discuss in our sequel – *The Templar Revelation: Secret Guardians of the True Identity of Christ*, published in 1997 – and which later inspired Dan Brown's depiction of Leonardo in *The Da Vinci Code*. In particular our understanding of the true nature of that most controversial secret society, the Priory of Sion, has developed almost out of all recognition: we now freely admit that originally we were somewhat naive in our dealings with them. As will become apparent from our 2006 book *The Sion Revelation*, our own discoveries about the Priory of Sion carry the whole subject to an entirely different level. The Priory of Sion is emphatically not what is claimed for it by many, but, nevertheless, it is dismissed at one's peril . . .

Originally, we tended to take its historical claims of an unbroken succession going back to the twelfth century more or less at face value, but since then our discoveries have led us to quite different conclusions and our attitude to the Priory of Sion has undergone something of a sea change. However, while its pedigree may not be what it claims, we have come to realise that the Priory still has some importance because of *what it represents* – an age-old tradition, whose deeply disturbing secrets may still threaten the very foundations of the Church. This is what lies behind the 'real da Vinci code': the Johannite movement, which, we now realise, holds the keys to many great mysteries not least that of the Turin Shroud – and indeed may also possess the answers to the most enduring questions about the founder of Christianity himself.

This book represents the beginning of what was an extraordinary journey for us. We hope it opens the way for you, too.

Lynn Picknett and Clive Prince
St John's Wood,
London
17 January 2006

1

More Questions than Answers

'The Shroud of Turin is either the most awesome and instructive relic of Jesus Christ in existence ... or it is one of the most ingenious, most unbelievably clever, products of the human mind and hand on record; there is no middle ground.'

John Walsh, *The Shroud* (1963)[1]

The modern Italian city of Turin is a sprawling industrial conurbation, a concrete hymn to the internal combustion engine. Yet it also is a place of pilgrimage, as it has been for many years – for Turin houses what has long been regarded as the most precious, inspiring and awesome of all Christian relics: the Holy Shroud of Jesus, miraculously imprinted with his image.

For over 400 years the Shroud has been the jewel in the crown of Turin Cathedral, which is dedicated to St John the Baptist. Today, it rests out of sight, beneath a fireproof gold covering, inside a box-like altar in one of the side chapels, behind glass and for most of the time behind pale blue curtains. Inside the altar the Shroud is laid out flat – rather than folded as it was kept for much of its history – and an ingenious arrangement allows it to be swung out, encased in a metal frame with bullet-proof glass, when required for one of the infrequent public displays, or expositions.

Such expositions are very rare, approximately once a generation. In the twentieth century, it was exhibited just four times: in
1931, for the wedding of the future King Umberto II (then
Prince of Piedmont); in the Holy Year of 1933; in 1978 to commemorate the 400th anniversary of its arrival in Turin and in
1998 to commemorate the centenary of the first Shroud photographs – which was, as we will see, a major landmark in its
history. It was also displayed in 2000 as part of the Holy Year celebrations. The Shroud is not due to be displayed again until 2025.

The exposition in 2000, between August and October, was the
longest ever – originally planned for ten weeks, it was extended
by another week because of serious floods that hit that area of
Italy – and attracted just short of a million visitors. Of course, this
is a respectable number, but even so it only represents approximately half the attendees who filed past the Shroud during the
eight-week display in 1998 and a third of the three million who
attended the 1978 six-week exposition. The reason for such a
marked decline can be summed up in two words: carbon dating.
As most people are aware, the Shroud was finally put to the test in
1988 and pronounced a medieval or early Renaissance fake. Even
so, a million is an impressive figure – clearly, to a great many
Catholics, it is still the miraculous Shroud of Jesus. So why does
that highly controversial piece of cloth still have such potent
appeal? What did all those pilgrims see? What is the Turin
Shroud?

It is a length of pale biscuit-coloured linen, over 14 foot long
by 3½ (4.25m by 1m). It bears various folds and blemishes accrued
throughout its long life. Most conspicuous are the marks of a
fire, in 1532, which burned through one corner of the cloth (which
was then kept folded), damaging it in several places, notably through
the shoulders of the image. There are other isolated burns from
specks of molten silver from the same fire.

There are also four sets of three round burn-holes dating from
before the 1532 fire – they can be seen in earlier copies – which

are generally known as 'poker marks', because that is what they are widely thought to be. The four sets line up when the cloth is folded, proving that they were made at the same time, possibly in an attempt to test the Shroud's authenticity by subjecting it to 'trial by fire'. One wonders what conclusion the poker–wielding vandals came to after the cloth burnt in the normal way. A less melodramatic explanation might be that the 'poker holes' were caused by a dripping torch.[2]

However, the burn marks, whatever their provenance, are not the reason that the pilgrim looks upon the Shroud. It is to the image that all eyes are drawn, and upon which all devout hearts feast, for is it not truly the image of the Lord Jesus Christ?

Down the centre of the cloth, taking up just over 13 feet (4m) of its total length, are two images showing the front and back of a naked, remarkably tall man, 'hinged' at the head. The cloth is believed to be a winding sheet, which means the corpse would have been laid on one half, and his front covered over with the other.

The man is bearded, with very long hair hanging down past the shoulders at the back, and stopping at shoulder-length at the front. The hands are crossed modestly over the genitals. The sole of one foot, dreadfully darkened with what appears to be blood, is clearly outlined on the image of the back.

The eye is drawn unmercifully to dark lines and splotches on the body; apparently blood from several atrocious injuries. There are small, pierced wounds on the head, and a round one on the only visible wrist – as if a nail had been driven through it. There is what appears to be a large stab wound in the chest, blood from which also runs across the small of the back, and there are small flows of blood on the front of both feet and a larger one on the sole of one foot. Some believe that the face appears to be swollen and contused, and over one hundred scourge marks have been counted on the back, wounds that also curl around the front of the body and legs.

Obviously, judging by these horrific marks the man on the Shroud was – or was supposed to be – Jesus Christ.

Under the Microscope

There are millions in the world who still believe in the sanctity of the man on the Shroud. At the forefront of the faithful is the international Shroud community, or 'sindonologists' (from the Greek *sindon*, a shroud), but who are known with more or less affection as 'Shroudies'.

Of the many organisations formed to study the Shroud throughout the world, most are overtly religious and primarily concerned with the 'message' of the cloth, such as the Holy Shroud Guild of the USA. Others were founded with – supposedly – more objective and scientific principles in mind, such as the Shroud of Turin Research Project, Inc (STURP) in the USA, the Centro Internazionale di Sindonologia in Turin itself, the Centre International d'Études sur le Linceul de Turin (CIELT) in France, and the British Society for the Turin Shroud (BSTS) in the UK.

Over the years there have been dozens of books, pamphlets and articles written about the Shroud, and the above groups regularly add to the literature with their own publications, the most important being *Sindon* (published by the Centro Internazionale di Sindonologia) and the Australian *Shroud News*.

Despite a characteristic reluctance on the part of the Savoys and the Church authorities to release part or all of the cloth for scientific research, it has nevertheless been subjected to such scrutiny several times. Experts from many different disciplines have been involved in studying the Shroud: historians, textile specialists, physicists, chemists, photographers, artists, art historians, anatomists, surgeons and forensic scientists – even botanists. It has been subjected to a whole host of tests, including X-ray photographs, infrared light and ultraviolet light, examination under a microscope, ultraviolet spectrophotometry, infrared spectroscopy and X-ray fluorescence. Samples have been taken and given a variety of chemical tests.

Despite all this, the Shroud has steadfastly refused to give up its secrets, although many clues have surfaced.

It must be remembered that serious interest in the cloth is little more than a century old. It had previously been viewed as a curiosity because the image is too faint to make out clearly with the naked eye; the body seems impossibly tall and thin, and the eyes look positively owl-like as if the man were wearing dark glasses.

But in 1898 a lawyer from Turin was asked to take the first photographs of the Shroud – Secondo Pia, a local councillor and keen amateur photographer. As the Shroud was being displayed as part of the festivities to mark the fiftieth anniversary of the unification of Italy at the time, this seemed a fitting and unique addition to the celebrations.[3]

Pia's ten Shroud photographs (although it was thought until recently that he only took two),[4] were undoubtedly the most significant of his career: seen in photographic negative for the first time the image suddenly leapt into focus. Instead of a vague outline of a bearded man, there is a massively detailed photograph of a terribly wounded, terribly real body.

It is a horrific, graphic catalogue of the grisly business of crucifixion; every nail-hole, every lash of the Roman scourge cries out for our compassion. However, although we are looking at the brutal proof of man's inhumanity to man writ large, even given the evidence of our own eyes we could well be making too many assumptions by immediately supposing that the man was actually Jesus Christ.

Yet all eyes are drawn to the face of the man on the Shroud. Long, lean and bearded, with a prominent and long nose (which may even be broken), it is a face of rather gaunt dignity. Moreover, to many it is an image of stunning and memorable beauty, its very serenity revealing a triumph over the worst of deaths.

Small wonder that Secondo Pia was one of many to look on the face of the man on the Shroud and become transfixed. Hitherto an unpersuaded churchgoer, the Turin worthy abruptly took to his religion with a passion. For surely this image, this torn and tortured man, could only be Jesus himself. The power of the Shroud is never to be underestimated.

Others also reacted quickly to the photographic image. It was now increasingly hard to dismiss the cloth as a crude medieval forgery, for several reasons.

No artist could have created what is known as the 'negative effect' (indeed, several abortive attempts have been made to replicate the image using standard artistic techniques).[5] And no known medieval artist had either the skill or the anatomical knowledge needed to create such an image; besides, realism was not part of their artistic canon.

There are many other practical reasons why the image could not have been painted, particularly its faintness when seen close up – which means that the artist would not have been able to see what he was doing.

For much of the century between Pia's discovery and the present day, researchers have had to be content with his photographs plus a second set taken by Giuseppe Enrie in 1931.[6] As it was not until 1969 that the Church allowed hands-on investigation of the cloth itself, researchers had to confine their studies to the physiology of the man on the Shroud and speculations about what kind of process might have caused the image, with its spectacular negative effect.

Enrie's photographs – generally deemed to be superior to Pia's – included several close-ups of different areas of the cloth, of good enough quality to be blown up. These were seized on for detailed study of the cloth, the image and the bloodstains.

Later landmark studies included those of Paul Vignon, a

wealthy French biologist and friend of the future Pope Pius XI who attempted to replicate the image-forming process. Another notable early Shroudie was the Parisian anatomist and surgeon Pierre Barbet, who in the 1930s devoted himself to studying the effects of crucifixion, using corpses. Although both men's work has a lasting interest, neither actually cracked the code of the Turin Shroud.

Then in 1969, Cardinal Michele Pellegrino, Archbishop of Turin, assembled a team of experts from various disciplines to report on the state of preservation of the Shroud; the team usually referred to as the Turin Commission.

The 1969 examinations were a preliminary investigation only; further tests were recommended, and were carried out four years later, the day after the Shroud was exhibited on live television on 23 November 1973. It was on this occasion that Swiss criminologist Dr Max Frei took his now famous pollen samples (see below), and when for the first time strips, approximately 1½ inches by ½ inch (40mm by 10mm), were taken from the main cloth and its side strip, plus fifteen individual threads from both image and non-image areas.[7]

Curiously – but characteristically – the work of the Turin Commission was carried out in strict secrecy. There seems to be no obvious reason why. When rumours of the 1973 tests leaked out, the authorities denied that anything more than a routine examination had taken place. Only in 1976 was it admitted that the cloth had been tested, and those who had carried out the tests were named. This information was even withheld from King Umberto, then the Shroud's legal owner.

The 1970s saw a quickening of scientific interest in the Shroud, particularly in the USA. In 1977 two key bodies were founded: the BSTS in the UK, and in the USA, following a conference on the Shroud held in Albuquerque, New Mexico, STURP. This last organisation went on to conduct the most extensive tests yet on the cloth, in 1978.

It was a major year for Shroud studies. The Shroud was exhibited to the public between 26 August and 8 October, which led
to a wave of popular interest, prompting several books on the
subject to be published. Most notably, Ian Wilson's seminal *The
Turin Shroud* was hailed as a significant breakthrough in making
the Shroud a household name, and became an international bestseller. There was also the BAFTA-award-winning documentary
film *The Silent Witness* by Henry Lincoln (later co-author of
The Holy Blood and the Holy Grail), from an idea by Ian Wilson.[8]
The book and film between them raised the profile of the
Shroud among Catholics and non-Catholics alike; the cloth
became a topical point of discussion among people everywhere in
Christendom, and the face of the man on the Shroud looked
out from thousands of bookshop windows, with the haunting
appeal of its curious serenity, straight into millions of faces – and
perhaps, secretly, into as many hearts.

Wilson's contribution to Shroud studies should never be
underestimated. Driven by an inner certainty that the cloth was
indeed the winding sheet of Jesus Christ, he rarely allows that
view to show too obviously in *The Turin Shroud,* and argues with
intelligence and style – if little conviction – that there may be other
explanations for its origins. To this day, his public pronouncements
on the Shroud are largely models of reason and balance, but perhaps
it would be naive in the extreme to be too swayed by such an
appearance of objectivity. His original script for *The Silent Witness*
was tellingly entitled *He Is Risen: The Story of the Holy Shroud
of Christ*.[9]

But for those of a strictly scientific bent, the most important
event of 1978 was STURP's series of tests, undertaken in con-
junction with a small team of Italian scientists and Max Frei. For
five days immediately following the October exposition,
STURP was allowed full access to the Shroud, and even to take
samples for later analysis.[10]

STURP's primary objective was to discover what the image

was made of, and whether or not it was of human manufacture. Despite all their efforts, however, they failed. They examined it under X-rays, infrared light and ultraviolet light, as well as by more conventional methods such as microscopy. Samples were taken by the simple expedient of sticking adhesive tape to the cloth and testing the loose threads that came away with it. Most of these tests were designed to reveal the presence of artificial pigments. In all, they spent more than 100,000 hours analysing the data, and the whole project cost around $5,000,000.

The conditions were far from ideal: the STURP scientists had effectively to take the laboratory to the Shroud and not vice versa, and there was a strict time limit that meant not only that they might easily have missed something crucial, but also by the very nature of the work, it could not be checked as the tests could not be repeated.

Date with Destiny

Only one of STURP's proposed tests was rejected by the Church authorities. STURP had wanted to radiocarbon date the cloth, the ultimate test of its authenticity. The Church feared that a large portion of cloth would be destroyed in the test, and permission was not granted. However, it was pointed out to the Church authorities that samples already taken by the Turin Commission in 1973 would do perfectly well for the purpose. On hearing this, the Church demanded that the samples be returned, whereupon they were locked up in Turin Cathedral. When they were loaned out to STURP in 1979 a legal document prevented the fragments from being carbon dated.[11]

Eventually, however, the Church ran out of excuses and had to give in to the pressure. In October 1986 Pope John Paul II, after a meeting of representatives of seven laboratories (later reduced to three to minimise damage to the cloth) with the Pontifical Academy of Sciences in Turin, gave his approval to the tests – if not exactly his blessing.

Carbon-14 is a radioactive form of carbon that is produced in the upper atmosphere by the action of cosmic rays. It is absorbed by all organisms and can be detected in them. The rate of absorption is constant during that organism's life, and when it dies, the carbon-14 decays over a great length of time and at a constant rate. The carbon dating process measures the amount of carbon-14 in a given sample; as the amount that would have been present in the living organism can be calculated, the difference between that and the existing amount shows the age of the sample.

It was only after intensive lobbying from several interested parties – including Ian Wilson – that the Vatican finally gave permission for the cloth to be carbon dated. Three laboratories were involved: the University of Arizona in Tucson, the Oxford Research Laboratory, and the Swiss Federal Institute of Technology in Zürich. The bluntly sceptical (and ultimately dismissive) Professor Teddy Hall of Oxford was appointed as spokesman.

Typical Church secrecy surrounded the taking of samples; although officially scheduled for 23 April 1988, the event was switched, with little warning, to 4 a.m., 21 April, when the Italian President was in Turin, diverting Press interest. Representatives from each of the laboratories, including Teddy Hall, were present, and the operation was overseen by Michael Tite of the British Museum Research Laboratory.

A piece approximately four square inches (25cm^2) was cut from one corner, and in turn three samples were cut from that. They were sealed in special containers, along with control samples, and one was given to each of the laboratory representatives. The whole process was videotaped.

(Curiously, after the samples had been cut off, Giovanni Riggi, the microanalyst appointed by the Church to remove the samples, secretly – but with the consent of the Shroud's official custodian, Cardinal Anastasio Ballestrero, Archbishop of Turin – removed some threads from the bloodstains on the head, which he deposited in a bank vault. Why he did this and why it was done in such secrecy remains a mystery. In late 1992 Riggi released them to Texan paediatrician and Shroud enthusiast Dr Leoncio Garza-Valdès in order that the blood could be tested for DNA. Apparently even Ballestrero's successor, Cardinal Giovanni Saldarini, was unaware of the existence of these samples until Garza-Valdès sent him a copy of an article about the DNA tests in 1996. Not surprisingly Saldarini furiously declared that Riggi had no authority to release – or even possess – the samples and demanded their immediate return. He also made it clear that the Church would deny the validity of any scientific tests carried out on the samples.[12])

The results of the carbon dating were released on 13 October 1988, although they had already been 'leaked' beforehand. (This was the tenth anniversary of the final day of STURP's examination.) They were first announced by Cardinal Ballestrero in Turin, and later that day by Dr Tite at a Press conference at the British Museum.[13]

The carbon dating showed that it was 99.9 per cent certain that the Shroud originated from the period 1000 to 1500, and 95 per cent certain that the cloth dated from between 1260 and 1390.

The Holy Shroud of Turin was a fake.

To say believers in the Shroud's authenticity were plunged into a state of shock is to put it mildly; their very world was being hammered by the iron fist of a reality too brutal to bear. The Shroud was so much more than a mere relic to them; it was the perfect and unique reminder of their Lord, and absolute proof of his holy, redemptive death. But now the deathly hush of shock spread throughout the Shroud community, its fragility being reinforced by Professor Hall's insensitive comment to the

Press: 'Somebody just got a piece of cloth, faked it and flogged it. I don't think the Shroud of Turin is of much interest any longer.'[14]

The Church did not pronounce officially on this result, but appeared to profit by its Jesuitical streak when Professor Luigi Gonella, scientific advisor to the Vatican, said: 'The tests were not commissioned by the Church and we are not bound by the results.'[15]

Almost immediately rumours began to circulate about conspiracies among the researchers, and the cream of the Shroudies, including Ian Wilson, began to issue statements that typically included such phrases as, 'While we have the greatest regard for scientific testing . . .' Their implication was that carbon dating could be wrong, terribly wrong, and that this had been the case where the Shroud was concerned.

Sceptics whooped with joy and more than a touch of 'I told you so', while the believers licked their wounds. Of course some merely left the Shroudie world without a backward glance, granite-faced with disappointment. Others were angry at being taken for a ride, at being duped at their most vulnerable level, that of religious faith — but who could they blame except the unknown medieval hoaxer? Those whose sole concern was to believe at all costs and damn-the-evidence began to regroup, although not without a huge loss of credibility.

The full significance of the test results was not lost on them; for the dates they had suggested pinpointed exactly the same period in history when a Holy Shroud first appeared, unannounced. To many Shroudies, this happy coincidence seemed deeply suspicious.

The post-carbon dating world of the Shroudies was very different from the one that preceded the devastating announcement of 13 October 1988.

For the Shroudies, the worst thing about the carbon dating was the ridicule. Cartoons began to appear, and jokes about it crept into television programmes, such as the irreverent satirical show *Spitting Image*. A full-length transparency of the Shroud was later to figure in the British Museum's exhibition 'Fake: the Art of Deception'. When Ian Wilson gave a talk to the Wrekin Trust on 5 November 1988, and was introduced as 'being best known for his book *The Turin Shroud*, the large audience of respectable, intelligent people laughed. He may have smiled back, but one does not have to try too hard to understand his feelings.

After the Fall

It is at this point that our own story begins, for the carbon dating intrigued us greatly. We had both been fascinated for some time with the Shroud, and the new information, as far as we were concerned, merely added to its appeal. We had previously taken the rather vague line that the cloth may have been imprinted with an image through some unknown form of energy release, but of course this in itself did not prove that the Shroud was Jesus' winding sheet. To us, the carbon dating simply added to its fascination. If there was any one moment when Picknett and Prince became Shroudies, the carbon dating was it.

We found ourselves rather ironically going along with the believers – at least in one respect. It seemed to us to be outrageous to dismiss the Shroud totally, overnight. There were an enormous number of questions to be answered – more, in fact, now it had been shown to be a fake. What about the negative effect? If it was a painting, as the carbon dating implied, then where was the paint? Had the man whose image it bore actually been crucified? And if so, who was the unhappy model? And what medieval faker had the skill, the brains – and the nerve – to have created such a shocking joke for posterity?

Above all else, there was a sense of shock involved, even for

those like us, whose spiritual centre had not been violated. This
was no crudely botched daub; this was no relic that would blend
in seamlessly with the tons of fake splinters from the 'True
Cross'. You could not even call it a 'work of art', for whatever art
was involved in its creation was totally unknown.

In fact, we realised that, as a fake, the Shroud of Turin had
become the ultimate *heretical* relic, something created with a kind
of perverse love for the job, an incredible eye for detail and a skill
that was matchless throughout history. If you could stomach the
implications, it was nothing short of wonderful.

We were hooked.

Yet here we must add a personal note that, despite rumours to
the contrary, we would have preferred not to. Unfortunately,
however, it is crucial to this story.

On the day that Ian Wilson was being laughed at for his
apparent gullibility about the Shroud, Lynn was part of the Wrekin
Trust's audience. To cut a long story mercifully short, within
three weeks of meeting there they had begun a two-year on/off
relationship. The only reason for mentioning this painful episode
is to show why Lynn became even more interested in the Shroud
in the year following the carbon dating.

It must be remembered that Wilson had been vociferous in his
support of the carbon dating before the event, writing in his
1978 bestseller: '. . . there is one scientific test . . . that could at
a stroke determine whether the Shroud dates from the fourteenth century, or is indeed much older.'[16] Two years before the
tests he wrote emphatically: 'A consistent fourteenth-century
date . . . should certainly be decisive enough to cause a massive
rethink among those who, in common with this author, support
the Shroud's authenticity.'[17]

Yet this was the same man who, three years after the carbon
dating, in *Holy Faces, Secret Places*, quoted Deuteronomy 6:16,
'You must not put the Lord your God to the test', adding: 'In a
very real sense they [the scientists involved in the carbon dating]

were aiming to demonstrate whether God had shown himself in
the form of the Turin Shroud. Is it too much to suggest that God
might have pulled down the blinds?'[18]

When something beloved dies – be it either a person or a
dream – there must be a time of bereavement, a period of adjust-
ment. But as the Shroudies never admitted there was a death in
the first place, is there any wonder that in the years following the
carbon dating their intensifying bitterness and fear turned them
into a veritable mafia? It is only too significant that all the doubts
about the technique of carbon dating have surfaced since, not
before, the actual tests.

Take the words of the late Rodney Hoare, then BSTS
Chairman. Before the tests he wrote: 'Carbon dating would
enable an estimate to within an accuracy of 150 years in 2000 . . .
the refusal of the Roman Catholic Church custodians to grant
permission is difficult to understand.'[19] But in a letter to Clive in
1993 he wrote: 'The carbon dating is likely to be too late rather
than too early, if contaminants were "pressure-cooked" into the
fibres by the fire of 1532 . . .'[20] And in that same year he wound
up an unusual AGM by appealing to members for suggestions on
how the carbon dating might be wrong.

Nevertheless, it is instructive to review the Shroudies' objections to the tests. As we have seen, many believers immediately
fell back on allegations of conspiracy. The right-wing luminary
of La Contre-Reforme Catholique au XXe Siècle, Brother
Bruno Bonnet-Eymard, claimed that Dr Michael Tite switched
the samples for parts of a late thirteenth-century cope (a ceremonial cloak).[21] He also hastened to point out that Tite got
Professor Hall's job at Oxford when the latter retired. In fact, the
cope was used, but only as a control sample.

What would be the motive of such a conspiracy? Bonnet-
Eymard thinks it is an attempt by scientists to undermine the
Christian religion. Leading sindonologist Professor Werner Bulst
goes further, and has spoken on German television of a 'Masonic

anti-Catholic plot'.[22] In 1988 Cardinal Ballestrero stated his belief in an interview for a Catholic magazine that Freemasons had been behind the carbon dating.[23] However, it is difficult to see what the conspirators would hope to gain. Discrediting the Shroud would do little to shake the faith of most Christians – especially in the last century, the Church has been careful to avoid endorsing it as genuine. On the other hand, proving the Shroud authentic might conceivably attract more followers into the fold. It is easy to imagine a conspiracy aimed at proving a first-century date, but not so easy to imagine the scientists risking their reputations and careers by plotting to brand it a fake.

In 1992, however, German researchers Holger Kersten and Elmar R. Gruber, in their *The Jesus Conspiracy* (published in the UK in early 1994), advanced a bold – and novel – variation on the conspiracy theme. They believe that the carbon dating was rigged by the scientists *in collusion* with the Vatican.

Kersten and Gruber believe that pieces of fourteenth-century fabric were switched for samples cut from the Shroud. This happened, they claim, when Michael Tite sealed the samples in their containers before handing them over to representatives of the three laboratories, as this was (suspiciously) the only part of the operation that was carried out in private and out of sight of the video cameras that were recording the event.

They base their belief on the apparent discrepancies in and vagueness of the scientists' reports regarding the size of the samples they received, and the apparent differences in the samples before and after they were sealed up.

Unfortunately, the samples themselves were destroyed by the testing process, and so Kersten and Gruber had to rely on photographs taken in Turin Cathedral when the samples were first cut from the cloth and on photographs taken at the laboratories. They claim that it is impossible to match the pieces of cloth as seen on the two sets of photographs, which should

have been identical. However, such comparisons are not as easy
to make as might be first thought: it was not simply a matter
of the original piece being snipped into three equal bits. The
samples were cut from the middle of the piece, leaving material
to spare.

Gruber and Kersten's cynical reconstruction of the sample-
cutting has been challenged – for example by sindonologist
Eberhard Lindner, who has shown that the samples *can* all be
matched up.[24] Kersten and Gruber's suspicions were raised by the
inordinate length of time that Michael Tite and the Vatican representatives were closeted away while cutting the samples. It does
seem that they were there for quite some time, but surely they
would not have needed very long to switch samples either, if that
was what they were up to.

The most unlikely part of this scenario is the alleged alliance
between the scientists – some of whom, like Teddy Hall, were
vehement atheists – and the Vatican. Kersten and Gruber realise
that the conspiracy they suggest can only work on the assumption that such a collusion actually took place, since Tite was
accompanied when the supposed switch took place.

Their suggested motive is ingenious and intriguing: they
assert that the Church wanted to discredit the Shroud because
it proves that Jesus was alive when laid in the tomb, and that
the Resurrection – the cornerstone of the Christian creed –
never took place. The Church, they argue, had long been keen
to acquire the Shroud so they could discredit it, but until it
was bequeathed to them by King Umberto in 1983, they were
powerless to do so.

This idea is not a new one. It was first published in the 1960s by
a curious individual called Hans Naber. He claimed that, in 1947,
he had had a vision of Jesus, who told him that the Resurrection
never happened and that a study of the Shroud would prove it,
and thereafter Naber saw it as his mission to bring this message
to the world. He first achieved international publicity in 1969,

when he learned of the Turin Commission's secret investigations and claimed that the Church intended to use the Commission to destroy the cloth in order to hide its secret.[25]

Since then, Rodney Hoare has promoted a similar thesis in books such as *The Turin Shroud is Genuine* (1994). His ideas are discussed later.

Kersten and Gruber, like Naber, point to the way that the blood appears to be still flowing from the wounds as proof that Jesus was still alive when the Shroud image was formed. However, there are weaknesses in their theory.

First, although the Church authorities did not legally own the Shroud until 1983, it was still in their power, so they could easily have arranged for it to be destroyed, say in a fire. In fact, there have been several attempts to steal or burn the Shroud, all of which have been foiled by the Church guardians. There was no need to go to such lengths to enter into a conspiracy with the scientists. Secondly, as we will see, there is a strong case against authenticity. And Kersten and Gruber never consider the possibility that the image might have been created by someone who was *deliberately* aiming to show that Jesus did not die on the cross.

Apart from allegations of conspiracy, since the 1988 carbon dating results the believers have been desperately trying to find ways to discredit them, coming up with a host of different processes that could have distorted the results – with varying degrees of plausibility (often quite the opposite). They include the effects of the 1532 fire, contamination from the handling the Shroud received during its various public expositions, and Dr Leoncio Garza-Valdès' hypothesis of the presence of a 'bioplastic coating' of bacteria and fungi. Effectively, this claims that what the carbon dating dated was this coating, not the Shroud.

At the beginning of 2005, much publicity was given to a new theory of how the carbon dating was botched: it was alleged that the scientists mistakenly took samples from a repair patch added in the Middle Ages or later and dated *that*, not the actual Shroud. In other words, the dating was accurate, but the cloth was wrong.

The idea was first proposed by Joseph G. Marino and M. Sue Benford at a conference on the Shroud held in Orvieto in August 2000. Their suggestion was that the samples cut from the Shroud included threads from a (hypothetical) repair. The presence of the more recent threads threw the carbon dating out, producing a date that was an average of the original two-thousand-year-old Shroud and the later repair. The reason for such a blunder, they suggest, is that the threads were from an 'invisible mend' and so were not obvious to those who cut the sample.[26]

There is much assumption-making and circular reasoning in their argument. There is no documented evidence of a repair at that place at any time (it was not damaged in the 1532 fire). And their conclusion that *if* the 1988 results are revised to exclude the repair material, then the date would have come out at the first century, is circular reasoning of the highest order since they have to guess at the amount of later material in the sample and its date (which they assume to be sixteenth century). And their claim can never be checked, as the carbon dating process destroyed the samples. For these reasons, Marino and Benford's theory was not taken particularly seriously.

However, their idea was followed up by STURP scientist Raymond N. Rogers – a chemist retired from the Los Alamos Research Laboratory – who published his own variation on the theme in the journal *Thermochimica Acta* in January 2005, a few months before his death. Rogers' credentials are such that his claims were taken much more seriously than Marino and Benford's.

Rogers was the custodian of material removed from the Shroud on three occasions: during the 1973 Turin Commission examination; during the 1978 STURP tests; and when some loose threads, given to him by Professor Gonella, were taken from the carbon dating samples in 1988 before they were handed over to the laboratories. Not only were the latter the only surviving pieces of the carbon dating samples – potentially providing a means of testing Marino and Benford's hypothesis – but the earliest, 1973, material was taken from an area immediately adjacent to them. (The 1978 samples were from other parts of the cloth.)

After comparing these samples, Rogers reached an even more extreme conclusion than Marino and Benford: he believed that the *whole* of the sample cut from the Shroud for carbon dating came from a repair patch. (As so often in Shroud research, Rogers played down the fact that his conclusions are incompatible with Marino and Benford's; the pro-authenticity literature makes it appear that the two theories support each other, whereas in reality they are mutually exclusive.) This was because he found significant differences in the visual and chemical characteristics, on the one hand, of the 1973 and 1988 samples, and on the other, the 1978 samples. In particular the former had a coating of madder root dye in a gummy residue that he thought was probably gum arabic, and which was absent from the latter. Rogers suggested it was a dye added to a repair patch to make it the same colour as the rest of the Shroud. (Rogers also found minute cotton fibres stuck to the 1973/1988 samples, suggesting, he proposed, that the linen came from a loom that was also used for cotton, something conspicuously absent from the Shroud as a whole.)[27]

On the other hand, those who did the carbon dating are adamant that they specifically avoided cutting the samples from any patches or seams. (The location for the sample was selected by two specially-chosen textile experts to ensure that it was genuinely part of the original cloth.) Both Marino/Benford's and Rogers' conclusions involve a serious questioning of the competence of the scientists and experts involved, who either failed to spot the presence of threads from a repair (in Marino and Benford's scenario) or who did not notice an entire patch of repair material (in Rogers' scenario).

The problem, as Rogers' critics have pointed out, is that he is basing his far-reaching conclusions on tests carried out on such tiny samples – just a couple of threads left over from the 1988 testing, given to him in circumstances that remain somewhat unclear – and comparison with the 1973 material.

Significantly, when Rogers' results were published, many Shroudies who had argued for years that the carbon dating results were wrong because of contamination of the samples and such-like, now quite happily admitted that the tests had been accurate after all – but the wrong piece of cloth had been tested!

While it must be admitted that carbon dating is by no means totally reliable, the most that Shroudies can ever hope to do by challenging it in this case is to prove that the carbon dating tests are invalid. But even by disproving them they would still fail to prove that the Shroud is 2000 years old.

The best that can be said is that some uncertainty remains about the carbon dating, which can only be resolved by repeating the process, something that seems unlikely to happen in the near future – if ever. However, as we were to find as our investigation into the Shroud proceeded, the carbon dating is not essential to see that the alleged relic is not genuine but is the product of human ingenuity.

But it was in the light of the carbon dating that we began our research, looking for the identity of the author of this extraordinary hoax in the evidence of the cloth itself, and in its complex and vexed history. It was perhaps rather like the little boy who saw through the emperor's new clothes setting out to write a history of fashion, but we certainly came to Shroud research with a new eye.

So what are the hard facts about the Shroud? What has all that

meticulous scientific research actually established? We went back
to basics.

Facts and the Figure

The fabric is bleached pure linen. The cloth measures 14 feet 3
inches by 3 feet 7 inches (4.4m by 1.13m) and is one thousandth
of an inch (0.03mm) thick, with a 3½ inch (8.9cm) strip on its
left-hand side. This strip is almost an exact match, and appears
to have been added to centralise the image; it has therefore been
assumed it was sewn on when the Shroud was put on display.
The weave is known as 'three-to-one herringbone twill' (the
same as in denim jeans), an unusually elaborate and costly weave
for a cheap fabric like linen. There is no evidence either way
for it being compatible with cloth produced in first-century
Palestine.

One of the details much quoted by believers is that of the
evidence of the pollen. Dr Max Frei, a famous Swiss criminologist and the only non-Italian member of the original Turin
Commission, took samples of pollen from the cloth in 1973 by
the simple method of attaching sticky tape to the cloth and
pulling it off. The particles were analysed under the microscope.

Frei published his results in 1976, claiming that he had
found – besides the expected European pollen – samples from
plants unique to Palestine, the Anatolian steppes and Turkey,
leading him to conclude that the Shroud had at some time been
in each of those areas. Despite the claims of some, Frei's work
cannot be used to date the Shroud, and in any case, as we will
reveal in Chapter 2, there are serious difficulties with his conclusions. We consider that his findings were remarkably selective,
to put it mildly.

The body image is so faint that many find it extremely difficult to make out at all. All photographs – not just negatives – effectively enhance the image, partly because they are reduced in size and therefore focus the image, and partly because film emulsion intensifies the contrast. Up close, or under a magnifying glass, the image seems to disappear.

All the tests have failed to establish what produced the image, although they have eliminated many possibilities. No substantial traces of pigment, ink or dyes have been found on the cloth (except by Dr Walter McCrone, see Chapter 4), although minute traces of pigment have been detected. This is said to be because painted images are known to have been placed on it to 'sanctify' them.

Under the microscope the colour of the image shows no sign of soaking along the threads (capillary action), as would most paints. No foreign matter adheres to the threads. The parts of the image next to the 1532 burn marks do not change in colour, neither do the parts where the tidemarks (where water was used to put out the fire) cross it.

Rather than being caused by something being added to the cloth, the image seems to have been created by something being taken away, some degradation of the structure of the linen. STURP scientists observed that the imaged parts of the cloth are structurally weaker than the non-image areas, and under high magnification the fibres can be seen to be damaged, with a corroded appearance. Some have likened the damage to that caused by a weak acid.[28]

The image does not penetrate the cloth. It is hard to imagine any artistic technique that would prevent the paint soaking through something that is just one thousandth of an inch (0.03mm) thick. Even individual threads can be seen, under the microscope, to be coloured on one side only.[29]

The image is completely uniform in colour. The impression of contrasting areas is an illusion due to the variation in the number of coloured threads per square inch. (It is hard to equate this with the artistic forgery so beloved of the dismissive sceptic.)

The negative effect is still the most puzzling, and the most fascinating, characteristic of the Turin Shroud. It is a concept that would have been completely alien to a medieval forger, besides being totally pointless when it could never have been appreciated in photographic negative.

There have been suggestions that the image might have been painted in positive and the effect of ageing turned it negative – something which happened to a fresco in the church at Assisi – but in the case of the Shroud the dark background of the negative is the cloth itself. For an Assisi-like effect the cloth would have had to have been dark at first and then changed colour, and the image would have had to be lighter than the cloth to start with.

In fact, sceptics have a hard time trying to explain the negative effect, and can only really do so by denying that it exists. They claim that it was merely a by-product of the artist's efforts to reproduce the contact points – the areas where the body met the cloth. Walter McCrone wrote: 'I feel the negative character of the image is a coincidence resulting from the artist's conception of his commission.'[30]

Equally intriguing, or so we once thought, is the claim that the image apparently exhibits '3-D information'. This means that there is a direct, measurable relationship between the intensity of the image and the distance of the cloth from the body.

This was first noticed by Paul Vignon at the turn of the twentieth century, and was demonstrated by two US Air Force physicists who were later instrumental in setting up STURP, devout Catholics John Jackson and Eric Jumper. Their most dramatic demonstration of this effect was when they used the VP-8 Image Analyzer, originally developed for NASA, which produced 3-D images. This effect is impossible to create with ordinary paintings as the unequal density of the colour fails to give the Image Analyzer anything to work on.

This 3-D effect is believed to be a highly significant characteristic of the Shroud image, although what it actually means is acknowledged to be unclear. To believers, it is proof of some form of radiation emitting from the body of Christ. Our own research, however, was to reveal something quite unexpected about this '3-D information' – as we will see.

From the earliest studies it was realised that, if authentic, the image was caused by a more complex process than simple contact between body and cloth. For example, Paul Vignon proved that if the cloth had been draped over a body that had been covered in paint, the image would be grotesque and bloated-looking when the cloth was straightened out.

The image shows parts of the body that could not even have touched the cloth. For example, the nose would have formed a 'tent' from its tip to the cheek, yet the image shows the nostrils and part of the cheek distinctly. In *The Shroud of Christ* (1902), Paul Vignon declares that the image is 'the result of action at a distance', or 'a projection'.[31]

There are a number of small flows of blood – or dark patches that appear to be blood – from the scalp, both back and front, which appear to be consistent with wounds caused by the Crown of Thorns. Blood also runs down the arms, and seeps from an apparent nail-wound in the sole visible wrist. There is a large patch of blood on the chest, which matches the centurion's spear-thrust in the Biblical account. Blood has gathered in the small of the back, perhaps pooling when the body was laid flat on the Shroud. Blood also leaks from wounds in the feet, and seems particularly concentrated on the sole of one foot.

However, there are significant differences between the image of the body and the image of the blood. Although the bloodstains appear to be similar in colour to the body image in indoor lighting, in natural light the blood is seen to be distinctly different –

a vivid red. The bloodstains themselves do not exhibit the negative effect.

Under the microscope the fibres are matted together by, and
encrusted with, the 'blood' that can clearly be seen to have been
added. The 'bloodstains' do penetrate the cloth, and there are
signs of capillary action along the fibres (although not as distinct
as it should be with liquid blood).

The conclusion is crucial: since the two images – the body
and the blood – are so different, then they must have been created by separate processes. Indeed, to the (unbiased) naked eye,
the blood does seem to have been rather crudely added, as if
overlaid somehow on the body image.

The Shroud literature often states as an established fact that
there is no body image on the cloth underneath the bloodstains.
If true, this would imply that the Shroud had been in contact
with a body, and the blood itself would have prevented the image
from forming. No forger would have applied the bloodstains first
and then painted the image around them. However, this so-
called 'fact' is based on a test by STURP scientist Alan Adler on
a single fibril taken from the Shroud – it takes more than a
hundred of these to make up just one thread. In order to determine whether the blood is genuine Adler took just one
'blood'-coated fibril and applied a chemical that would dissolve
any blood protein present. The 'blood' did dissolve – suggesting,
but not proving, that it is blood – and afterwards Adler observed
that the fibril showed none of the discoloration found on the
body image.[32] However, to extrapolate from this that there is no
image at all under the blood is to exceed the data by miles. We
have already seen that many individual fibres within the imaged
areas are not coloured. Other STURP scientists have admitted
that this question is open.[33]

But is it blood? Real blood dries brown, not red – in fact, tests
by STURP concluded that it was not blood. However, when
Italian scientists claimed to have proved that it was, and had also

isolated the blood group (AB), STURP changed their minds and agreed that it was blood after all.

The question of blood on the Shroud has led to some remarkable claims about human DNA being discovered on the relic.

In 1992 Dr Leoncio Garza-Valdès took the samples given to him by Giovanni Riggi to Dr Victor Tryon, Director of the Center for Advanced DNA Technologies at the University of Texas. Tryon was able to isolate gene segments indicating that the samples contained DNA from a human male. However, because of the very degraded nature of the samples, it was not possible to go further and determine any of the other characteristics of the individual concerned, such as their hair or eye colour. Nevertheless, Garza-Valdès has had no compunction about describing this as 'the DNA of God', although his book of the same title does admit to a question mark.

(Incidentally, if the Shroud is genuine, the presence of both X and Y chromosomes in the Texan DNA would tend to show that the individual was the product of normal human procreation, and not a miraculous Virgin birth.)

The existence of DNA in samples taken from the blood-stains on Shroudman's foot in 1978 was also announced in 1995 by a team at the Institute of Legal Medicine in Genoa. These results are usually given short shrift in the Shroud literature, partly because of their customary bias in favour of American research but mostly because the Genoa team reported that they had found both male *and female* DNA. Cardinal Saldarini quickly distanced the Church from these conclusions, saying:

> The DNA findings may well have been based on minute samples which were taken, with official consent, in 1978. But the presence of feminine DNA on these, even if it is accepted, cannot be regarded as a significant finding. All it shows, as is

already well known from the Shroud's history, is that the Shroud has been handled by a variety of people. In 1534, for example, it was for two weeks in the care of the Poor Clare nuns of Chambéry, in order for them to repair the damage caused by the 1532 fire. To pinpoint any particular DNA on the Shroud as definitely deriving from the crucifixion would be a very long shot indeed.[34]

Saldarini may have a point. A nun may have cried over the cloth – indeed, it is likely that hundreds of nuns would have sobbed at the sight of that horribly tortured body over the centuries. However, in accepting the validity of Dr Tryon's research, Shroudies such as Ian Wilson argue that his results can only be wrong if someone had happened to bleed on exactly the same spot as the original bloodstains – a most unlikely eventuality. But the Genoese results are dismissed out of hand, because of course, to them, the Shroud cannot contain female DNA.

Although nothing here is absolutely conclusive, the weight of evidence is that the bloodstains on the Shroud are, or at least contain, real human blood. But there are still many questions to be asked about this: does the blood necessarily belong to the same individual whose image appears on the cloth? And does it confirm that the Shroud was once in contact with a real, bleeding human body?

The answer to both questions must be no. If the Shroud is a forgery its creator may well have used real human blood to add verisimilitude. The blood might have been taken from several people, which would account for the presence of both male and female DNA and, as we will see later, there are several anomalies with the bloodstains that strongly suggest that they were added artificially.

The Eye of the Beholder

The image has been studied by many anatomists and forensic scientists who agree that the physique is consistent with a real human body. Some have gone so far as to say that it is too flawless to be the work of an artist.

The man on the Shroud is generally taken to be around 5 feet 11 inches (180cm), but there are estimates as low as 5 feet 4 inches (162cm) depending on assumptions made about the lie of the cloth – and, as we will see, evidence that he was *much* taller . . .

The physique is usually taken to be that of a healthy well-developed male, who was not given to manual labour. Harvard ethnologist Carleton S. Coon pronounced the features to be ethnically those of a Sephardic Jew or an Arab, but it is impossible to be dogmatic on this issue. This assumption has been added to by the 'evidence' of the long hair on the back image, which is often described as being the 'unbound pigtail' of the young Jewish male of the first century.

The man appears to be between forty and fifty years old; it is possible, according to one school of thought, to make a case for Jesus having been older than the accepted thirty-three years at the time of his crucifixion.

Pierre Barbet, working on freshly amputated arms, demonstrated that the only way that the weight of a nailed body can be supported is by nailing it through the *wrists* (the 'space of Destot'), as here. He also discovered that the nail hit the median nerve, which causes the thumb to contract into the palm. The thumbs of the man on the Shroud are invisible.[35]

However, it would be untrue to say that this somewhat specialist knowledge is modern; the nailing of the wrists was actually mentioned in the first work specifically devoted to the Shroud, by Cardinal Gabrielle Paleotti, Archbishop of Bologna, in 1598. He wrote that this was 'proved by the experiments carried out by talented sculptors on corpses with a view to making a picture.'[36] Van Dyck (1599-1641) and Rubens (1577-1640) also depicted Jesus as being crucified in this way. It was not, however, known in the pre-Renaissance period in which the Shroud is assumed to have been faked.

Analysis of the angles at which the blood flowed on the arms shows that it is consistent with that of a man being crucified with his arms held above his head, forming a 'Y' shape rather than the usual 'T' shape of artistic depiction. The blood flows along the arms, with occasional downward drips due to gravity. These run at two slightly different angles from the line of the arms and there have been claims that this fits exactly what would have happened in crucifixion.

There are two main theories as to how crucifixion kills. Pierre Barbet believed that death is caused by asphyxiation, as it would be impossible to breathe with the arms in that position unless there is support for the legs. The victim could only raise his chest by pressing down on the nails in his feet, which in turn would be agonising, causing a sort of see-saw motion: rising to draw breath, falling from the pain, rising from pain to yet more pain. Barbet claimed that the two angles of the blood flow are consistent with the two positions. It does, however, require that the only lower support for the body is the nail or nails in the feet, there being no crotch support (sedile).[37]

Another school of thought, supported by Rodney Hoare, is that there was a sedile, and that death was caused by some other factor.[38] The arms would be kept in one position while the victim was alive, changing as he lost consciousness and slumped to one side. This school also claims that the angles of the blood flow support their view.

The course the blood has taken does seem to be realistic. The most noticeable of all the flows, which forms the shape of a figure '3' on the forehead, for example, behaves exactly the way blood wells up from a puncture-wound, and even shows changes of direction over the furrows of the brow. Some have even seen signs of the separation of serum from the blood – although it could equally well be the separating out of the components of artificial blood.

Some have seen the clearer patches in the middle of the chest wound as indications of the 'blood and water' that is said to have issued from Jesus (John 19:34), and have even worked out medical explanations for just how it happened. However, any forger working from the Biblical account would have been careful to have included this detail.

The spear wound is curved on one side, apparently corresponding to examples of the Roman *lancea*, the weapon specifically referred to in John's Gospel. Although frequently cited as evidence for the Shroud's authenticity, it is inadmissible as no-one has ever shown that the wound does not match those caused by weapons of any other place or period, such as Renaissance Italy. No-one had ever thought to look. (However, even a cursory glance through an encyclopedia of weaponry shows that similar lances were used in almost every period – there are, after all, limited possibilities for the design of such an object.)

The facial wounds are a contentious area. Most researchers agree that the man shows signs of violence here, but they disagree as to how much his face suffered.

Secondo Pia's original photographs seem to show a far greater degree of bruising and swelling than those since. Giuseppe Enrie found that this was because Pia had failed to lay the cloth flat, distorting the image. His own view, interestingly, was that the face shows no marks of violence at all.[39] At the other extreme are those such as Dr David Willis (a British physician, and devout Catholic, who made a special study of the wounds), who lists a horrific catalogue of facial injuries, such as swollen eyebrows, and a torn eyelid – an injury virtually impossible to sustain, even in the most severe beatings.[40]

In fact, this is a perennial problem: while the image is astoundingly life-like, attempts to focus on minute detail only result in very subjective interpretations, rapidly becoming a kind of Rorschach inkblot test. The weave of the cloth itself acts as a barrier – beyond it no detail can be seen, although this does little to prevent many seeing the most amazing patterns, which their minds then transmute into proof of their own hypotheses. Another problem is that researchers always use hugely enlarged photographs, never the real thing, and there are of course limits as to how far an image can be blown up while preserving the detail. Not only does it become progressively more blurred, but the grain of the film itself can make deceptive patterns.

Over one hundred marks, as of scourging, can be detected, mainly on the back of the image. Forensic scientists have been able to calculate the number, height and position of the scourgers. The claim has been made that the shape of the wounds matches that of the Roman flagrum, a whip with dumbbell-shaped metal tips. However, no comparable studies of scourges used in other times and places have been made, although it is known that the Flagellants during the Black Death in the fourteenth century used very similar whips,[41] and from the mid-fifteenth century onwards the 'Florentinian Flagellants' provided rich street theatre with their al fresco demonstrations of athletic masochism.

Different explanations have been offered as to why we can see the sole of one foot. Some, such as Rodney Hoare, assume that the body was lying completely flat, and speculate that the cloth was folded up around the feet, which were pressed against the wall of the tomb.[42] Or it may be that the body simply retained the position it held on the cross, with its knees raised slightly, allowing the feet to be placed flat on the ground when taken down.

The Hungarian-born American religious artist Isabel Piczek has made a special study of the Shroudman's anatomy, particularly with regard to the apparent foreshortening of the image. She concluded that the body shows the position of crucifixion, presumably retained by rigor mortis, with the arms being forced down across the body. The foreshortening is accurate to a degree that argues against it being the work of an artist of merely average skill.

The VP-8 Image Analyzer work caused great excitement when John Jackson claimed that the 3-D images showed what appeared to be small coins over the eyes. Soon, an enthusiastic researcher, Francis Filas (a Jesuit theologian from Chicago), claimed to be able to read part of an inscription around the edge of a coin – just four letters, UCAI, which could be the middle of a Greek version of 'Tiberius Caesar' (*Tiberiou Caisaros*). He was the emperor in Jesus' day, and this was an inscription known from leptons in use during Pilate's governorship. However, most other researchers ascribed this to Filas' imagination, and when STURP made a special search for the coins, they could not find them.[43]

Perhaps surprisingly, a believer in the Shroud's authenticity, a retired priest, Father Charles Foley, criticised Filas' claims. He pointed out that he had used enlargements of Giuseppe Enrie's 1931 photographs and that his film was very grainy, which would have been exacerbated by the process of enlargement. Foley believes that Filas simply imagined a shape in these grains.[44] This conclusion is supported by the fact that the photographs taken by STURP in 1978 using better quality film do not show any trace of coins. A leading supporter of Filas – and, as we will see, of many other extreme claims concerning the detail of the Shroud image – Dr Alan Whanger, argues that this is because the threads in the eye area had been 'pulled or rotated' during the 1973 examination.[45] Not only is this somewhat desperate, but very unscientific – if details can only be seen on one set of photographs and not on others, then scientifically speaking, they must be invalid.

We are back to the problem of trying to see patterns in the weave of the cloth and enlarged photographs – a process very similar to seeing recognisable shapes in the clouds. This problem also pertains to another set of widely publicised claims made in 1997: researchers at the Institute of Theoretical and Applied Optics in Paris claimed that they could discern Greek and Latin letters on the Shroud. Even diehard Shroud supporters were unimpressed. Leading BSTS member Mark Guscin, in a report on the 1997 Shroud Symposium in Nice at which the French researchers delivered a paper, said that it was 'most unconvincing' and that 'the so-called "letters" they "see" could be anything with a bit of imagination.'[46]

However, this did not prevent Swiss enthusiast Maria Grazia Siliato, based on the French research, claiming that she could read the Greek words for 'Jesus' and 'Nazareth' on the cloth in one-centimetre-high (0.39 inch) letters – and that this proved that the Shroud is authentic . . . While obviously little comment is required, how a label, which could have been written at any time, proves the Shroud's authenticity, is beyond us. (In fact, it would even argue against it, as it is now generally recognised that 'Nazareth' is a mistranslation of 'Nasorean', meaning member of a specific sect. The town of Nazareth did not even exist in Jesus' day.[47])

Such extreme claims aside, however, there are still many enigmatic features about the Turin Shroud: the 'negative effect', the anatomical perfection and the sheer realism of the image.

Refusing to Lie Down

So we are faced with an astonishing enigma. The carbon dating tells us that the Shroud is a fake, but if it has been pronounced dead then this is one relic that resolutely refuses to lie down. In fact, most of the above characteristics are as incompatible with a fourteenth-century origin as they are with a first-century date.

Although we were determined to solve the mystery of the Shroud, at first our task seemed daunting, to say the least. If it were not for the carbon dating, we might have been tempted to fall in with the believers, for the evidence – as listed above – still appeared to be on their side. And had it not been for the astonishing events that were to come our way, we might still have been part of that uneasy coterie whom the rest of the world too glibly describes as 'flat earthers'.

But first we had to look at the known history of the Shroud, to glean from an often biased and selective story where the most awesome relic in Christendom could possibly have begun its career. Had it actually originated in a cold tomb in first-century Palestine – or was it created much nearer to our time, and even nearer to us geographically?

Where did the Turin Shroud come from?

2

The Verdict of History

'The case [against the Shroud's authenticity] is here so strong that . . . the possibility of an error in the verdict of history must be accounted as almost infinitesimal.'

Herbert Thurston, Society of Jesus, 1903[1]

The believers' biggest problem has always been that there is no historical evidence that the Shroud is older than – at the very best reckoning – 650 years. It simply appears, unheralded and without the slightest explanation of how it got there, in the middle of France some time in the second half of the fourteenth century. Both the mystery of its previous whereabouts and the very manner of its appearance tell against the Shroud's authenticity. If it is genuine, where was it for the thirteen centuries after the crucifixion? And how could the relic to end relics just drift casually into history? Surely something so potent, with so much potential for seizing the hearts and minds of the masses, would have been ushered in with fanfares, prayers and feasting.

Those worried by this glaring gap have made several suggestions to account for it, while others take the stance that the missing years can just be ignored, since the scientific evidence alone (apart from the carbon dating, of course) is, they claim, enough to guarantee the Shroud's authenticity. Before the carbon dating, the believers could argue that the weight of evidence was in favour of the Shroud being genuine, but now the scales have tipped the other way, and the only way in which the results can be undermined is by showing that the Shroud existed at least before the earlier date-limit of 1260.

As we have seen, another line of attack is to point to examples of the unreliability of carbon dating, or to argue that the samples taken were contaminated in some way. It is true that carbon dating has provided a good few howlers in its time, and that the tests are so sensitive that contamination is a recognised and constant problem (exposure to cigarette smoke, for example, renders a sample useless).

On the other hand, the same dates were arrived at by three separate laboratories, and the carbon dating pinpoints exactly the time of the Shroud's debut in the historical record – which many believe cannot be a coincidence. Nor can it be anything other than desperation that makes the same believers who argued most vociferously for the carbon dating tests the very people who are now most active in criticising the technique.

The pro-authenticity lobby, then, sees the Shroud's history in two parts: first the period of total mystery from the first century to its appearance in fourteenth-century France, followed by its accepted history from that time to the present day. But we were to discover that there are grounds for disputing even the second part. However, first we had to familiarise ourselves with the main events of the accepted history, especially those surrounding its sudden and dramatic appearance.

Out of Nowhere

Until 1983 today's Turin Shroud was the property of the House of Savoy, Italy's royal family. Their ownership can be traced back to the mid-fifteenth century, when they acquired it from the de Charnys, minor members of the French aristocracy, who owned it in the last part of the fourteenth century. The first documented reference to the de Charny Shroud dates from 1389. Before that there is total silence – nothing to show where and how the de Charnys had come by it.

Clearly that first document is critical to our understanding of the Shroud's origins. It was a letter from the Bishop of Troyes, Pierre d'Arcis, to Pope Clement VII – and it unequivocally denounces the Shroud as a fake, a cynical forgery created to defraud gullible pilgrims.[2]

The circumstances that compelled d'Arcis to pen his letter (which is generally known as the 'D'Arcis Memorandum' among Shroud researchers) were as follows: in his diocese was the insignificant village of Lirey, the family seat of the de Charny family and the site of a small collegiate church (one that houses an endowed chapter of canons). Those canons, with the approval of the head of the family, Geoffrey de Charny (known as Geoffrey II to avoid confusing him with his more illustrious father) had just begun to hold public expositions of a cloth that they claimed was the Shroud of Jesus, and upon which his image could be seen, miraculously imprinted. After investigating the matter, d'Arcis was convinced that it was a hoax and, incensed by such blatant exploitation, wrote to the Pope demanding that he ban the expositions.

They were certainly theatrical; lit by torches, the Shroud was held up by priests on a specially erected platform, high above the heads of the huge throngs eager to see the wondrous image. Later, to demonstrate his support for the canons in their dispute with d'Arcis, Geoffrey II took to raising the cloth with his own hands. The bishop's description of the image is all too brief, '[it is] the two-fold image of one man, that is to say, the back and the front,' but it does sound like today's Turin Shroud.

D'Arcis denounced it in the most forthright terms, accusing the Dean of Lirey of deceit and of being 'consumed with the passion of avarice', even going so far as to accuse him of hiring 'pilgrims' to feign miracle cures when the cloth was raised aloft.

He was also angry because in gaining Pope Clement's approval for the displays Geoffrey had gone over his head and made the request directly to the Papal Nuncio to France. When d'Arcis tried to intervene and threatened the Dean with excommunication, Geoffrey appealed to King Charles VI of France for a warrant to confirm his right to exhibit the Shroud – which he duly received.

But for later historians the most damning claim made by d'Arcis was that the image was painted. One of his predecessors, Henry of Poitiers, had carried out his own investigations and, d'Arcis said, 'discovered the fraud and how the cloth had been cunningly painted, the truth being attested to by the artist who had painted it, to wit, that it was a work of human skill and not miraculously wrought or bestowed'.

Unfortunately for d'Arcis, Pope Clement was related to the de Charny family – Geoffrey II's stepfather was his uncle – and instead of supporting his local representative he sided with the de Charnys, going to the remarkable length of commanding the bishop's 'perpetual silence' on pain of excommunication. He did, however, compromise to the extent that he decreed that the cloth could only be displayed as a 'likeness or representation' of Christ's Shroud.

The whole episode could be dismissed as a local dispute over just one of the many alleged holy relics that proliferated in Europe at the time – feathers from the wings of angels, countless splinters from the True Cross and a whole wardrobeful of the Virgin's chemises – were it not for the fact that seemingly the same relic would, 600 years later, still perplex modern scientists.

Even at this stage there seems to have been something going on behind the scenes beyond a mere tussle over a lucrative relic, or a local power struggle between bishop and lord. Geoffrey II's direct approach to the Pope, even given their kinship, was unusual and suggests it was a tactical move on his part. And Clement's threat of excommunication has a distinctly malodorous air of downright blackmail. As Ian Wilson remarked in his first book, 'One cannot escape the feeling that there is something missing, something more to the affair than meets the eye.'[3]

For those opposed to the Shroud's authenticity, the 'D'Arcis Memorandum' is proof that the Shroud was, and is, a painted fake. Believers have countered that it is equally correct to interpret that most damning phrase of d'Arcis as meaning that Henry of Poitiers had found not *the* artist who had painted the image, but *an* artist who had merely made a copy of it.[4] It is, however, a specious argument; it is true that the original Latin does allow for such an interpretation, but in the context the accepted version must be correct. What possible reason would the bishop have had for mentioning it otherwise?

Nor was d'Arcis the only one to make the claim that the image was painted. At one stage in the dispute Charles VI sent the Bailiff of Troyes to confiscate the Shroud, pending a judgement. (The Dean refused to hand it over.) The Bailiff's report survives to this day – and it, too, states bluntly that the image was a painting.[5]

The memorandum also yields another clue. The bishop states that the exhibitions were a revival of earlier displays that were held 'thirty-four years or thereabouts' before – that is, around 1355. It was on that occasion, according to d'Arcis, that Henry of Poitiers found the guilty artist and stopped the expositions. If true, this would make the first known owner of the Shroud Geoffrey II's father, also Geoffrey, in his day a famous knight and war hero of France.

There is no direct corroboration of the existence of the Lirey Shroud in Geoffrey I's day, and there are several reasons to doubt that it was being displayed in 1355. It was that Geoffrey who founded the Lirey church, and the records of its original endowment in 1353 (which still exist)[6] make no mention of the Shroud among the relics he donated. The church was consecrated by Bishop Henry of Poitiers in 1356 (again with no mention of the Shroud in the records),[7] something that seems unlikely if Henry had only a year before disciplined the canons over such a serious offence. However, d'Arcis' 'thirty-four years or thereabouts' does allow some leeway. Geoffrey I was, in fact, killed in battle less than four months after the consecration ceremony, dying a hero's death at the battle of Poitiers while shielding his king, Jean II, from an English lance-thrust with his own body. He had no opportunity to present the church with the Shroud in the intervening months, and public pilgrimages could not have been organised in such a short space of time. Some have therefore speculated that it was actually his widow, Jeanne de Vergy, who, left in financial difficulties after her husband's death, first displayed the Shroud to swell her coffers – even though Geoffrey himself had sought to keep it secret. This would put the date of the first expositions at 1357 or 58.[8]

The only independent testimony that the Shroud was exhibited at Lirey during the time of Geoffrey I or Jeanne de Vergy is a solitary pilgrim's badge recovered from the bed of the Seine in 1855 and now in the Musée de Cluny, Paris, which shows a Shroud-like image (unfortunately too small for any of the details to be properly made out). It has not been dated precisely, but because it includes the coats of arms of both the de Charny and de Vergy families – they were only united by the marriage of Geoffrey I and Jeanne – it has been suggested that the badge belonged to one of the first pilgrims who made the journey to Lirey to see the Shroud.

Throughout the historical dispute, however, neither the first nor the second Geoffrey de Charny ever described – at least in writing – how the Shroud came into his family's possession. How could the ultimate relic have virtually *sidled* into their hands? If it had been a trophy of war, they might be expected to have boasted of their bravery in capturing it. If they had bought it, or even won it in gaming, they might be expected to seek some congratulation, if only for their shrewdness. Even if the de

Charny family made a fetish out of modesty – and there is no
evidence that they did – surely they would have spoken out to
clear their names when accused of maintaining a hoax by d'Arcis
and Henry of Poitiers. But of the Shroud's provenance there is
silence. It is almost as if they had found it lying in the attic – or
as if they had conjured the image up through the skills of an
unscrupulous artist. After all, similar hoaxes happened before and
will no doubt happen again.

Fire, Flood and Fakery

After the Pope silenced the bishop with his threat of excommunication, Geoffrey II continued to exhibit the Shroud at Lirey
(although as 'a likeness or representation' only) until his death in
1398, when it was inherited by his daughter Margaret. She was
married and widowed twice – her first husband falling at
Agincourt, her second being the wealthy Humbert of Villersexel
(whose other titles included Lord of St-Hippolyte-sur-Doubs
and Count de la Roche). She remained childless.

In 1418 Margaret and Humbert removed the Shroud from
Lirey Church, ostensibly for safekeeping during the troubled
times following the English victory at Agincourt – and were
promptly sued by the canons for making off with what they
regarded as their property. Until 1449 the relic was kept in a
chapel on Humbert's land at St-Hippolyte-sur-Doubs in the
Franche-Comté region, where annual expositions were then
held.

Humbert died in 1438; eleven years later Margaret took the
Shroud to Belgium, where it was displayed at Liège. The local
bishop appointed two professors to investigate the Shroud who
concluded it was a fake.[9] Three years later it was exhibited back
in France, at Germolles. It is usually assumed that, despite being
seventy and presumably frail, Margaret insisted on travelling

because she was seeking a suitable guardian for her family's treas-ured possession – she was the last of her line, after all – but this is just speculation.

Finally, some time before 1464, she gave the Shroud to the wealthy dukedom of Savoy, then headed by Louis and his wife Anne de Lusignan, Queen of Jerusalem, in return for a castle and land. At least, it is presumed that they were exchanged for the Shroud; selling a holy relic would have been regarded as improper, so there is no proof of this supposed grand barter. (The land may have been a gift, however, for Margaret's second husband was known to have been closely associated with the Savoys.)

Was Margaret genuinely concerned that the greatest relic of all should find a good home? And if so, is that in itself evidence that she believed it to be authentic? Or was she merely lining her pockets as the chill of her declining years began to bite? We will never know, but each action of the historical guardians of the Shroud has been – and will continue to be – mulled over and interpreted in strikingly different ways depending upon the beliefs of the interpreter. There are many such examples of this selective reading of history.

For example, in the pro-authenticity literature, the Shroud's subsequent owners – Louis, Duke of Savoy and his wife Anne – are usually described as being extremely pious and noble; Anne especially being singled out for her spirituality. The reason given for this uncritical view is simply the fact that they surrounded themselves with monks and priests. Historians generally, how-ever, are less kind – and less naive – seeing Louis as a weak man completely under the thumb of his dominant and ambitious wife. Indeed, one commentator goes so far as to call her 'the evil genius' of the Savoy family.[10] The *Encyclopaedia Britannica* describes Louis as 'indolent, incapable and ruled by his wife',[11] while the Siennese poet and diplomat Aeneas Sylvius states that Anne was 'a wife incapable of obeying married to a man inca-pable of commanding'.[12]

The House of Savoy had grown steadily in wealth, influence and territory since the early eleventh century, until by Margaret de Charny's day they controlled large areas of the old kingdom of Burgundy, covering parts of modern France, Switzerland and Italy. Louis' father, Amadeus VIII – who died in 1449 – was the first to be granted the dukedom (until then the Savoys were mere counts), and was one of the most remarkable characters of the period. An archetypal early Renaissance prince, Amadeus was a patron of the arts who was equally respected as a soldier and peacemaker, and was renowned throughout Europe for his piety. In 1434 he renounced his title in favour of his son and went into retreat at the monastery of St Maurice at Capaille. But five years later he reluctantly came out of retirement when he was declared Pope Felix IV, despite the fact that he had never taken holy orders.

Louis clearly had a lot to live up to; no doubt he felt the strain of maintaining such notable piety. But for aspiring noble families of the Middle Ages the best status symbols were undoubtedly the rarest of holy relics; what could be better than the Holy Shroud itself?

Unfortunately, Anne's scheming, Louis' weakness and the continued war between the countries on either side of Savoy, France and Italy, meant that the family suffered a decline. And so did the Shroud. Between the year they acquired it and its public exposition at Vercelli on Good Friday, 1494, it seems to have virtually disappeared from public view, precisely at a time when its pulling power might have helped them financially.

Although it was known to have remained among the Savoys' possessions, it was remarkably quiescent during a full forty-year period. It is not even certain where it was kept, although it was certainly at the forefront of their minds – they enlarged their principal church at Chambéry between 1471 and 1502 specifically to house the Shroud. *Or perhaps it was to be the home of a new, and better, Shroud?* Could it be that arrangements were underway throughout this 'silent' phase to provide the world with a more impressive holy relic?

Certainly, following its 'reappearance' in 1494 there was an enormous change in the way it was publicly perceived. Until then the only official line was that it was merely a 'representation' of Jesus' Shroud. However, during the 1470s this view was challenged by Pope Sixtus IV (Francesco della Rovere), who championed it as the true Shroud in his book *On the Blood of Christ* (written in 1464, but not published until 1471, after he became Pope). On his election he accorded special honours and privileges to the Chambéry church, to him the last resting place of the cloth that had held Christ's body. It was especially important to him because he laid great emphasis on the redemptive power of Christ's actual blood – and was not the Shroud itself imbued with this potent and mystical power?

It is unlikely, however, that Sixtus ever saw the Shroud. Its real apotheosis came when his nephew, Julius II, granted the title 'Sainte Chapelle of the Holy Shroud' to the chapel at Chambéry and gave the cloth its own feast day, 4 May. Annual expositions followed, on a far grander scale than those at Lirey a century and a half earlier. All this, of course, proved extremely lucrative for the dukes of Savoy and the clergy of Chambéry; huge revenues from pilgrims and gifts from Europe's nobility poured in to swell their coffers. Fifty years on, Louis of Savoy's investment had finally begun to show a dividend. Not surprisingly, the Shroud became the family's most prized possession, almost taking on the role of a protective talisman.

But disaster – almost – struck. During the night of 3–4 December 1532, a great blaze swept through the Sainte Chapelle in Chambéry. The Shroud was kept in a locked silver casket, which was itself locked behind a metal grille. Ironically, this elaborate security arrangement nearly brought about the relic's destruction – the fire spread too quickly for the terror-stricken nuns to fetch the key-holders. Luckily, the town blacksmith managed to reach the chapel in time and prised open the grille. The precious casket was carried to safety by one of the Duke's officials and two priests. The silver casket had, however, begun to melt in the intense heat, and a drop of molten silver had set the cloth alight. The flames were quickly doused, but the scars of the fire, and the tidemarks of the water, are still clearly visible.

The fire is important, not only because of the damage it caused to the cloth, but also because it is constantly cited as evidence for some theory or another about how the image was formed, and it is regularly quoted as a reason for the 'freak' carbon dating results. Some have speculated that before the fire the image had been painted, and that the image visible today was caused by a reaction in the pigment or some other effect due to the heat.[13] More recently there have been claims that the chemical changes in the linen interfered with the carbon dating results, making the cloth appear much younger than it was.[14] It has also been proposed that the original Lirey Shroud was destroyed in the fire, and that today's Turin Shroud was a Renaissance replacement. The idea is not new.

Rumours circulated within weeks of the fire that the Shroud had not survived, and they grew to such proportions that a papal commission was sent to investigate. It was almost a year and a half later that the Shroud, with patches over the burnt parts and a new backing cloth of a coarse linen known as holland, was returned to the Sainte Chapelle. But the Shroud had not been destroyed in the fire: the Lierre copy, made in 1516, shows the 'poker marks', which must have been made before 1532, and other earlier evidence of damage.

In 1578 the Shroud was transferred to the Cathedral at Turin – which is dedicated to St John the Baptist – something that, in the light of our later discoveries, was to prove enormously significant. Turin was the new capital of the Savoy lands, and the Shroud was to remain there except for the years of the Second World War, when it was taken to the Abbey of Montevergine at Avellino in the south.

The Duchy of Savoy gradually shifted its affiliations, becoming steadily more pro-Italian, a process finally complete in the middle of the seventeenth century when Savoy became an independent Italian state. On the unification of Italy the House of Savoy was elected to be the new state's royal line. The Shroud remained their greatest treasure, even after the monarchy was abolished and the family exiled in 1946. Even when living in Portugal, the last king, Umberto II, continued to be consulted about its care and display, while the clergy of the cathedral acted as its custodians until Umberto's death in 1983, when he bequeathed it to the Vatican. (His widow, as we shall see, was considerably more sceptical about it, and had no hesitation in denouncing it as a fake.) The Pope is now the Shroud's official custodian, although in practice this role is delegated to the Archbishop of Turin.

The Shroud was moved to a specially built chapel, designed by Guarino Guarini, in 1694. In its early Turin days it was displayed on its feast day – 4 May – but later it became the custom to do so only for special occasions, often with a gap of decades. It remained there, locked away above the altar in its silver casket, for exactly 300 years, until, during repairs to the Royal Chapel in 1994, it was moved to the main body of the cathedral. There – still in its casket – it was placed in a bullet-proof glass case that weighed some three tons.

Ironically, not for the first time in the Shroud's history, the security precautions – taken to prevent it being stolen or vandalised – nearly led to its demise. Shortly after 11 p.m. on 11 April 1997, the cathedral was the victim of an arson attack, and by the time the Turin fire brigade arrived, the Royal Chapel – where the fire had started – was completely gutted and the conflagration was taking hold in the main part of the building, threatening to engulf the Royal Palace of the Savoys, which is attached. Luckily, a banquet in the palace for some 130 distinguished guests – including guest of honour United Nations Secretary General Kofi Annan, the ex-Prime Minister of Italy, Giulio Andreotti, and the head of Fiat, Giovanni Agnelli – had finished only ten minutes before the fire broke out.

At any moment the domed roof threatened to collapse on the cathedral's – not to mention Catholicism's – most precious relic. Apparently after a curious delay of an hour, the fire brigade was summoned: by then the fire had taken hold and it seemed that the arsonists would succeed. But they had reckoned without fireman Mario Trematore who, with the fire raging around him, battered the thick bullet-proof glass with a sledgehammer until it gave way, allowing him to carry off the casket to safety.

While the heroic Trematore had been battering the glass case until his hands bled, a crowd of 3,000 people had gathered in the darkness outside, many praying for the safety of the Shroud. Perhaps their prayers were answered – certainly, Cardinal Saldarini was in no doubt about it, declaring the rescue of the relic to be 'a miracle'.

After that traumatic event, the Shroud (now permanently unfolded) was, for a time, put into a huge mobile display case, also of bullet-proof glass, which was kept at a secret location. However, in March 2001 it was (at least so we are told) put in its new permanent home within the side chapel.

In 2002 the Shroud itself experienced the most radical change in the way it is kept since the previous fire that nearly destroyed it. On 20 June 2002, as usual under conditions of the strictest secrecy (nothing at all was revealed until the work had been completed), the Swiss expert on textile conservation Mechthild Flury-Lemberg began a thirty-two-day examination of the Shroud. During this she removed the holland backing cloth (in place since 1534, except when it was partially removed by STURP so that the underside could be examined) as well as the many patches over holes (mostly those over damage caused by the 1532 fire). At the end of the exercise, Flury-Lemberg stitched on a new backing cloth of raw linen but did not replace the patches.

The revelation of the secret examination of, and modifications to, the cloth sparked off the predictable heated row in the Shroudie world, as it rapidly divided into two camps: on the one hand, those who believed that removing the old cloth and patches had destroyed vital clues and evidence about the Shroud's past, or had even contaminated the cloth itself – for example, they alleged that Flury-Lemberg and her assistant failed to wear sufficient protective clothing or gloves during their work, and did not adequately protect the Shroud from exposure to light or the Turin air – and questioned why all this work had been done in secret and without any consultation with outside scientific institutions; on the other those who approved of the Church's actions. Typically, this seemingly inoffensive difference of opinion led to real acrimony and many bitter exchanges.

A Suspicious Silence

The Shroud's journey through history was not all smooth, and there were many sceptical voices raised at every opportunity. One of the most frequently voiced objections to its authenticity is the fact that a miraculously imprinted Shroud is not mentioned in the New Testament at all. It does not figure either in the story of the Resurrection, which relies heavily on miracles, nor is it mentioned in the Acts of the Apostles or in the Epistles, where every possible evidence of Jesus' divinity is harnessed as propaganda. Surely, say the sceptics, if such a thing had existed, it would have been one of the most heavily promoted aspects of the whole Christian story. Yet it is not there at all.

With distinctly Jesuitical logic, some have even managed to use this argument in support of the Shroud's authenticity. They argue that a medieval forger would not have faked a relic that was not mentioned in the gospels[15] – although quite how this accords with the popularity of, say, Our Lady's chemises, is not explained.

As usual, interpretations of the original Greek gospels are combed for supporting material. The Synoptic Gospels of Matthew, Mark and Luke describe Jesus being buried in a single piece of cloth. The Gospel of John – arguably the only eyewitness account of the burial[16] – has the body being wrapped in several 'linen bands' or othonia, and a soudarion (sweat cloth) which was separate from them. No-one knows how big these bands were, or their precise function. It seems unlikely, however, that a strip of cloth would match the dimensions of today's Turin Shroud, which is a quite massive 14 feet (4m) long.

Some contend that the soudarion fits the bill, while others shrink it to no more than a sort of holy facecloth. But the real point about the Gospels is that they never describe the cloths as blood-stained, nor do they mention a miraculously imprinted Shroud at all. On these grounds alone are we justified in condemning the Shroud as a fake? Many think so, but there are several other objections.

Debate also rages about whether or not the image of the corpse conforms to, or contradicts, first-century Jewish burial practice. It is unlikely, however, that any conclusion will be reached, as our knowledge of this esoteric area is limited, and again, somewhat speculative. More significantly, there were no relics bandied about in the earliest days of the Church – a fact that in itself immediately casts doubt on those that surfaced abruptly in the golden age of relics, some 1300 years later.

Then again, believers claim that the image – perhaps due to some anomalous chemical reaction between the body and the spice-impregnated cloth – could have 'developed' over time, and may not have been visible for months, even years, after Jesus' death. But in this case, why would the bereaved disciples have kept it in the first place, when there was nothing remarkable to see on it? The 'developing' process would hardly take over 100 years, roughly the time it took for the New Testament to have been written. Surely a miraculous image of Jesus would have deserved even the most last minute of 'stop presses'?

If a miraculously imprinted Shroud had been somehow accidentally omitted from the New Testament, might not a rumour of such a relic have circulated among the wonder-hungry early Church? But there was not so much as a whisper about such a holy artefact. The early Church was Shroudless.

Then again, did Jesus actually look like the man on the Shroud of Turin? There is no physical description of him in the New Testament, but the Biblical commentator Robert Eisler has found evidence in the Apocryphal texts to show that Jesus was short, possibly even hunchbacked. This is not, of course, our idea of what Jesus looked like. Enter almost any Western church and you see a proliferation of statues, engravings, stained-glass windows and so on showing a tall, strapping man with a handsome, narrow face, forked beard and hair parted in the middle: an image that has entered the collective unconscious, but which almost certainly came at least in part from the Turin Shroud. The fact that it owes nothing to historical accuracy is almost neither here nor there. To most people, this is what Jesus looked like, and to challenge it, perhaps putting in its place a pitiful hunchback, is to chip away at the very foundation of the emotional hold of Christianity. Whoever faked the Turin Shroud created a template for our concept of Jesus, either deliberately or accidentally. Whoever faked the Turin Shroud used a model who was to become in time the Jesus of our very dreams.

The Rivals

The Shroud only surfaced in 1357. If it is genuine, where was it before that? If it had existed, it would have been the most prized and sacred relic in Christendom; how could it have remained anonymous and unmentioned for well over a thousand years?

However, between the sixth and thirteenth centuries there were references to supposed shrouds of Jesus. Relics of the Son of God himself were naturally the most sought after, but seeing as he was believed to have ascended bodily into heaven, believers had to make do with associated items, such as bits of the True Cross or the Crown of Thorns, and such things as his alleged milk teeth and his strangely numerous foreskins – all seven of them – went the rounds.

Bits of shroud, or mummy-like wrappings, had been venerated since the fifth century, when one such relic had been taken to Constantinople, and another was seen by a Frankish bishop in Jerusalem in the mid-seventh century. Others were brought into Europe by returning Crusaders, such as the Shroud of Cadouin (shown recently to be an eleventh-century Muslim cloth). Another European contender was the Shroud of Compiègne in France, acquired by Charlemagne at the end of the eighth century and preserved until its destruction during the French Revolution in 1789.

Naturally the two greatest collections of relics in Christendom would not have been considered complete without their own 'Shrouds'; that of the Byzantine Emperor in Constantinople boasted one from the late eleventh century, and the thirteenth-century collection of Saint Louis IX housed one in the Sainte Chapelle in Paris. Altogether there were more than forty rival claimants for the title of 'Holy Shroud' – and the claims of every one of them have been minutely examined by historians.[17] Yet in only one case – an isolated reference dating from 1203 – is there any possibility that it might have been the Lirey or Turin Shroud in an earlier guise. In all the other cases, the dimensions are completely different and, most significantly of all, in no instance (except in that 1203 reference) is there any mention of a miraculous image. In other words, alleged shrouds of Jesus may have been relatively thick on the ground, but in almost all cases they were blank pieces of cloth. Clearly this was because the exhibitors did not know they were supposed to fake an *image*, and because the story was completely unknown.

Of course that single 1203 reference has excited interest in predictable circles as the only potential precursor of the Lirey Shroud, providing answers to why the Shroud had managed to remain completely unknown for so long.

In the Middle Ages, the single greatest collection of relics was kept not in Rome, but in the centre of the Eastern Orthodox Church – in the Pharos Chapel of the Byzantine Emperor, in the grounds of his imperial palace in Constantinople. In 1204 the city was looted by soldiers of the Fourth Crusade – fellow Christians – and soon afterwards Europe was flooded with stolen relics. Shortly before the ransacking of Constantinople, the French knight Robert de Clari recorded, in the church of St Mary of Blachernae: '. . . the *sydoine* in which our Lord had been wrapped, and which stood up straight every Friday so that the *figure* of our Lord could be plainly seen there.'

He goes on to say that, after the city was sacked six months later, this *sydoine* disappeared. Was it destroyed in the fighting or was it absorbed into the booty of some European knight?

De Clari's memoir is beloved of Shroudies everywhere, for it is seen as proof that a shroud bearing an image existed well before the time of Geoffrey de Charny, and therefore before the period indicated by the carbon dating. But there are problems with it.

The chronicler is not regarded as reliable; the preferred account of the Fourth Crusade is that of Geoffrey de Villehardouin. Not only was he a meticulous observer, but he was also a veteran diplomat who actually worked with the leaders of the Crusade. And he never mentions such a *sydoine*.

Although de Clari describes a shroud complete with image, he gives too few details for it to be compared at all objectively with today's Turin Shroud. There is even some dispute over whether the Old French *figure* refers to a full-length image or, as in modern French, simply means a face. (The consensus is, however, in favour of the former.) It is not even certain that de Clari is claiming that he actually saw the *sydoine* with his own eyes, since he only describes visiting the church 'in which it was displayed' – he might simply have been told about it.

At the same time a plain – unimaged – Shroud was among the relics catalogued for the Pharos Chapel, which had definitely been there since the 1090s. Like all of the most sacred relics of the Byzantine Empire, this Shroud was deemed too holy for the masses, being kept for the eyes of the privileged only and never shown publicly.[18] The very fact that de Clari's *sydoine* was displayed on a weekly basis shows that – whether it was today's Turin Shroud or not – it was certainly not regarded as a major relic. And just to confuse matters further, Geoffrey de Villehardouin[19] states that St Mary's Church escaped the looting of the city. So, tantalising though de Clari's story may be, it is inadmissible evidence for the existence of the Shroud before the time of the Geoffreys of Charny.

Shroudies are not so easily put off; all attempts to reconstruct a pre-Lirey history for the Turin Shroud still include de Clari's note. But how did the Shroud find its way from first-century Palestine to the Constantinople of 1203, then on to Lirey in the 1350s – and all against a background of its official (that is, Biblical) non-existence? There is one idea that may just save the day for the Shroudies here: Ian Wilson's famous Mandylion theory, which was developed from the work of Father Maurus Green.

'Not Made by Hands'?

In his 1978 bestselling *The Turin Shroud*, Wilson claims the Shroud had indeed appeared throughout those early years, but under another name, that of the Holy Mandylion of Edessa. (Henry

Lincoln's film, *The Silent Witness*, based on an idea by Wilson, also makes this claim.)

The Mandylion was a cloth that bore a miraculous image of Jesus' face – an object referred to from its first appearance as *acheiropoietos*, Greek for 'not made by human hands'. Like the Turin Shroud, some of its history is documented fact, while some remains in the realm of legend. It emerged as the most sacred relic of the city of Edessa in what is now Turkey in the second half of the sixth century, where it remained until 944. It was then forcibly removed – despite violent protests from the local faithful – to Constantinople to join the Emperor's huge collection of relics in the Pharos Chapel. There it stayed until the looting of 1204, when de Clari's *sydoine* also vanished. Superficially at least, it does seem as if the hypothesis that the Mandylion and the Turin Shroud were one and the same has something going for it. After all, neither was 'made by hands'. (Although even here the holes in this evidence are clear: the shared *acheiropoietos* label is a matter of faith, and trying to prove similarities between two things that were *missing* seems to be clutching at straws!)

The immediate objection is that the Mandylion bore the image of Jesus' face only – the word implies a small, handkerchief-sized cloth. It was supposed to be a towel imprinted during his lifetime, unlike the Shroud image that was created after his death and bore the likeness of his whole body. Although Wilson has supplied counter-arguments, some background is essential.

During the life of the Mandylion, relics had a different function in the Middle East from their European counterparts. In Europe they were officially objects of devotion, while being enormously lucrative for the Church. In the Middle East they represented political status and power, and often had a talismanic potency, being seen as protectors of the city that owned them, warding off foreign invasions and natural disasters alike. Known as *palladia*, every city had such a holy prophylactic, and Edessa's was the Mandylion – a fitting honour for the first city to be evangelised in Byzantium.

The relic was first mentioned by the chronicler Evagrius in the 590s when he told how its miraculous powers repelled an attack by the Persian army fifty years previously. To explain its provenance, there are only legends that link the cloth to a King Abgar V of Edessa – a contemporary of Jesus.

According to the legends, Abgar wrote to Jesus asking him to come to Edessa to cure him of a terrible illness. Jesus' written reply was itself deemed Edessa's most holy relic – until the Mandylion appeared. Shortly after the crucifixion the Apostle Thaddeus travelled to Edessa and cured the king, converting him to Christianity.

In fact, once the cloth was established as the primary relic towards the end of the sixth century, the legends were adapted to link it with King Abgar. There are two versions: in one Jesus had caused an image of his face to appear on a towel with which he wiped his face, and which he then sent along with his letter to King Abgar. The second is that the image was created during the Agony in Gethsemane, and it was taken by Thaddeus to Edessa. Either way, it was a miraculous cloth that healed Abgar and brought about his conversion. Abgar's successors, however, reverted to paganism, so the Mandylion was hidden – bricked up in a niche above one of the city's gateways. Here it remained for 500 years until it was rediscovered and came to the aid of the city.

The story can be dismissed as a fable that had been concocted after the discovery of the cloth to give it a suitably holy and miraculous pedigree. But if it does have similarities to the Turin Shroud, it may be argued – as Wilson has – that the legends preserve a memory of genuine events involving an imaged cloth taken to Edessa shortly after Jesus' death.

While it was in Edessa the Mandylion was deemed too holy to be copied, and was never displayed publicly, so there are no eyewitness accounts of it. Even in Constantinople it was kept strictly for the Emperor and his honoured guests. There are no known firsthand copies, so it is impossible to reconstruct its true appearance.

Although this relic showed only a face and not a whole body image, Wilson argues that before it was hidden, the cloth had been folded so that only the face was visible. It is a fact that if the Turin Shroud were folded in half four times, the face would fit exactly into the uppermost section, showing nothing of the body. If the Shroud were then fixed to a board and covered with some kind of ornamental metalwork – and there is some evidence that the Mandylion was – the cloth could easily have gone through history without its owners knowing that it was a full-length shroud.

Support for this theory comes from one of the earliest texts to describe the Mandylion, the late-sixth-century Acts of Thaddeus.[20] Telling how Jesus dried his face on a towel, the cloth is described as *tetradiplon*. This is a totally unknown and untraceable word – indeed, this is its only known use – and because of the context it is usually translated as 'towel'. But its literal meaning is 'doubled in four', according to Wilson.

He argues that the later Abgar legends are based on the true event of the Shroud arriving in Edessa soon after the crucifixion, and that it really was preserved bricked up in a city gateway for 500 years. He believes it was discovered thanks to rebuilding work needed after the great flood of 525, and that the city fathers kept its discovery a secret until the Persian attack nineteen years later.

During its time in Edessa, the Mandylion was not known to be merely part of a larger image, but some time after its arrival in Constantinople – says Wilson – its true nature was rediscovered, although not made public. It then became the *sydoine* seen by Robert de Clari in 1203. Looted by Crusaders in the next year and brought to Europe, it eventually made its way into the hands of Geoffrey de Charny in the 1350s.

The plausibility of this theory hangs on the veracity of Evagrius' story, and Professor Averil Cameron of King's College Ancient History Department in London has pointed out that there is every reason to treat his account with caution.[21] Evagrius said that the Mandylion was used to repel the Persians in 544, but he was writing fifty years after the event. And another chronicler, Procopius, writing just five or six years after the event, makes no mention of it at all. Even more significant is the fact that Evagrius based his account on that of Procopius. Presumably Evagrius invented the story to give Edessa's holy relic more eminence than those of rival cities, and therefore there is no proof that the Mandylion existed in 544. In fact, all the evidence suggests that it did *not* exist – at least at that time (and, indeed, for many years afterward).

Other cities used their *acheiropoietos* images in the years between the accounts of Procopius and Evagrius: for example, one at Memphis in Egypt in the 570s and another at Camuliana, Cappodocia in the 560s. If the Mandylion had been discovered in 544 it may well have been the original that inspired them, but the 590 date makes it just another in a long line of similar relics. And if the story was an invention, then there was no link between Abgar and Jesus.

The term *acheiropoietos*, however, does appear to indicate that the image was mysterious, until one realises that even quite blatantly manufactured images were also said to be 'not made by hands' – one of the quainter traditions of the medieval Church. In the Lateran Palace in Rome, for example, a painting of Jesus is known as 'The Acheropita' (the Latin equivalent). Even a mosaic was given this title. Obviously it came to refer to a specific genre of religious art; it cannot be used to uphold the authenticity of the Mandylion or of anything else.

There is also a serious contradiction in Wilson's argument about the meaning of the word *tetradiplon* in the Acts of Thaddeus. According to Wilson, when this was written in the sixth century no-one knew that the Mandylion was actually the folded Shroud. Why then does the writer of the Acts of Thaddeus call it 'doubled in four', especially as he is clearly talking about a facecloth?

'Mandylion' derives from the Latin *mantile*, which means 'hand-cloth', to which the diminutive ending -ion has been added.[22] Both stress that this was a *tiny* thing. Yet Ian Wilson dismisses the etymology of the word as being no more significant than the nickname of Robin Hood's side-kick Little John[23] – in which case this must be the only example of heavy ecclesiastical irony being applied to a holy relic! As the Turin Shroud is 50 square feet (5m²), surely it would have been somewhat bulky for a facecloth? Even the most dimwitted removal man would have wondered at its sheer weight.

There are other problems with Wilson's hypothesis. He says that at some stage the Mandylion was discovered to be the full-sized cloth bearing the image, and it then became the *sydoine* recorded by Robert de Clari in the St Mary of Blachernae Church. But the inventory of relics for Constantinople's Pharos Chapel listed the Mandylion *and* an unimaged shroud – so the *sydoine* could not have been the Mandylion.[24] In fact, de Clari actually mentions the Mandylion in an earlier passage about the Pharos Chapel.[25] Wilson counters that after the discovery of the full image the Mandylion became the *sydoine* and a false Mandylion was put in its place, although there seems to be no earthly reason for this elaborate subterfuge, especially as the *sydoine* was regarded as the lesser of the two relics. If you have the real thing, why try to make it something else?

In fact Wilson himself relies on the Shroud having been worshipped as just a head in his reconstruction of what happened to it between 1204 and its appearance at Lirey 150 years later. He says it became the infamous idol head worshipped by the Knights Templar (a chivalric order founded in about 1118 and suppressed in 1312) – although according to our research Jesus' shroud image would be the very last thing the Templars would want to worship. In other words, Wilson fills the Shroud's missing years by equating it with three equally mysterious objects – the Mandylion, the *sydoine* and the Templar idol. But to do so he has to assume that it was originally believed to be just a head. Then, according to his theory, the full image was discovered and displayed, but then the Templars seemed to forget that it had a body, reverting to displaying it to members of their own order as just a head. Depending on Wilson's argument, it is either a head or a full figure. He wants it both ways.

Another episode in the Mandylion's career indicates that it was a simple painted image. It was pawned in the eighth century by the Edessan rulers to pay taxes to one Athanasius, a member of a rival Christian sect, the Monophysites. But when it was redeemed he gave them a copy he had had painted and gave the original to his Monophysite baptistry.[26] As the Edessans were completely fooled by his trick, was the original just such a painting? Significantly, the best modern artists have failed to reproduce a convincing Shroud image, and a painted copy would be very obvious immediately.

Philip McNair, a professor of Italian with an interest in the Shroud, has objected to the Mandylion theory. He suggests that if it had been the Shroud with just the head section on display, then the cloth would have yellowed, the image faded, and the difference would be noticeable today.[27] In fact, although the background of the cloth is evenly coloured, the head image itself is actually darker than the rest.

An Ill Wind

Is there any way of proving the Shroud's history? A great many people we have talked to during the course of our research have cited the work (published in 1976) of Dr Max Frei, the forensic scientist, as ultimate proof of the authenticity of the cloth. (In fact, at one point the phrase 'but what about the pollen?' was, not entirely seriously, considered as a title for this book.) Frei's palynological work was, however, as we hope to show, very flawed from a scientific point of view.

Frei identified pollen trapped in the fibres of the Shroud as belonging to species of plants found only in Palestine, the Anatolian steppes surrounding Edessa (modern Urfa) and around Constantinople (Istanbul). From this it was reasonable to conclude that the cloth had, at some time in its chequered career, been in each of those three places – exactly, in fact, the places proposed by Wilson. This was not a coincidence.

Accounts of Frei's work give the impression that he took his samples from the Shroud and identified the plants from which they had come by comparing them to catalogued pollen from around the world. Then, it is assumed, he compared the identified samples to their known geographical distribution, and independently arrived at the same conclusion as Wilson. Not so.

Before Frei's work there had been virtually no systematic collection and classification of pollen, so he himself had to build up the database with which to compare his own samples. Although one of the most important criteria of scientific investigation is that results should be verifiable by others, in this case it was impossible to do so.

There were also no controls to which his results might be compared. Frei's work was based on the premise that pollen grain husks are virtually indestructible, and this also implies that they could be carried great distances over a period of millennia. Any ancient piece of cloth would be bound to pick up stray pollen husks from a great many places. With this in mind, finding grains from, say, Urfa is not significant unless they exist in such a proliferation on the cloth that they are definitely above the level that might find its way there by accident over the years.

No-one knows where the cloth was woven. Neither is it known where and when it was kept before being imprinted with the image. It could have been kept directly in the path of a wind blowing straight in from Urfa almost constantly, for all we know.

There are also some clues as to how Frei's work seems only too neatly to reinforce Wilson's reconstructed history of the Shroud in the background to his research. After taking the samples in 1973, it seems Frei's work ground to a halt for lack of funds. Then in 1976, producer David Rolfe began to work on the film *The Silent Witness*, based on a script by Ian Wilson, with the Mandylion theory at its centre. Rolfe and Wilson roughed it in various inhospitable parts of the Middle East (heroically coping with the puzzling but complete lack of sanitation at Urfa), looking for locations for the film: Rolfe paid for Frei to go with them. It was from samples collected on this trip that he completed his work and presented his conclusions.[28]

True, Frei did match pollen found on the Shroud to plants unique to the three locations suggested by Ian Wilson, but then he *only looked in those three places.* The Mandylion theory demands that the Shroud had been in those three places – and those three only. If, for example, there was evidence that it had been in Toledo, the entire theory would be invalidated. Yet for all we know there is Australian pollen on the Shroud: Frei did not look for it. Both Wilson and Rolfe, however, must have been pleased with his work, which justified the gamble of Rolfe's funding of Frei's trip, and one could easily conclude that the latter may have regarded it as a loan repaid. Perhaps his sponsors would not have been so keen to enlist his help if they had known that he was, in the years to come, to be the man who disastrously authenticated the 'Hitler diaries'.[29]

Frei's work has been criticised by other experts as being too selective. And it received scant support from STURP – they found 'very few pollen' on the samples that they took.[30] This is one of the lynchpins of the case for the authenticity of the Shroud. Although it has never been claimed that this dates the Shroud, Shroudies love the pollen because it appears to make the all-important connection with both Jerusalem and Ian Wilson's Mandylion theory. However, the more one looks into it, the more Frei's case falls apart.

Astonishingly, although he published his conclusions, his detailed paper showing how he reached them remains unpublished, even after thirty years, despite the fact that making all the data publicly available is normally a prerequisite for publishing a scientific paper.[31] (Frei died in 1983, but his manuscript is owned by the American pro-Shroud group ASSIST – the Association of Scientists and Scholars for the Shroud of Turin, Inc. – who also have his original tape samples.) To accept any conclusions without seeing all the relevant data is simply not science, but even without it, there are severe problems with Frei's work.

He claims to have identified 58 specific plant species based on his visual analysis of the pollen. Other specialists, such as Smithsonian Institute botanist Richard H. Eyde and Dr Oliver Rackham of Corpus Christi College, Cambridge have pointed out that this is *impossible* using current methods. It is only possible to identify the genus or family of the plants to which the pollen belongs, not the species. Eyde says: 'This is so well known, that the burden of proof is on the one who says he's identified a species by its pollen. The identifier must say what traits separate the identified grain from grains of related plants.'[32] And, as Rackham points out, Frei's claims to have pinpointed species that grow only in specific geographical areas are crucial to his case.[33] In fact, his whole case depends on it.

Ian Wilson argues that Frei *may* have devised a new method that enabled him to identify species, and that the secret of this new technique *may* be contained in his unpublished papers.[34] Or, of course, it may not. We may never know one way or the other.

Incredulity has also been expressed that the majority of pollen grains found by Frei come from Palestine and Turkey.[35] As the Shroud has, according to the accepted history, been in France and Italy for the last 650 years, we should expect most of the pollen to come from European species. This has prompted many to have grave suspicions about Frei's work as a whole.

But the most serious allegations against him were made by the noted American Shroud sceptic Joe Nickell and the micro-biologist Walter McCrone (of whom more later), a friend of Max Frei. Both examined his tapes when they were acquired by ASSIST in 1988 and were puzzled by the fact that the pollen samples were in the wrong place on the tapes – on the leading edges, rather than in the middle. McCrone initially put this down to 'contamination' but later wrote to Nickell: 'At the time I remember saying diplomatically that they were "contamination . . ." It is very doubtful that they were present on the Shroud itself and sampled by Max [Frei]. The fact that they are then present indicates that the tape had to be pulled back so that they could be introduced and I see no good reason for that except skul-duggery.'[36]

If Frei's samples were adulterated with pollen from the Middle East, how did it get there? Perhaps it should be remembered that in between taking his samples from the Shroud and publishing his conclusions, Frei had been to Israel and Turkey with Ian Wilson and the producer of the film *The Silent Witness*. Perhaps he picked the pollen up then. But whatever happened on that trip, allegedly finding pollen from those particular places on the Shroud was to provide the *only* evidence to link it with Palestine, and the sole physical evidence to support Wilson's Mandylion theory.

Adoration of the Templars

The Shroud is not, then, another incarnation of the Mandylion. But where was it from 1204 to its sudden appearance in Lirey in the late 1350s? Again, Wilson endeavoured to provide the answers. He believed that the Shroud was taken to France by Crusaders who sacked Constantinople. To explain the bewildering silence on the subject that followed, he invokes that most enigmatic military order, the Knights Templar.

The Templars were, ostensibly, an order of soldier-monks founded to safeguard the passage of pilgrims to the Holy Land in the early twelfth century. Soon they became influential and wealthy, with branches in most European countries, but as their power increased, so did the machinations of their enemies.

With varying degrees of plausibility they have been put forward as custodians of the Holy Grail, the progenitors of Freemasonry, protectors of the bloodline of Jesus – and, most recently, they have been persuasively implicated in the search for the lost Ark of the Covenant. Although historians complain that the Templars are all too often employed to plug gaps in history, their background is so murky, and the rumours surrounding them are so extraordinary, it is no wonder that they are invoked by anyone keen to find answers to the most enduring of mysteries.

The Order of the Poor Knights of the Temple of Solomon – to give the Templars their proper title – was founded in Jerusalem in around 1118, shortly after the First Crusade, by just nine knights. The Templars soon grew to immense wealth and political power, acting virtually as a separate European state during the twelfth and thirteenth centuries. It was a mixture of military/chivalric and monastic orders, each member being bound by strict oaths of loyalty, personal poverty and celibacy, while also being the most highly trained and feared fighting force of their day.

Proud and aloof, acknowledging only the Pope as superior, the Order owned lands and fortresses across Europe, and operated the first international banking system. But on Friday, 13 October 1307, every single Templar knight in France was arrested and imprisoned on the orders of Philip IV, on – even for that day – quite sensational charges of heresy and diabolical practices. They were tortured, and confessions that supported the charges were wrung out of them.

Over the following months, under the orders of Pope Clement V, much the same happened in other European countries, and the Order was dissolved by 1312 – as far as most historians are concerned, that was certainly the end of that. However, the authorities in countries outside France tended towards greater leniency; the detained knights were released – as long as they rejected the order and repented of their 'crimes'. But those who insisted on their innocence were burnt to death. This included the Grand Master of the Order himself, Jacques de Molay.

History has it that Philip simply wanted their money, but were the charges against them trumped up completely? It is suspicious that so many knights, even given the horrific circumstances of their confessions, told tales that tallied in detail. The most serious accusations levelled at them were that they denied Jesus as Christ, spat at and trampled the cross, indulged in ritual homosexual practices, and that they worshipped a mysterious idol known as 'Baphomet', whose exact form differs depending on the confession, but which is generally taken to be a demonic head.

Ian Wilson's theory is based on the fact that one of the highest ranking Templars – the Preceptor of Normandy, who was executed with Jacques de Molay – was called Geoffrey de Charnay. This is, of course, the same as that of the first recorded owner of the Lirey Shroud forty years later (the variation in spelling is not significant). Wilson's original speculation about a possible family connection between the two Geoffreys rested on just the similar name – there was no genealogical evidence one way or the other. But in 1987, genealogist and BSTS member Noel Currer-Briggs established that there was a relationship between the two historical figures; Templar Geoffrey de Charnay was the uncle of the Geoffrey of Lirey fame. On this, Wilson was proved right.[37]

For him, this relationship helps to explain where the Shroud/ Mandylion was between 1204 and the 1350s. If the cloth were in the possession of the Templars then no wonder its whereabouts were unknown – the Order was obsessed with secrecy. And after the fall of the Order, the relic passed into the possession of the de Charny family, whose failure to explain its provenance may well have been a natural reluctance to have the Shroud linked with the disgraced Templars.

There is, of course, one immediate objection to Wilson's theory. In his eagerness to find the Shroud a pre-1350 location, he seems to have unavoidably linked it with Baphomet, the demonic idol head of the Templars. We shall come to our own understanding of that order and its beliefs later, but for Wilson, with his own well-publicised Roman Catholic views, this is an astonishing connection.

Suspending disbelief for a moment, how did the Shroud get to France after the sacking of Constantinople in 1204? The Templars were not involved in any action there during the Fourth Crusade. Building on Wilson's ideas, Currer-Briggs suggested that it could have found its way into Europe through the good offices of the former Empress of Constantinople, Mary-Margaret of Hungary.[38]

She was of a Frankish noble family who were related to some of the Crusade's leaders, and was the widow of the deposed Byzantine Emperor Isaac II. It was his overthrow (for reasons that are not relevant here) that led directly to the sacking of Constantinople. Within a month of the fall of the city, Mary-Margaret married one of the Crusade leaders, Boniface de Montferrat – with whom she went to Greece – then after his death, with yet another husband, moved to Hungary. Currer-Briggs believes that it was this Elizabeth Taylor of the Byzantine world who took the Shroud/Mandylion out of the sacked city, possibly giving it to the Templars as security for a loan.

An ingenious retrospective – but it is a theory about an article

that may well not have even existed, or which was being deliberately kept secret, so it must remain speculation. And, throughout
the unwinding of these elaborate historical theories, one must
always bear in mind that, for the reasons given above, the
Mandylion could not have been the Shroud.

The Mind's Eye

In the absence of any hard-and-fast evidence for the existence of
the Shroud before the Lirey displays, several researchers turned
instead to indirect clues.

For example, many believers say that because the man on the
Shroud fits the image of Jesus in pre-fourteenth-century Christian
art, it must prove the cloth's authenticity. True, before the
sixth century there were many variations in the depiction of
Jesus – he was sometimes shown beardless, for example – but the
sudden consensus image does not itself prove that the Shroud had
come to light and inspired all art thereafter. Of course if the
Shroud is a forgery it could well have followed established
artistic traditions, especially if the forger had a keen eye for detail
and was a meticulous master hoaxer.

Some researchers, however, have claimed to locate specific
characteristics on the Shroud itself that establish that it influenced
artists before Lirey. Frenchman Paul Vignon, one of the most
celebrated sindonologists, claimed that some characteristics of the
face of the man on the Shroud match depictions of Jesus dating
back to Byzantine times, which have now become known as
'Vignon marks'. The most famous of these is the downward
pointing 'V' shape between the brows, which Vignon believed
matched exactly the tradition in early iconography of showing
Jesus with what looks like a distinct frown-mark. Vignon claimed
to have isolated twenty similar marks which he matched with
those on early Christian paintings. No icon had them all – a

twelfth-century Sicilian painting had the most at fourteen – but it was enough to convince Vignon that the Turin Shroud had been around since at least the eighth century.

The marks identified by Vignon are not unique to depictions of Jesus in Byzantine icons: for example, the 'V' features on the foreheads of saints and even the Virgin Mary. More significantly, most of Vignon's marks can only be seen in the photographic negatives of the Shroud – so how could the artists of old have seen them?

There are other difficulties here: as we were to find out to our cost, there are indeed none so blind as those who won't see, and nowhere is this adage more relevant than when applied to Shroudies. They have seized on Vignon's work with great excitement, taking it as yet more evidence for the Shroud's authenticity. But an objective appraisal of it is nowhere near as conclusive. They point, for example, to similarities of one raised eyebrow – and of course the 'V' shape – between the Shroud image and earlier icons. But where the more obvious detail is concerned, earlier icons show a marked difference from the Shroud. For example, they show the shape of Jesus' face as anything from long and narrow (as on the Shroud) to full and round. Why do such minute things become part of a tradition, whereas the major things do not?

The minute inspection of the cloth went on: after Vignon came Alan Whanger, Professor of Psychiatry at Duke University, North Carolina. Using a device for superimposing one picture on another that he had developed specially for the purpose, he compared the face of the Shroudman to various pre-thirteenth century paintings of Jesus. He concluded that they fit with such precision that the pictures must have been copied faithfully from the Shroud.[39]

Whanger's criteria were the 'points of congruity', such as those used by US police forces to judge whether or not two pictures are of the same person. He claimed that some of his examples actually showed more points of congruity than are required by the police and the FBI to establish identity. The trouble with this kind of work – as we were to find out for ourselves – is that it is very subjective, and rapidly becomes a kind of Rorschach inkblot test. The other problem is that such fine detail tends to blend in with the weave of the cloth (again, we speak from experience). And, of course, in order for any of these observations to be valid, they have to be applicable to the image as seen by the naked eye, and not using the negative.

Again, subjectivity ran riot in Whanger's work. One of his most congruous 'fits' (matches for the Shroud image) is that of Christ on a Byzantine coin from the reign of Emperor Justinian. He has found no fewer than 145 points of congruity here – surely a superhuman feat, for the image on the coin is only ⅓ inch (9mm) high (smaller than the Queen's head on a 5p piece). But if Whanger showed virtually paranormal powers of observation, then what about those of the putative Byzantine copier, who slaved away without benefit of computer microscope and super-strength contact lenses? And even if this unknown genius of a draughtsman had the technical prowess to do such a thing, why would he have needed to, when a much vaguer copy would have done just as well?

Perhaps not surprisingly, Whanger's claims have been met with some scepticism from the more objective of Shroud scholars. As Ian Wilson joked in a lecture to the BSTS in April 1991, 'all this [Whanger's claims] from a psychiatrist . . . !'

Whanger, who works closely with his wife Mary, has also revived the botanical evidence for the Shroud's origins. This is not about looking for pollen – the Whangers claim that it is possible to see imprints of petals and leaves on the Shroud image, which came from bouquets of flowers being placed on the body. The Whangers, poring over enlargements of Enrie's 1931 photographs, claim to have identified 'hundreds' of such images on the Shroud, mostly around the head but also 'many others including several bouquets extending down to the level of the waist'. They go on to identify no fewer than 28 species of plants from these petal images, and – to their great satisfaction – found that all of them grow in modern-day Israel. Indeed, one species – a variety of bean caper – grows exclusively in Israel, Jordan and Sinai.[40]

Checking the Whangers' hypothesis against their own book and website, we are frankly at a loss to understand what they are talking about. For example, we are presented with a picture of a chrysanthemum, and asked to find it on the enlargement of the image. This has to be the most unsatisfactory 'Magic Eye' puzzle ever: vague splodges seem to whirl before one's gaze, making no sense. Perhaps one can understand that flowers may have been laid on a burial shroud, but here we are being asked to 'see' all sorts of objects – a veritable hardware shop of things such as a nail, a hammer, a broom, a rope, a die, the Crown of Thorns and a reed attached to a sponge . . . (Of course all of them figure in the New Testament story – puzzlingly, apart from the broom.) Quite apart from the highly subjective nature of these findings, it seems very curious that the disciples chose to enshroud Jesus with all this ironmongery, especially the instruments of torture. Even many fellow Shroudies have the good grace to be deeply embarrassed by the Whangers' claims.[41]

Remarkably – indeed incredibly – the Whangers' work has received the backing of two Israeli academics, Dr Avinoam Danin of the Department of Evolution, Systematics and Ecology at the Alexander Silberman Institute of Life Sciences, and Dr Uri Baruch of the Antiquities Authority in Jerusalem. Danin and Baruch even managed to link their and the Whangers' work with Max Frei's claims based on pollen samples.

Danin and Baruch – who later collaborated with Alan and Mary Whanger on *Flora of the Shroud of Turin* (1999) – combined the Whangers' claims of being able to see plant images on the Shroud with Frei's pollen analysis, using the samples that Frei himself took in 1973. Their key claim is that they could match two plants, Tournefort's gundelia and the Syrian bean caper, which are found growing together only in Israel, thereby (in their view) proving that the Shroud had once been in that region. The more significant is Tournefort's gundelia (*Gundelia tournefortii*) – a kind of thorny tumbleweed that comes from a family of plants (the asteraceae) which includes the sunflower – as they claimed to have identified both its pollen in Frei's samples *and* an image of its flower on the Shroud itself. (The bean caper – *Zygophyllum dumosum* – was identified only by the alleged image of its leaves on the Shroud.)[42]

Danin and Baruch's methods are open to question – for example, Danin made some of the observations using binoculars during the 1998 exposition (besides looking at enlargements of various photos from Secondo Pia's onwards). Like Frei, neither is a palynologist – and, as with Frei, experts in that discipline doubt that it is possible to do what Danin and Baruch claim to have done.

Vaughn M. Bryant of the Palynology Laboratory of Texas A&M University, with over thirty years' experience of palynology, the last ten of which have been on the forensic side, declared that their data is 'not convincing' and, like Richard Eyde in the case of Frei, states that visual examination of a pollen grain under the microscope, especially when it is stuck to sticky tape, is an extremely unreliable way of identifying it as from a specific species of plant.[43] Most damningly, Bryant disputes that it is possible to distinguish the pollen of Tournefort's gundelia from the 19,000 other species of the asteraceae family by visual examination alone, stating:

> If *Gundelia tournefortii* pollen were associated with evidence in a forensic case, I would not be willing to state under oath that I could confidently separate it from all other composites. If the authors of this current new book can do this, and can identify

this pollen taxon [classification based on structure] to species, as they claim, then they should provide convincing evidence and a list of the techniques and criteria they used to do this.[44]

The Tantalising Paradox

Other researchers look for characteristics that are *different* from artistic convention, arguing that these show that the Shroud image was genuine. One such is the nakedness of the man on the Shroud and the unusual and unnatural way his hands are crossed. Wilson cites examples to underline this, such as an illustration in a late twelfth-century manuscript in Budapest — known as the Pray Manuscript — and a tapestry sent to Pope Celestin II at about the same time: both show Jesus' hands crossed as on the Shroud, and the former also shows him completely naked.[45]

The trouble with this argument is that there are also paintings showing people other than Jesus with these characteristics. In a church at Berze-la-Ville in south-east France, for example, a wall painting dating from 1110 shows St Vincent naked and in a pose exactly like that on the Shroud.[46] Using Shroudies' logic, this proves that the man on the Shroud is in fact St Vincent.

The fact that believers have to fall back on such minutiae and ludicrous arguments highlights the essential problem. There is no documentary evidence of the Shroud's existence before, at best, the 1350s, but there are isolated references — such as de Clari's — to objects that might be the Shroud if the data is manipulated hard enough. Neither are there any unambiguous written descriptions or visual representations of anything that might be today's Turin Shroud.

If the Shroud existed before the fourteenth century, it would have been the greatest thing ever where Christendom was concerned, and we today would have been left in no doubt about its existence. But its modern supporters have to scrabble around for titbits that may or may not even be relevant and to pick out of the hundreds of thousands of Christian icons and relics the handful that bear some slight resemblance to the Shroud image.

For example, a favourite of Ian Wilson and other Shroudies is an illustration from the above-mentioned Pray Manuscript – from a Hungarian Benedictine monastery in the 1190s – which shows Jesus' body being prepared for burial by Joseph of Arimathea and other male disciples. The body is shown in a similar pose to that of the man on the Shroud, particularly the crossed hands. Beneath this scene, with Mary Magdalene and the women, is an angel who is holding a cloth, presumably a shroud in which the body is about to be wrapped. The cloth has three mysterious dots on it which Ian Wilson and others argue are supposed to depict the three 'poker marks' that can be seen on today's Turin Shroud.[47] But how did that particular illustrator know about this detail when no-one else seemed to at the time? And why was he hinting at his knowledge by putting three dots on the cloth? Why not simply depict the Shroud as such and have done with it? There is another problem for Shroudies: according to Wilson's theory, this is precisely at the time when the Shroud was supposed to be the Mandylion, folded up as small as a facecloth.

All this evidence, especially when set against the carbon dating, is simply speculation – in some cases fuelled by the near desperation of the believer to prove the cloth authentic. None of it shows that the cloth we call the Turin Shroud existed before the later limit of the carbon dating – indeed, before the 1350s.

Perhaps there was a series of 'Holy Shrouds'; today's Turin Shroud being just one of a line of them . . . but whatever the background of the fake's emergence (and we will be coming to that shortly), there was no doubt that the time was absolutely ripe for producing such a thing.

Although there was no early report of an imaged shroud ever being exhibited to pilgrims, there had long been traditions of cloths imprinted with Jesus' face. Apart from the Mandylion, there was also the Veronica.

Again, although significantly omitted from the New Testament itself, the story of its creation figured largely in early Christian tradition, and is part of the Catholic Stations of the Cross. It was said that, as Jesus staggered up Calvary under the weight of the cross, a sympathetic woman rushed out of the crowd and wiped away the sweat from his face with her handkerchief. It was then seen to bear the imprint of his image. The woman's name was Veronica.

A cloth said to be the same one, and which is called the Veronica, had been kept in Rome since at least the twelfth century. It was seen publicly very rarely, but one of those rare occasions was just a few years before the first appearance of the Lirey Shroud – in the Holy Year 1350 – when it was displayed to a rapturous audience of pilgrims. It was the talk of Europe.

But it was only Jesus' face. Imagine how gullible Christendom would react to a cloth bearing the image of his entire body; one that showed him crucified, about to come into his godhood through the final glory of the Resurrection. How could the unscrupulous and avaricious resist such a temptation? And we believe that all the evidence points to such a fraud – or a series of frauds – being perpetrated.

There remains, however, the Shroud's essential paradox. On the historical evidence alone no-one should have the slightest hesitation about dismissing it as a fourteenth-century fake. But on the scientific evidence – at least on its superficial appearance – alone, we have to admit that there is something truly strange and inexplicable about the image. What arguments about how the image was formed do believers in the Shroud's authenticity put forward to underpin their beliefs? And if the Shroud is not the winding sheet of Jesus, how else could the image have been created?

3

Theories

'The dilemma is not one of choosing from a variety of transfer mechanisms but rather that no technologically-credible process has been postulated that satisfies all the characteristics of the existing image'

Lawrence Schwalbe and Raymond N. Rogers,
STURP scientists, 1982[1]

If the Shroud of Turin is authentic, how could the image have been formed? And, conversely, if it is a fake, by what process could it possibly have been made? These are questions that have vexed thousands of thinking people since the true extent of its detail became known in 1898.

Surprisingly, however, few Shroudies regard the image as literally a miracle. Of course, if it were, all the effort put into the scientific studies would be pointless, since, by definition, miracles are outside the scope of science. If God can accomplish anything simply through an act of Divine will, he could easily have caused an image of the crucified Jesus to appear spontaneously on a piece of medieval French linen, or hurled the genuine burial cloth through a time-warp from first-century Jerusalem to fourteenth-century Lirey, thus bypassing 1300 years and skewing the carbon dating.

There have been similar images reported by the faithful over the years. The most holy relic of Mexican Catholicism is the image of Our Lady of Guadalupe. It is a cloth bearing the image of the Virgin Mary, which was said to have appeared on the cloak of an Indian who had an encounter with her in 1531 (conveniently for the Church, she appeared complete with Indian features and dress and urged the natives to convert to the religion of their new overlords). Although the relic is known to have been overpainted, there is still some mystery about the underlying image (there is, in the USA, an Image of Guadalupe Research Project). Although the arguments are outside the scope of this book, many do point to this relic as a clear example of miraculous imprinting. And if it could happen in the case of this cloth, why not in the case of the Turin Shroud? Yet nobody has felt the need to trace this particular icon back to the earthly life of the Virgin Mary.

Part of the Shroud's appeal to the believers is that it is, apparently, something between a miraculous and a mundane object, a souvenir left by Jesus that is now open to the scrutiny of the twenty-first century. More than one writer has suggested that this is deliberate, a conundrum set by God to bring the atheistic age of science back to the right path. Why, they ask, would the Shroud display characteristics that could only be appreciated in our technological age, when photography and computer-aided image analysis are available? One leading researcher, while advocating a strictly scientific approach to the enigma, has even stated that the Shroud has been divinely protected throughout its long life for just such a purpose.[2]

Labelling the Shroud 'a miracle' is perhaps a fail-safe – or just an excuse – for those who wish to ignore the carbon dating, but those who have devoted themselves to its investigation and uphold the laws of science will have no truck with the easy way out.

Paranormal Images

Some see the origin of the image on the Shroud as paranormal, rather than miraculous. They suggest that supernatural, rather than Divine, forces may be at work. Mexican parapsychologist César Tort has raised the possibility that the image is a 'thoughto-graph'. There is evidence – controversial, but not easily dismissed – that some psychics can create recognisable images on film by the power of thought alone. The most famous case is that of Ted Serios, an alcoholic Chicago bellhop, whose abilities were studied intensively in the mid-1960s by the eminent researcher Jule Eisenbud. If it exists, the ability of the mind to affect the highly sensitive chemicals of photographic film would seem to be a natural variant of psychokinesis (PK) – the alteration of the state of a physical object by mental influence alone – as exhibited most famously by Uri Geller.[3]

Tort points to a similar phenomenon, that of images appearing spontaneously on the walls and floors of buildings. He cites a well-documented case from the 1920s, when the image of the late Dean John Liddell appeared on a wall of Oxford Cathedral. Such pictures are usually of people of special sanctity, but not always. In one case in Bélmez de la Moraleda in Spain, which was investigated by the veteran parapsychologist Professor Hans Bender, one-time mentor of Elmar Gruber, co-author of *The Jesus Conspiracy*, leering, demonic faces have appeared regularly on the walls and floors of a house for more than twenty years.

César Tort's starting point was the paradox between the historical and scientific evidence that we had already noted: the image on the Shroud is more consistent with actual crucifixion (and so, to most people, with the first century), than with a medieval artistic forgery, but the carbon dating and the documented history show it to be medieval. How, asked Tort, could a fourteenth-century cloth show a first-century image? So he speculated that it was a thoughtograph, projected onto the cloth by the collective minds of the pilgrims who came to meditate on a (then plain) cloth that they believed had wrapped their risen Lord.

Tort admitted the main objection to this scenario: even suspending disbelief about the reality of thoughtography, we would expect the image to conform to the beliefs and expectations of those who unconsciously created it. To a medieval mind, there should be nails in the palms (not the wrists), Jesus should look younger, and he would certainly not be naked as here. To explain this, Tort has to invoke another paranormal phenomenon – retrocognition – where the past can be psychically perceived.

The pros and cons of these phenomena are outside the scope of this book, but in the case of Tort's hypothesis it is enough to say that neither effect has ever been reported as working on the scale needed to make the Shroud image, and that the use of two such unknowns – thoughtography and retrocognition – is simply stretching credulity far too far. Neither does it explain why a negative image was projected, or why the bloodstains should be so different from the rest of the image. It is a bold and open-minded attempt to reconcile the contradictory elements of the Shroud, but in the end it creates more questions than answers.

Fire From Heaven

One of the favourite theories of scientific Shroudies is that the image is not in itself a miracle, but that it was the by-product of one – the Resurrection. This is the 'nuclear flash' theory, promoted by STURP co-founder John Jackson (a physicist with the USAF) and taken up enthusiastically by many others.[4] They suggest that, as the image resembles a scorch mark, it was caused by a split-second burst of high-energy radiation emanating from Jesus' body as it regenerated. Since the carbon dating, believers have hastily capitalised on this theory: they claim that if the Shroud had been subjected to a blast of radiation, the amount of radioactive carbon-14 would have increased and the Shroud would appear to be much younger than it really is.

We have heard variations of that theory from virtually every Shroudie we have talked to – and it seems crazy. We think it is astonishing that such a theory could have been seriously advanced by a trained physicist, and supported by other scientists, since it should be obvious to anyone with even the most elementary understanding of the nature of radiation that this hypothesis violates the very laws of physics that it invokes.

For the 'nuclear flash' theory to be valid, the energy released would have been so great it would have destroyed not only the cloth itself, but also a large part of Jerusalem. But even if we accept, for the sake of argument, that the phenomenon was somehow controlled by Divine will, there are still fundamental objections to be considered.

Such a process could never have imprinted the kind of image we see on the Turin Shroud. All radiation – nuclear, thermal or electromagnetic (which includes light) – spreads out from its source in all directions, and therefore would have scorched all parts of the cloth equally. Even if the cloth were in close contact with the body, the best that could be expected is a scorched silhouette of a human form, featureless and of equal intensity – certainly not the detailed and recognisable Shroud image. If the cloth were draped over a body, we should be able to see the sides and the top of the head. As it is, they are not there.

It is like holding a sheet of photographic film a few inches away from a light bulb and expecting to see a picture of the bulb itself when the film is developed: all that would be seen is a fog where the light had uniformly hit the film. Light shining from any source is known as incoherent, with the rays spreading out equally from the point of origin. Without some mechanism for turning it into coherent light – where the rays are made to travel in the same direction, towards a specific point – no image can be captured. We can see the light bulb because the eye has such a mechanism, its lens; as does a camera. These laws hold good for any kind of radiation.

To produce the Shroud image, the radiation would have had to travel directly up, perpendicular with the body, and also directly down to produce the back image, and in no other direction. This breaks the laws of physics. But even if the radiation behaved in this way, it could never have reproduced such fine detail of the man on the Shroud. Radiation can only make a picture by being blocked by something, thus creating a shadow. Different kinds of radiation are blocked by different materials; visible light will not pass through a human body, whereas X-rays will pass through the skin and internal organs but not through bone. If the 'nuclear flash' theory were correct, we ought to see the same effect as an X-ray – a skeleton – not the detailed outer body. Proponents of this view have pointed out that the fingers do appear to be skeletal, but in that case why is the rest of the body natural in appearance? It can be argued that the hands have that look due to 'degloving' – the draining of the blood from the hands during the process of crucifixion.

Some books on the Shroud reproduce pictures of images produced by the aftermath of the atom bomb at Hiroshima – for example, the 'shadow' of the wheel of a hand valve etched onto the wall of a nearby gas tank – and attempt to draw a parallel with the Shroud image.[5] In fact, they are no such thing. These images are literally shadows – the wheel was between the source of radiation and the wall, blocking or altering its passage. In the case of the Shroud the theory is that the source of radiation was within the body. We are seriously asked to believe that it was blocked only by the skin and hair, which it then faithfully reproduced.

The only way in which a recognisable image can result from

a three-dimensional body, using any form of radiation, is if the radiation is reflected from its surface, not shining through it. The source would have to be outside the body. Take this example: imagine making a glass model of a human head with a bright light bulb in its centre. Turn the light on and what do you see? Only the shining shape of the head: the features would not be distinguishable. Now imagine a solid bust lit from an external source, reflecting the light. Everything about it would be clearly visible. Even so, we can only make it out because our eyes focus the rays of light; a cloth coated in light-sensitive chemicals and suspended in front of the bust would never capture the image.

Moreover, – as pointed out by BSTS member Peter Freeland – the process would have burned away, or at least caramelised, any blood on the cloth.

Finally, in the last paper he wrote before his death in March 2005, STURP's Raymond Rogers poured more cold water on the radiation theory. His rejection was based on tests on fibres from the cloth, which showed none of the effects that such a burst of radiation should have had on the structure and composition of the fibre.[6]

So, the much-quoted 'nuclear flash' theory is the least tenable of all, and would deserve less attention even than the thoughtograph hypothesis of César Tort, were it not for the fact that it continues to be taken seriously in Shroud circles: for example, a paper was given on the subject at the 1993 Rome Symposium. Many unscientific Shroudies accept it as the most likely explanation, or at least as a serious contender. But the scientific Shroudies also tend to cling to this theory, which surely says more about their desperation to believe than their faith in the laws of science. The theory is as full of holes as the Shroud would have been, had it been exposed to such a process.

Blood and Sweat

There is a second category of theories to account for the formation of the image: rare natural processes, chemical reactions between the body of Jesus and the cloth of the Shroud.

The first such idea was Paul Vignon's 'vapourographic' theory, put forward in the early years of the twentieth century. He speculated that the cloth was impregnated with aromatic oils that contained myrrh and aloes that reacted with ammonia gas given off by the body. (The corpses of people who die after prolonged torture are covered with sweat with an unusually high urea content, in which ammonia is abundant.) Vignon carried out some experiments with these substances and, after much trial and error, he was able to produce vaguely Shroud-like stains, but with nothing like the detail of the real image.

Recently Elmar Gruber and Holger Kersten returned to this hypothesis, and in their experiments, which are described in their book *The Jesus Conspiracy*, they applied concentrated heat to Kersten's body, which had been soaked in a mixture of aloes and myrrh. This was to test their idea that Jesus was still alive while in the Shroud. They managed to obtain images, but had to admit, because of the resulting distortion, that 'the original could not have been formed in this way'. Despite this failure, they still believe that some similar process must have been responsible for the formation of the image on the Turin Shroud.

Since Vignon's experiments, many other reacting agents have been suggested, which include an extract from the soapwort plant used to clean fabrics in Roman times, a turpentine-like extract from the terebinth tree, and even common salt. Fortunately it is not necessary to discuss them all individually as they all share a basic flaw.

Any chemical reaction would have continued through the cloth as the rising vapour seeped through, whereas the Shroud image is only on one side of the cloth. (This was not known in

Vignon's day.) And to produce the perfectly graded image, the gas would have had to travel in parallel lines and lessen in density the further it moved from the body. Gas does not behave like that: it diffuses in all directions. The best that we would see is a uniformly coloured, man-shaped silhouette.

To deal with some of these problems, Rodney Hoare introduced what he called the 'thermographic correction'. As we have seen, this also formed the basis of Gruber and Kersten's hypothesis. Noting that all chemical reactions need some degree of heat, he argued that perhaps Jesus was actually alive in the tomb and warmer than his surroundings: from this he developed the idea that the Resurrection was, in fact, simply a recovery from coma, which led him to make some extraordinary claims for the 'message' of the Shroud.[7]

Hoare argues that, if the body were warm, the inside of the cloth would have been warmer than the outside, which would explain why only one side is darkened. The fabric closest to the skin would have been warmer than that slightly further away, hence the grading of the image. Both arguments, however, fail to convince: the fall off in temperature would, once again – by some uncanny coincidence – have to have been exactly right to produce the recognisable human form. The fact of the back image also presents a problem. If the man's back were pressing down on the cloth it should have trapped the warmth, or at least pushed the cloth nearer the body, making the image visibly darker than the front. Yet both back and front images are of equal density. Critics have also pointed out that, had the man been alive, the cloth around the nose and mouth would have been distorted – and therefore so would the image – where it had been sucked in as he breathed.

A serious objection, which applies to all the chemical theories, was raised by STURP. If the image is composed of chemical by-products from the original reaction, it should (as with pigment), have changed colour near the areas that were burned in the fire of 1532. (STURP also made a specific search for the chemical by-products predicted by Vignon's theory, and failed to find them.)

Any process involving vapour rising from the body would depend on factors such as the texture of the body in any given spot. For example, for Vignon's theory, the entire body must have been uniformly drenched in urea-laden sweat, otherwise the intensity of the image would vary. Conceivably, the skin was, but the hairs of the beard and the head do not perspire – and even if they were soaked in sweat they would still have got in the way. The vapour would also rise at a different rate from the hair than the skin, so the image of the face and the beard should be very different. They are not.

The chemical vapour theories also fail to explain the lack of distortion of the image. Attempts to reproduce the image by putting a cloth over a model covered with paint have ended up with a distorted, unlife-like image when the cloth was flattened out. The same would apply to an image created by any chemical reaction.

None of these theories accounts for the presence of the blood. If it is real blood, it must have transferred to the cloth through contact with it, yet we know that the body image was, at least in part, the result of action at a distance. (We will discuss this highly significant point in greater detail below.) So a second, equally rare process would have to be invoked, and the odds against two such phenomena coming together are astronomical. Significantly, the believers frequently say at this point, 'But it is Jesus we are talking about – anything could have happened.' Perhaps this is true, but then they have no right to cite known scientific laws as any of their evidence. They cannot have it both ways.

A case cited as support for the 'natural process' hypothesis emerged in 1986, from a hospice in Thornton, Lancashire. Five years before, a patient, identified only as 'Les', died there of cancer of the pancreas. On stripping his bed, the nurses found a stain on the mattress, forming the clear outline of the back of the unfortunate man's body: shoulders, back, buttocks and upper legs, and, most strikingly, the left arm and hand on which he had been lying. A faint, distorted image of part of his face could also be seen. Remarkably the image had formed on the mattress through the man's pyjamas and the bedsheet (both of which were routinely burned before the image was discovered, although the imaged mattress cover was kept). Although it was five years before the case was brought to the attention of medical and forensic experts, Professor James Cameron of the London Hospital, who had studied the medical details of the Shroud image, was able to show that the image was due to the action of enzymes present in alkaline fluids. Because of the condition of the patient's pancreas, they were released in his urine and, due to his incontinence, collected in the hollows created by his body.[8]

The case caused a stir in the Shroud world, but in fact the parallels between this case and that of the relic are merely superficial. Les's image was clearly made through contact, and was distorted by the weight of his body pressing against the mattress. The difference between the two images is that between a face looking through a window at you from a few feet away, and one pressed up against the glass.

If the two cases were truly the same phenomenon, the back of the Shroud image ought at least to show similar evidence of contact. It does not. The Thornton image is that of the outline and hollows of the body only, where the liquid collected, whereas the Shroud shows all areas of the body equally. If the image on the Shroud were caused by similar enzyme action, the fluid would have had to jump across the gap between body and cloth where the cloth was not actually in contact with the man's flesh.

The two images do not even look alike, and the enzyme theory cannot be applied to the Shroud. The case does, of course, demonstrate that human bodily fluids can create images that do not wash off – in the Thornton case even bleach failed to budge it.

Another intriguing parallel, this time from the plant world, is that of the 'Volckringer patterns'. These were described in 1942 by Jean Volckringer, a chemist colleague of Pierre Barbet at the Saint-Joseph Hospital in Paris. He discovered that when plant specimens are kept pressed between sheets of paper in botanical collections, negative images sometimes appear on the paper – even, on occasion, upon a second undersheet. Like the Shroud image they are negative and sepia in tone, and show parts of the plant not in direct contact with the paper. They can take years – sometimes decades – to appear, yet the image must have been 'caught' early on, since they show the sample as it was when first pressed, even though it later shrivelled up. The patterns also appear without exposure to light.

The cause of the Volckringer patterns remains unknown, as indeed does their relationship to the Shroud image. Certainly they represent the only parallel found in nature, yet on a much smaller scale and involving vegetable, not human, tissue. The 'action at a distance' exhibited here also involves far smaller distances, and pressed plant samples are of course much flatter than a human body, so helping to create an undistorted image. It is hard to see how the Shroud image could be created by the same process. And although the time it takes the Volckringer images to appear might explain why no image was described as being on the empty burial linen in the Gospel stories, it also provides no reason for the cloth to have been kept and treasured in the first place – especially by Jews, for whom burial linen was deemed so unclean as to be untouchable.

This phenomenon did inspire some original work by BSTS Honorary Chairman Dr Allan Mills, a lecturer in planetary science at Leicester University. He suggested that the Volckringer patterns were due to the effect of free radicals, unstable atoms that are given off by some substances and which, after running loose for a brief life, bind together with other molecules, causing a reaction. He thinks that free radicals are given off by plants and

react with lignin, a polymer present in plant and vegetable products such as paper. His experiments showed that lignin was
particularly sensitive to the effects of free radicals. And as it is also
present in linen, he proposed that the Shroud image was caused
by what he terms Free Radical Catalyzed Polymerization – stable
currents of warm air rising from the body that carry with them
free radicals, which then permeate the cloth. (He disagrees with
Hoare about warmth necessarily implying life; he suggests that
the warmth of a living body would produce currents that are too
turbulent to create a sharp image.)

When Mills gave a talk on this effect to the BSTS in October
1991, however, he did admit that his theory could not explain
the back image. And discussing some other aspect of his research
he also said, 'I stopped the experiment when I realised it wouldn't
work in a tomb . . .' As an increasing number of people point to
a studio of one sort or another as the original location of the
Turin Shroud, for Mills's work to be at all valid, he should at least
have considered this possibility.

All the problems discussed above go to prove that no single
known chemical process could create the Shroud image, at least
not without requiring highly controlled and/or coincidental
conditions. So we are left with only one possible category of
explanation: forgery. But even this is almost equally problematic.
Even setting aside the stylistic arguments discussed in Chapter 1 –
the un-medieval realism, the anatomical excellence, the negative
effect and so on – there are still enormous difficulties.

The Art of the Fake

Most of the experiments conducted by the STURP team were
designed to detect artificial pigments – inks or dyes – on the
image. The results were negative, except in the view of one
member of the team, Dr Walter McCrone. He received a good

deal of publicity in the months after the testing by claiming that
he had not only found and identified paint that made up the
image, but also that he had worked out the actual method used
by the forger. (The qualification 'that made up the image' is
important: there is no dispute that there are microscopic traces of
pigment on the Shroud. It is known to have been in contact with
painted copies, which were often held against it to 'sanctify'
them.)

Walter McCrone was a microanalyst with his own research
company, Walter C. McCrone Associates Inc., based in Chicago.
His method of identifying substances was to study them under
high magnification, and sometimes to supplement that with
chemical tests. He was involved in the forensic work of many
criminal cases and often consulted by art dealers about the
authenticity of their *objets.* An independent, even abrasive
character, McCrone seemed to revel in controversy and
publicity.

The case that established his international reputation and
brought him to the attention of the Shroud world was his
unmasking of the 'Vinland Map' forgery. In Barcelona in 1957
an American antiquarian book dealer found a map, apparently
dating from the fifteenth century and copied from an earlier
Viking one, which showed parts of North America. For years
there had been speculation that two tenth-century Norse sagas
telling of the discovery and colonisation of an unknown land
to the west were in fact describing America. This would mean
that the Vikings had beaten Columbus to it by over 500 years –
and the Barcelona discovery seemed to be proof of this at
last. At first sight it appeared to be genuine: wormholes in it
matched those in two books of known fifteenth-century provenance, indicating that the map had once been bound between
them (a common practice of the time).

Yale University bought the map in 1965, but after some historians had expressed doubts about its authenticity, they decided

to bring in Walter McCrone. He removed particles of the ink and examined them under an electron microscope. His conclusion, announced in 1974, was that the ink contained a substance – anatase (titanium dioxide) – that had only been invented in the 1920s. The map was therefore a forgery.[9] The case brought McCrone international publicity, and it was this that led Ian Wilson to approach him on the possibility of applying his techniques to the Shroud.

Ironically, serious doubts have recently been raised about McCrone's debunking of the Vinland Map.[10] In 1987 physicists at the University of California examined the map using a well-tried technique for analysing chemicals, particle induced X-ray emission, and found that the ink contained only minute amounts of titanium – more than 1000 times less than that claimed by McCrone – which one would expect to find in medieval ink. It appears that the Vinland Map is genuine after all, but (perhaps predictably) the finding has been almost completely ignored by the archaeological world, even though, before McCrone's announcement, archaeological discoveries in Newfoundland had proved that the Vikings had indeed discovered the New World.

This case is interesting because of the insight it offers into McCrone's character. He dismissed the University of California's results as mistaken. Contrary to the detachment supposedly exhibited by scientists, he appeared to take their findings as a personal attack, writing to the Californian team that their work was 'the first shot in a declaration of war'.[11]

Despite his field of expertise, McCrone's interest in the Shroud initially centred on the possibility of carbon dating it, and it was to this end that he first began to work with STURP. However, in 1977 he made an independent approach to King Umberto II to try to get permission for the tests, which effectively antagonised both the custodians in Turin Cathedral and STURP itself – and as a result, he was banned from the tests when they did take place.[12]

After the 1978 STURP tests he was given access to the samples of threads that were taken back to the USA, examining them
first under a conventional microscope before turning to the more
powerful electron microscope. His conclusions were extremely
provocative and profoundly distasteful to the believers: he
claimed he had found artificial pigment – paint – on the threads
taken from the Shroud. And predictably, although challenged by
all the STURP team and the Italian scientists present at the tests,
McCrone received more publicity than all of them put together.[13]

His final conclusion was that the samples contained a pigment
known as Venetian red, which was made by grinding iron oxide
into a powder. He claimed that this alone was responsible
for the Shroud image. The ground pigment would have been
mixed with a liquid medium for application; his chemical tests
revealed the presence of a protein, collagen, that he interpreted
as being just that medium. To reinforce these observations,
he got an artist, Walter Sanford, to reproduce the Shroud face
using the same materials, with tolerably good results, although
nowhere near the quality of the original. But McCrone's
findings were good enough to convince David Sox, then
General Secretary of the BSTS (and up to that time a supporter
of the Shroud's authenticity), that the image was painted. As a
result of his sudden conversion to the anti-authenticity camp,
Sox left the BSTS, in the words of Ian Wilson, 'amid a brouhaha
of publicity'[14] – but as we were to discover to our cost, Sox was
neither the first nor the last to fall foul of that supposedly neutral
organisation.

The dispute between McCrone and the rest of STURP turns
on two questions: the origin of the particles of iron oxide on the
threads, and whether or not they were responsible for the creation of the image.[15]

Iron oxide – ordinary rust – is one of the most common substances on earth. It is present in dust, and so it is hardly surprising
that it was found on the Shroud. But from ancient times it has

been ground down by artists as pigment; McCrone's opinion was that the particles were of a shape and size that indicated they had been ground, and that they were present in too great a concentration to be due to accidental contamination.

It was not the presence of iron oxide that was disputed by the STURP scientists (chiefly biophysicist John Heller and chemist Alan Adler), but rather McCrone's belief that it actually created the image that led to their disagreement. So they tested it without resort to microscopy to see if it was present in sufficient quantities to account for the image. X-ray fluorescence scans during the 1978 tests had revealed traces of iron, but there was no detectable difference in its density between the image and the non-image areas – although there was more in the bloodstains.[16]

Several suggestions were made to account for the iron oxide; it could have come from the blood, spreading across the cloth due to years of folding and rolling. On the other hand it could be a by-product of the manufacture of the linen itself (probably the most plausible explanation),[17] or it could have been due to atmospheric contamination. In view of these objections, STURP declined to include McCrone's two papers in their final report. Their selectivity raises some interesting questions about their own position.

The tests that McCrone had used to detect the protein medium were criticised on the grounds that they produce false positive results when used on cellulose, a component of linen. Alternative tests were tried by Adler. They failed to find protein in the area of the body image; although, again, they did in the blood areas.[18]

Many harsh criticisms have been levelled at McCrone's method and conclusions. Most cynically, some have pointed out that, of all the STURP team, he was the only one to have benefited financially from the tests – due to the publicity for his research company. Others have noted that his papers were published only in his own journal, *The Microscope*, whereas other members of STURP chose to publish theirs in independent peer-reviewed journals, thus fulfilling a major criterion of scientific respectability: all papers have to be examined and the results confirmed by a panel of experts before being accepted for publication. McCrone said that he published in his own journal only because it could guarantee the necessary high quality colour reproduction of his photomicrographs.

Of all people, we admit to some fellow feeling for McCrone. Even before his findings were complete he had to endure a barrage of criticism from the Italian scientists that verged on pure abuse.[19] Even so, it has to be admitted that his work is open to serious question. To start with, McCrone produced figures showing the number of particles of iron oxide present in the image areas compared to those in the non-image areas.[20] They appeared to indicate that there was much more iron oxide in the image than elsewhere on the cloth, supporting the idea that it was the result of faking the image.

However, he made no distinction between those particles from the body image and those from the blood, having concluded that the difference was simply due to the amount of pigment applied. However, this is an oversimplification: the blood has many other different characteristics, most of which cannot be explained in this way.

When John Heller pointed out that the number of iron oxide particles quoted by McCrone, even on the image area, was so low that an image made by them would be too faint to be seen, McCrone's response was that, in that case, 'there must be more'.[21] Ian Wilson also challenged McCrone's published data, pointing out that it appeared to contradict the scientist's own conclusions by saying that there was less iron oxide on the blood image threads than on those of the body image. McCrone admitted that the apparently precise numbers of particles he had given previously, were in fact estimates.[22]

The most reasonable conclusion is that McCrone was wrong.

In any case, there are good logical reasons against the Shroud being a painting. For example, the 1532 fire would have made the paint crack and the subsequent dousing it received would have caused water damage that could be compared to that in other paintings. History has shown that the image, unlike any known painting, is not changed by either fire or water.

After McCrone, the leading pro-painting voice is that of American Joe Nickell. He is a private investigator, and a member of the Committee for the Scientific Investigation of Claims of the Paranormal (CSICOP), a scientific pressure group that campaigns against belief in any form of paranormal phenomena. In 1983 he published *Inquest on the Shroud of Turin* (revised in 1987), in which he proposed his own method for reproducing the Shroud image.[23]

Nickell soaked a cloth in hot water and then pressed it over a bas-relief statue. When dry, the cloth was fitted closely over the statue's contours. He then rubbed the cloth with powdered pigment of the type suggested by McCrone (although before he read McCrone's hypothesis he had tried powdered myrrh and aloes). He claimed that the result is an image that looks very like that of the Shroudman. It has a similar negative effect, but no three-dimensional quality.

It must be said that Nickell's results, like those produced by Walter Sanford under McCrone's direction – although more recognisable in negative – are nowhere near as impressive as the Shroud, even though both attempts were produced by modern artists deliberately trying to create a negative image. Although they were much more familiar with negatives than any medieval artist would have been, the hypothetical early hoaxer managed to outdo them.

Nickell's suggestion has been criticised for being too convoluted for any putative medieval artist and as having no parallel in art of that period. César Tort also points out that Nickell cites McCrone's work in support of his own. In fact, apart from the link with iron oxide pigment, McCrone's method is totally incompatible with Nickell's – McCrone believed he had found evidence that the pigment had been applied as *liquid* paint.[24]

Although they do reproduce some of the characteristics of the Shroud image, neither McCrone's nor Nickell's method – nor that of any other technique yet suggested – is satisfactory, and both researchers are forced to deny or belittle the significance of some of the Shroud's features, such as the negative effect.

Techniques other than painting have been proposed. One idea is that the scorch-like effect was created by heating a life-sized metal statue and wrapping the cloth round it. But the end result, once again, is a distorted and bloated image. Others have suggested that the image was the result of block printing using clay, and yellow ochre, or that it was drawn in red chalk. None of these work – although the last two ideas invoke Renaissance, not medieval, techniques.

To be fair, we found that the believers (who have the lion's share of Shroudie literature on their side) were often too quick to dismiss such ideas. For example, at one time a suggestion was made that the scorch effect could be due to something like 'invisible ink' – lemon juice or something similar – which looks clear when applied, but darkens when heated. This was dismissed, not illogically, on the grounds that it would be impossible to paint such a huge and detailed picture in invisible ink. The suggestion that some of the characteristics could be explained by some form of block printing was turned down because STURP had looked specifically for inks, and had found none.

However, nobody (to our knowledge) has ever put the two ideas together and realised that you can print with invisible ink. Not that we think this was the method used by the creator of the Shroud – even though, as we shall see, the invisible ink idea does have some bearing – but it just shows how wary one should be about accepting the believers' arguments unquestioningly.

The Crux of the Matter

We had looked into all the theories, both for and against – including some too bizarre to be mentioned – and in our view none provided a watertight case. We had noticed, however, that the same problems came up time and time again, whether one was examining the pro or the anti material.

The most significant problem was the lack of distortion of the image. No process put forward to explain its creation – be it contact with the body, heating a metal statue or even the nuclear flash theory – would provide a totally undistorted image. And why do we see only the front and back of the body, not the top of the head or the sides?

The inescapable conclusion is that the Shroud had never been draped around a body, living or dead. *However the image was formed, the cloth had to have been perfectly flat at the time.* This has long been recognised by the believers, but they have rather cannily played it down. To explain it they have argued that the Shroud must have been supported by something on either side of the body. The most popular idea is that the corpse was surrounded by blocks of spices, intended for use later when proper burial rites could be carried out after the Sabbath – and so the Shroud was stretched across the top of the blocks and kept flat.[25] But this can only work if the body was laid on one half of the cloth, the blocks placed round it, and then the top half pulled over the front. Given the haste that the Gospels tell us surrounded Jesus' burial (because of the imminent approach of the Sabbath), why choose such a complicated arrangement?

Another version, proposed by Rodney Hoare,[26] that the body was in a lidless stone sarcophagus and the cloth stretched over the top, is even more absurd. Presumably it would still be under the body – in direct contact with it – yet there is no difference in quality, colour, intensity or 'focus' between the back and front images.

The absurdity of these suggestions just goes to show to us that faith often moves even the mountain of common sense with seamless ease. If the cloth had been supported over the body, there are immense problems with the bloodstains. Unlike the body image, they were caused by some substance – real or fake blood – being added, so they could not have somehow been transferred across the gap from body to stretched, flat cloth. Yet the bloodstains are arguably the most perfect of all the anatomical details. They could only have been put on the cloth by direct contact.

Time and time again in our reading of the previous research, we kept coming back to the difference between the body and the blood images. The nuclear flash theory, for example, might explain the scorch-like nature of the body image, but the temperatures needed would probably have destroyed all blood (and flesh) within miles, let alone that on the cloth. And none of the chemical reaction theories explains how the blood got there.

Some theorists, as we have seen, try to invoke two unique processes working at the same time, rather like Tort's double paranormal phenomena. But not only are the processes different, as cited by their apologists, they are *mutually exclusive*. Any process that could explain the formation of the body image would actually prevent the blood image from forming, and vice versa. These anomalies could only be reconciled if someone deliberately put them together in faking the Shroud.

Other oddities about the bloodstains reinforce the idea of a fake, many of which were suggested in the late 1970s by BSTS member Peter Freeland – but which have been studiously ignored by the believers.[27] The bloodstains are just too perfect. Yes, they behave exactly as one would expect, given the nature of the wounds, but what state would the blood have been in when the image was formed? If the blood had congealed, then it could hardly have been transferred to the cloth. On the other hand, if it was liquid, it would have soaked into the cloth and run along the fibres. And it certainly would not be so sharply defined in the way that has impressed – and puzzled – the forensic scientists.

As might be expected, the believers have a ready answer. They suggest that the body was wrapped in the Shroud at the very moment that the blood was the right consistency; not too congealed to stick to the cloth, not so wet as to lose its definition. But we know that the blood soaked through the cloth, so it must have been fairly fluid. And their argument assumes that all the blood, from all the wounds, had reached exactly the same consistency at the same time. But even if the body had been wrapped in the Shroud immediately after being taken down from the cross, some of the blood would be fully congealed, some semi-congealed and some still fairly liquid. After all, according to the Gospel accounts, the various wounds were made at different times of the day.

The Crown of Thorns wounds were made in the morning, as were the marks of flagellation (which show traces of blood). The nail wounds, obviously made when Jesus was first put on the cross, would have continued to bleed throughout the day, and the angle of the blood flows confirms this. The last wound was the largest, caused by the centurion's spearthrust to the ribs; the blood flow there was so liquid that it ran across the back, apparently as the body was laid on the Shroud.

Yet all these bloodstains, regardless of their condition, look exactly the same on the Shroud. And the case against their authenticity is underlined by a closer look at the scalp wounds, as suggested by Peter Freeland: yes, they are particularly impressive at first sight, hardly the rough-and-ready daubs one might expect from an artist. The blood wells up from pin-sized wounds, filling out into large drops. And blood from the largest forehead wound has even stained the creases of the brow over which it trickled. Doctors have confirmed that real blood behaves just like this when running from real wounds of that size, on that part of the body.

Yet, as every reader of crime fiction knows, blood does not run from the wounds of a dead man. Here, however, it appears that fresh blood is welling up almost as the observer looks on. This feature, so often conveniently ignored, is central to the story. Even so, there is something terribly wrong with the blood on the scalp. Those 'perfect' blood flows, particularly on the back of the head, are *visible through the hair*. This is, of course, impossible. Blood running from pricks in the scalp would mat the hair and the stains would lose their definition; all we should be able to see would be a bloody smudge. Instead, on the Shroud, we can actually see the tiny head wounds individually. Equally puzzling is the fact that some of the blood flows appear to extend well beyond the face.

Whoever did this was no journeyman artist. Whoever did this, however, was – at least where the blood flows are concerned – just too much of a perfectionist. For once with this amazing image, aesthetic considerations overrode strict accuracy.

There are other anomalies where the blood flow is concerned. The scourge wounds, as Joe Nickell pointed out, have considerably less blood on them than they should have.[28] Anthony Harris, author of *The Sacred Virgin and the Holy Whore*, makes the same point, but more crucially notes that these wounds do not overlap, suggesting they were carefully positioned for either aesthetic reasons or dramatic effect.[29]

There is a similar problem with the blood flow from the wrist. While this wound is famous as an example of the anatomical accuracy of the image – not just because it is in the wrist, but also because of the angle at which the blood flows down the arm – much less attention is paid to the fact that its very accuracy cannot be reconciled with the Shroud being authentic. As Australian physicist Dr Victor Webster pointed out to Ian Wilson in 1978, the back of the wrist would have been pressed up against the wood of the cross and the blood coming from it would be badly smeared.[30] But did the blood come from the wound being re-opened when the body was taken down from the cross? The Shroud's supporters can't have it both ways – they have already argued that the change in angle of the flow demonstrates that when the blood ran down the arm, the man was actually nailed up.

In his 1998 book *The Blood and the Shroud*, Wilson explains this by arguing that traditional representations of crucifixion are wrong, and that the victims were really crucified *facing* the cross.[31] Perhaps they were, but the interesting thing here is that Wilson only brings the subject up to overcome a serious problem with the Shroud. And significantly, no other Shroudies agree with this method of crucifixion – they deal with the anomaly by studiously ignoring it.

Then there is the back image. It has the same intensity as the front. If it was authentic, the back must have been in direct contact with the cloth and the image should show some distortion, as in the Lancashire hospice case. It does not. And if it were due to some kind of chemical reaction, it should be darker than the front, since the body would have pressed harder on the cloth and would have trapped whatever vapours were responsible for the image. But it is exactly the same shade as the front. And some theories – such as that of Allan Mills – allow for no back image at all.

As we have seen, various theories have been put forward to explain away the carbon dating, reopening the possibility the Shroud could be genuine. However, the carbon dating is not necessary to show that the image is a fake – admittedly, a unique and brilliant fake, but a fake nevertheless. The most tell-tale clues that it is man-made are:

- The lack of any pre-fourteenth century references to an imaged Holy Shroud, and the flaws in theories put forward to account for this omission, such as the Mandylion hypothesis.
- Lack of any mention of such an object in either the New Testament or early Christian records.

- The fact that the Shroud must have been flat when the image was formed, otherwise it would be distorted. This applies to both the front and the back image. *The Shroud never wrapped a body.*
- The fact that two separate, and equally unique, processes are necessary to create the image of the body and the blood.
- The anomalies in the blood flows. They are almost perfect, but not quite.

As we came to look at the evidence of the Shroud as it stood in 1988, its mystery seemed more perplexing than ever. Everything points to it being a fake – the carbon dating, the historical evidence, the tell-tale anomalies in the lie of the cloth and the bloodstains. Yet it is not a painting. We could not ignore the work of STURP and other scientists. And while most other Shroudies are influenced by their own religious bias, it was not the case with us. Neither are we known as sceptics in matters paranormal (which includes so-called 'miracles'); put simply, we had no axe to grind one way or the other.

We kept coming back to the data. The sheer realism of the image and its anatomical excellence is totally at odds with what might be expected from a medieval forger. It was the 'nuclear flash' theory that helped to steer us towards a certain path by making us realise two major factors. The first was that, if the image really was created from a human body, whatever energy was used – nuclear radiation, rays or just ordinary light – had to be *reflected* from the body, not emitted from within it. The second was that the energy must have been directed or focused in some way, otherwise there would be no recognisable image.

In summing up the results of the 1978 tests, STURP scientist Lawrence Schwalbe wrote: '. . . elimination of all known methods does not prove that a clever artist or hoaxer did not think of a method unknown to us.'[32] Those words were to prove prophetic where our work was concerned, although the description of the hypothetical forger as 'clever' was, we discovered, definitely something of an understatement! Even at that early stage, we realised that even if the Shroud was the work of an artist, it was still far from being the simple fake that was dismissed so brusquely by detractors such as Teddy Hall. Whoever created it possessed knowledge far, far ahead of his time, and had used a method so effective that it continues to confound even the cream of twenty-first-century scientists. Clearly this was no ordinary artist – and no ordinary person.

In the months that followed the announcement of the carbon dating results, we were to discover that the creator of the Turin Shroud was much more than even a brilliant artist. He possessed, in ways hitherto unguessed at, one of the most extraordinary minds the world has ever known.

4

Correspondents

'The shroud is still an object worthy of contemplation and the identity of the unknown, brilliant author is the greatest remaining mystery.'

Professor Paul Damon of the Arizona
radio-carbon laboratory[1]

So far we have dealt with the historical and scientific background of the Shroud, and with all the theories put forward to account for the image as objectively as we can. But this story is inevitably also our own, and this is where it really begins.

The carbon dating results were announced on 13 October 1988. And within two months, Lynn was to begin a two-year on and off relationship with Ian Wilson. During this time she was asked to be consultant for an exhibition of images from the world of the paranormal at the Royal Photographic Society in Bath, which was entitled 'The Unexplained'. The Society's Administrator, Amanda Nevill, and Lynn spent many hours discussing the content of the exhibition, and their conversations often spilled over into other topics. They agreed that the carbon dating made the Shroud more, rather than less, fascinating, but Lynn was unprepared for Amanda's sudden instinct that the Shroud image should be included in the exhibition. By this time Lynn felt as if she were somehow being invaded by the thing – with Wilson's presence in her life and thoughts it seemed that everywhere she turned the Shroud was also there. At first, she was adamant that it should not be part of the exhibition.

However, very soon Lynn – still somewhat grudgingly – agreed not only to its inclusion, but to its being the focal point of the entire room. Of course the cloth itself remained firmly in its holy casket in Turin, but Wilson arranged for the RPS to borrow a full-sized transparency. Amanda had a lightbox specially constructed on which to exhibit it: as the image is over 14ft (4m) long, it cost approximately £900 to build (and was later bought by the British Museum, where the transparency was shown in their exhibition 'Fake: the Art of Deception', some months afterwards).

A life-sized photographic negative of the image was fixed on an adjacent wall, so visitors could check the detail after seeing the 'real' thing on the lightbox. It was an enormous success. In the first few days of the exhibition Lynn often fluttered nervously around like a mother hen, and many visitors came up to her and chatted about the exhibits. The Shroud replica, in its place of honour, was the first thing visitors saw on entering the exhibition, and, so soon after the 'disgrace' of the carbon dating, was a favourite topic.

A few visitors expressed their doubts about the carbon dating, saying that the image was obviously miraculous and that scientists could be wrong. Lynn could only nod in part agreement, having some strong views on the arrogance of scientists herself. But several visitors she talked to told her, rather vaguely, that they had 'heard somewhere', or 'read somewhere' that the Shroud had been faked by Leonardo da Vinci, or by 'his studio team'. It was an odd phenomenon: many people seemed to know that Leonardo was connected with the Shroud but could not remember where the information came from. One person who did, however, was Lynn's neighbour Helen Moss who said she clearly remembered being *taught* by her teachers at her Jewish School in Leeds that the Maestro had faked the Shroud.

Clive came to the opening of the exhibition and to other activities connected with it. For both of us, the groundswell of the various visitors' opinions about Leonardo and the Shroud meant very little in those early days. We both reflected, however, that it did make sense that almost the only known man clever enough to have perpetrated this astonishing fraud may actually have done it.

The exhibition had caused a minor flurry of publicity, and Lynn found herself on radio and television doing a whistle-stop tour of the exhibits. Having appeared many times on the Clive Bull and Michael van Straten shows on London's LBC Radio she felt at home with a microphone. John Sugar from the BBC World Service was one of the interviewers who came up to Bath, and after they had breezed through the exhibition on tape, they had a long discussion about the Shroud. As a result of her growing enthusiasm about it, he invited her to appear on a magazine programme specifically to discuss the post-carbon dating Shroud. Little did we realise just what fate had in store, thanks – perhaps – to that broadcast. We say 'perhaps' as at the same time Lynn had also expressed much the same views on LBC, and subsequent investigation has failed to isolate which one of those broadcasts initiated the coming events.

Over the years, like anyone who has appeared a few times on radio and television – and especially someone who dealt in the paranormal – she has had more than her fair share of crank letters. Some of them are obvious: written in three different coloured inks, for example, and on neatly cut-out, minute squares of paper; while others appear to be perfectly sane until the punchline. Suspicion of an alien intelligence that lurks in their television set is usually something of a giveaway, we find.

Shortly after doing both these broadcasts, Lynn received a letter from a complete stranger. She was more alarmed, to begin with, by the fact that this mail was addressed to her home, than with its contents. She was furious: heads would roll at LBC or at

Bush House! But both sets of staff emphatically denied giving out her personal details to any of their listeners.

The letter was intriguing. Signed simply 'Giovanni' it dealt with Leonardo and the Shroud, but took the story much further into the realms of what appeared to be fantasy. On the radio Lynn had simply said that the Maestro may have been implicated in the fake, but this man claimed to have inside knowledge that Leonardo had been responsible. Giovanni said that she should read *The Holy Blood and the Holy Grail* by Michael Baigent, Richard Leigh and Henry Lincoln, as background to the story of Leonardo and the Shroud, and that he would be in touch again.

We have to admit that, both of us having read the book, we were no wiser about Leonardo and the Shroud, although he does figure in the story as Grand Master of a secret society. The only reference by those authors to the Turin Shroud is found in their second book, *The Messianic Legacy* (1986), when they muse on a strange phenomenon among their readers:

> There were . . . numerous people who, quite inexplicably, persisted in confronting us with the Shroud of Turin. 'What about the Shroud of Turin?' we were asked repeatedly. (What indeed?) Or, 'how does the Shroud of Turin affect your thesis?' It was extraordinary how frequently this non sequitur occurred.[2]

Clearly there was a feeling that the events and theories outlined in *The Holy Blood and the Holy Grail* had some connection with the Shroud, although quite what it was eluded everyone. In due course, however, we made that connection . . .

Our mystery man, Giovanni, had made some astonishing claims about Leonardo and the Shroud. When we first read his letter there was, of course, a lot of nervous laughter. However, there was also a distinct feeling under it all that what he said would really start the ball rolling. As we have seen from the views of visitors to the exhibition, Giovanni's claim that Leonardo had faked the Shroud was hardly news. There appeared to be a rumour circulating in the collective unconscious to that effect. But Giovanni had much more dramatic details to flesh out this story. He offered extraordinary pieces of information that, although seemingly outrageous, gave us real food for thought.

He said that Leonardo had put the image of his own face on the Shroud. That serene, gaunt, bearded face so widely believed to be that of Jesus himself was in fact Leonardo da Vinci, perpetrating a sacrilegious joke on posterity. If this were not enough in itself, he went further, much further. He claimed that the body on the Shroud from the neck down at the front and all of the back image was that of a genuinely crucified man, a fifteenth-century victim of the first-century legacy of man's inhumanity to man (or to God, depending upon your views of the nature of Jesus). But Giovanni had no information on the central question: had Leonardo actually tortured someone to death in this horrific manner for the sake of historical accuracy, or had he used an already-dead body?

Still more was to come. Our informant also told us that Leonardo had not created the Shroud image by painting or any other known technique such as brass rubbing. He said that it represented the Maestro's greatest and most daring innovation, as the image had been created using 'chemicals and light, a sort of alchemical imprinting'. In other words the Shroud image is actually a *composite photograph* of Leonardo da Vinci together with some hapless crucifixion victim whose every contusion had been recorded for posterity by a fifteenth-century camera!

At least he had not claimed that the Shroudman was an alien from Betelgeuse, but we felt that what he had alleged was so outrageous as to belong in that category. Besides, why the semi-anonymity of signing himself just 'Giovanni'? At this stage we kept his letter in a file marked 'Loonies and Cranks', where we felt it deserved to be.

However, his words niggled away at us. The idea of the Shroud image being some kind of a photograph did make sense – after all, the most inexplicable feature of the Shroud is that it *behaves* like a photograph.

Whoever Giovanni was it soon became evident to us that he had made comments we should take seriously. As we have seen, several visitors to the exhibition had expressed the idea that Leonardo had been involved in faking the Shroud, and Giovanni just took the idea further. Although we were never to make up our minds about him or his true motives, and to this day we are healthily sceptical about everything connected with him, we are grateful for his tip-offs, which provided us with valuable short-cuts to the research that culminated in this book.

Face of the Master

There was another special moment, another sort of tip-off, and one that we look back on with a certain wonder and a great deal of affection. Walking round the exhibition in a daze some days after having received the first Giovanni letter, Lynn invited Amanda Nevill's then seven-year-old daughter Abigail to join us. An intelligent and lively child, she was delightful company and made considerably more pertinent comments about the exhibits than most of the adult visitors rolled into one. We rounded a corner and found ourselves staring straight at the life-sized negative of the man on the Shroud on the opposite wall. Lynn thought perhaps the image of such great physical torture was not appropriate for a child (having Cathar-like views on images of martyrdom), and tried to steer her away from it. But Abigail cocked her head to one side and stared at it solemnly.

'Why is his head too small – and why is it on wrong?' she asked immediately. Lynn looked at the image and felt distinctly faint. Suddenly this was like the critical moment in the story of the Emperor's New Clothes. 'It doesn't *fit*,' Abigail announced emphatically, with a certain disgust at the bad handiwork that was presumably involved. Then she lost interest. Lynn did not. Somehow she managed to turn the conversation and keep Abigail's remarks to herself for a short while. But inside she was exulting at what was clearly a highly significant insight – a real breakthrough. If you want the truth, ask a child.

This insight appeared to reinforce Giovanni's comments about the Shroud image being a composite. If Leonardo had superimposed his own face over someone else's body, it may not, of course, have made a perfect match. (At this stage we had no idea just how difficult his technique was: later, when we tried to replicate it, we got a taste of his problems.)

Clive was also stunned by Abigail's comments and at the speed that so many things were falling into place. Yet if we were ever going to present anything like a coherent case for this radical viewpoint, we had a very long way to go.

We got on with our lives, although Lynn admits to sneaking into a library and looking Leonardo up. She really wanted to know what he looked like: to her shame, her long years of education had not provided her with even a vague mental picture of the Florentine Maestro. She had to check; after all, if he was fat and bald he would be an unlikely candidate for the thin-faced bearded Shroudman! Lynn remembers clearly having to take a deep breath as she opened a standard art history book and flicked the pages. But there he was: thin-faced, bearded, beautiful.

Some weeks after this, Lynn went into a shop to buy a birthday card and was puzzled to see a vivid image of Leonardo on a stack of cards out of the corner of her eye. Intrigued as to why anyone would want them – perhaps there was a sudden craze for the Old Masters she knew nothing about – she investigated. In fact, what she was looking at was a reproduction of the 1935 portrait of the man on the Shroud by Ariel Aggemian. On the back of the postcard it read confidently 'You are holding a picture with . . . the Holy Face of Jesus . . . taken from the Holy Shroud of Turin.' Lynn certainly could not fault the last statement, but as for the first, her initial reaction was, even at this early stage, a vehement: 'Oh no I'm *not.*'

We hurriedly arranged a lunch, and Lynn presented a Leonardo reference book and the postcard. She had no need to point out the purpose behind this impromptu show of visual aids – Clive could see for himself.

A pattern was clearly emerging, but even so we had to go very carefully indeed. We needed some corroboration by someone who was totally unconnected and unconcerned with the Shroudie world. At the time Lynn was a freelance feature writer on a women's magazine, and that afternoon they were organising a mammoth photo shoot for their fashion pages. She took the portrait of Leonardo and the postcard into the models' dressing room, knowing that anyone connected with women's magazines is used to being asked odd questions, whether it be about their most intimate personal habits or their views on the latest mascara. So Lynn just showed them the two pictures and said, 'What do you think?'

The response was instant, and extremely gratifying. Out of fifteen who came and went during the afternoon (Lynn did manage to do some work from time to time!), eleven of them said straight away: 'It's the same man.' Two said words to the effect of, 'I don't know what you want me to say . . . apart from the fact that it's the same man.' One said she didn't know what Lynn was after and was busy, and the last one said she recognised the man on the Shroud because she was a Catholic and she hoped Lynn wasn't going to say anything upsetting about it. If she is reading this, which we doubt, we apologise.

This unofficial vox pop was hardly evidence, although it is true that the human eye is a better judge than almost any other monitoring, imaging or matching equipment, from the camera to the computer. Lynn had been careful not to give the models any clues as to what reaction she was looking for. We regret not having taken their details for future reference, but even so that episode certainly added to the growing enthusiasm we felt for further investigation into Leonardo and the Shroud. And it certainly made us smile when, months afterwards, Rodney Hoare and Michael Clift of the BSTS said, respectively, 'I can't see the similarity myself,' and 'The man on the Shroud looks nothing like Leonardo.'

On the other hand, even other believers have no difficulty seeing the resemblance. One of the most priceless moments in our career came in 2001 during the filming of a documentary about our work for the National Geographic Channel. The programme also included a piece about the Italian sculptor Luigi Mattei, who specialises in life-size sculptures of — as he firmly believes — Jesus based on the image on the Shroud. During filming Mattei spontaneously declared that he had often remarked on the striking resemblance between the Shroud image of 'Jesus' and Leonardo da Vinci . . .[3]

Sion Revealed

Over the months we received a total of thirteen letters from Giovanni, which gave us a great deal of information about Leonardo and the Shroud, most of which we have shown to be accurate through independent research and our own experiments. To sum up, these are his main points:

Leonardo faked the Shroud in 1492. It was a composite creation: he put the image of his own face on it together with the body of a genuinely crucified man. It was not a painting: it was a projected image 'fixed' on the cloth using chemicals and light; in other words it was a photographic technique.

The Maestro faked it for two main reasons. First, because he had been commissioned to do it by the Pope, Innocent VIII, as a cynical publicity exercise. But the reason he invested it with such concentration, daring and genius was that it represented for him the supreme opportunity to attack the basis of Christianity from within the Church itself (and perhaps he rather liked the idea of generations of pilgrims praying over his own image). He imbued it with subtle clues that, if understood, would be profoundly challenging to the Establishment. However, Giovanni said Leonardo was never paid for his work on the Turin Shroud because, to the naked eye, it was very disappointing! Perhaps Leonardo can now be said finally to have collected his reward.

All this information had been given to us as a statement of fact. But was there any evidence to back this up?

We have seen that Giovanni's first letter urged Lynn to read *The Holy Blood and the Holy Grail* by Michael Baigent, Richard Leigh and Henry Lincoln. In fact she needed no urging, having finally got round to reading it shortly beforehand: years previously, when she was Deputy Editor of the weekly publication *The Unexplained*, it had carried a short series about the book, but at the time it held no interest for her and, as she did not actually edit the series herself, she failed to read it.

Fate can be very quirky: the story of that book was to parallel ours to some extent, and was to be the background for much of our research. *The Holy Blood and the Holy Grail* begins with the mystery of Rennes-le-Château, a remote village in Languedoc in southern France, close to the Spanish border. In the last years of the nineteenth century its priest, François Bérenger Saunière, began renovating the church and allegedly found some documents in a pillar. The parchments were in code, and seemed to point to the involvement of local aristocracy in some kind of plot. Whatever else Saunière found, it seemed to be extremely valuable, for quite abruptly he became immensely wealthy, attracting the cream of Parisian high society to his parish – although, again, we can only guess what the attraction was. Saunière rebuilt the church to house many extremely bizarre decorations, including a plaster demon guarding the entrance, over which there is a sign that reads: 'This is a terrible place'.[4]

The priest died on 22 January 1917.[5] His corpse was set in a sitting position, and many mourners, including some from as far away as Paris, who seemed to have prior knowledge of this death-day, filed past, each plucking a red pom-pom off his robe. The priest who had been called in to hear Saunière's last confession had, it was rumoured, fled in horror, and Rennes' priest went to his grave unshriven.

In the 1970s Henry Lincoln had researched this story for three BBC television programmes,[6] and had uncovered possible connections with other murky groups in history, including the Knights Templar. Some years later he and his colleagues Baigent and Leigh collaborated on a book project that set out to research this bizarre story yet further. It was to be something of a Pandora's box, eventually leading them through a maze of secret societies and controversy, and which culminated in *The Holy Blood and the Holy Grail*, an international bestseller.

Their research led them to uncover the existence of a shadowy organisation called the Priory of Sion, which allegedly had existed since the eleventh century. Members of the Priory, including the then Grand Master, Pierre Plantard de Saint-Clair, had made themselves known to the three authors and had helped them in their research, which rapidly widened in scope until the original mystery was almost forgotten. The avowed aim of the Priory was, the authors agreed, to uphold the bloodline of Jesus and Mary Magdalene, who they believed had been married. They claimed that Jesus had not died on the cross, but had perhaps lived for many years afterwards, and that the Magdalene had taken their children to the south of France, where she lived out her long life. Their descendants became the Merovingian dynasty of Frankish kings. It is a strange, compelling – but of course 'heretical' – story and has received considerable criticism and downright abuse. (Ian Wilson always provides the prefix 'notorious' or 'infamous' when forced to discuss *The Holy Blood and the Holy Grail*.)

The Priory of Sion boasted that over the centuries it has had many great names as Grand Master.[7] In fact, a few of them had been women, for the Priory had always been an equal opportunities secret society. Among the male Grand Masters listed in the organisation's documents known as the *Dossiers secrets* were Sir Isaac Newton, Victor Hugo and Leonardo da Vinci. Leonardo, it seemed, took over the leadership in 1510 until his death in 1519 when he was a guest of Francis I at his château at Amboise in the Loire valley.

Like many other readers of *The Holy Blood and the Holy Grail* we felt twinges of scepticism about some of its claims, although we thought that the logical structure of the book was convincing enough. On the surface it did seem too good to be true that the Priory had as its Grand Masters some of the most famous names in history; others included Claude Debussy and Jean Cocteau, for example. However, in recent years less celebrated people have taken over that lofty role, including Pierre Plantard de Saint-Clair.

Giovanni also claimed to have been high in the ranks of a schismatic faction of the Priory of Sion, claiming that his faction were purists who believed that the modern organisation had moved too far from its original aims and beliefs.[8]

Many critics of *The Holy Blood and the Holy Grail* have underlined its reliance upon often mysterious – and therefore uncheckable – sources. Although we had been tempted to take the critics' side at first, very soon our own situation began to parallel that of those three authors to some extent, and we were rapidly humbled by it. As we found out the hard way, a mysterious source does not necessarily mean a fictitious one, although there is never any lack of critics to hint otherwise.

What evidence is there for the existence of the Priory of Sion? Opinions vary between two extremes. The first is that the claims made by the organisation – namely, that they have existed since the eleventh century and that they are the custodians of secrets from long before that – are literally true. The other extreme is that it is entirely and utterly a hoax, and that it was invented in the 1950s.

The middle ground is that the Priory is a modern group which is trying to claim a lengthy history for motives best known to themselves. Some writers on esoteric subjects have expressed scepticism that the Priory could have remained unknown for so long – the existence of even the most secret political, religious and occult societies eventually becomes known. The American writer and expert on secret societies Robert Anton Wilson has concluded that the Priory is of twentieth or perhaps late-nineteenth-century origin, and was created as a form of elaborate practical joke.[9] A similar view seems to prevail within today's esoteric circles.

There is a major problem here: proving the existence of a secret society is similar to trying to prove a negative. Logically, the most successful secret society is the one that nobody knows about, and it seems that when we are dealing with the Priory, we are at least up against past masters in manufacturing misinformation, cover stories and mischief. Yet in their case, there is evidence – albeit indirect – that backs up certain of the Priory's claims.

In the sequels to this book, *The Templar Revelation* and *The Sion Revelation*, we explore the extraordinary machinations of the Priory of Sion in greater detail and arrive at firmer conclusions about it. We came to realise that the Priory of Sion is, as its critics have claimed, a modern invention, dating back only to 1956. But that is not to say it is merely some kind of elaborate hoax: it acts as a 'front' for a network of related esoteric groups that do boast a much longer pedigree. These include the Martinist Order, a system of occult Freemasonry called the Rectified Scottish Rite, and the 'Egyptian Rites' of Freemasonry, the Rites of Memphis and Misraïm, which were united in 1899 under the great occultist Papus (Gérard Encausse).[10]

These societies, all founded in the eighteenth or nineteenth centuries, can be traced back to the same Masonic system called the Strict Observance that certainly existed in the 1740s but which – controversially – claimed to be the heirs of the medieval Knights Templar. So, in fact, the modern Priory of Sion is aligned to a tradition that goes back to at least the middle of the eighteenth century. But can it really, via the Strict Observance, trace its roots back to the Templars of the twelfth century?

We found that there were indeed common threads, the most important by far being that they share the 'Johannite tradition', which places special emphasis on the importance of John the Baptist – to say the least. In fact, we discovered that the Johannites actually believe him to be superior to Jesus. They also share a common involvement in alchemy and underground heresy.

We found that this Johannite thread was not only shared by the modern network of societies to which we linked the Priory of Sion, but was also a major part of the beliefs of the original Knights Templar. Not only did they specifically revere John the Baptist, but their secret rituals – for which they were to be per-secuted – included the veneration of a bearded severed head. (The Baptist was of course beheaded.)

So while the modern Priory of Sion's historical claims – as detailed in the *Dossiers secrets*, a series of enigmatic documents deposited in the Bibliothèque Nationale in Paris between 1964 and 1967 – should not be taken literally, they do seem to incor-porate long-running esoteric and heretical tradition.

The Priory of Sion claims Leonardo as one of its own, which means that if he had been a member of one of the Johannite groups in their network, it is possible that some inside knowl-edge of his involvement in the Shroud forgery could have filtered down to the present – and Giovanni.

In all of the thirteen letters from Giovanni, one phrase cropped

up more than any other, and that is 'For Those Who Have Eyes
To See, Let Them See'. We discovered that this was not only a
version of the well-known Biblical quotation, 'If any man have
ears to hear, let him hear,' (Matt. 8:16) but also an alchemical
adage. We were being told to look beyond the surface, to accept
no standard texts, no glib answers. We soon came to realise that
where the work of the Priory is concerned we were dealing with
people who had – and still have – the finest of minds, and with
an organisation that is as intelligent as it is 'heretical'.

On one level, these bits of information from an anonymous
source were not any more significant than, say, receiving the
answers to crossword clues (without always knowing the clues
themselves) through the post. There was something rather disturbing, however, about being picked out by a stranger who had
decided to unburden himself of some rather murky historical and
religious secrets. For some time Lynn was in danger of becoming
paranoid; unexpectedly hearing a male Italian voice behind her
would make her jump – she jumped a lot during the tourist season
in London – and she was not over-keen on hearing her letter-
box snap open and shut. She was not exactly scared by Giovanni's
letters – indeed they often enthralled her – but she wondered
what it was all leading up to.

'Not a Game for Children'

Then in March 1991, we met Giovanni. Somehow he had discovered Lynn's home telephone number, although it is
ex-directory, and to her utter amazement, got in touch. We met
him in the bar of the Cumberland Hotel off Marble Arch in central London for three hours of rambling conversation over drinks.

Giovanni was not a disappointment, although he could be said
to be too good to be true. Looking like a rumpled Tom Conti,
with a creased designer suit and a shock of greying black hair plus

beard, he was an Italian of middle age and middle height. Talking to Giovanni was like talking to the Queen: there was no small talk. After providing us with a bottle of very good Muscadet, he launched immediately, if idiosyncratically, into what our friend Craig Oakley was later to describe as 'heavy stuff'.

If we thought that we were being flattered by this attention, then we were rapidly disabused of this illusion. Giovanni seemed not to be interested in us personally, as his repeated questions about Ian Wilson revealed. Strangely, while he did know that Lynn was no longer in touch with him, he also seemed to think that this was merely a temporary state of affairs. Whenever he brought up the subject of Ian Wilson he scrutinised Lynn's face and mannerisms very carefully, being particularly satisfied – or so it seemed – when she once found herself blushing. It began to dawn on us that Giovanni's prime interest was not in us, but in Wilson, and that the reason he had been feeding us all the information about Leonardo and the Shroud was in the hope that it would get back to him.

After some long silences and exchange of glances between us, Clive asked Giovanni whether or not this was the case. With a private chuckle, our Italian contact admitted this was so. We asked why he had not approached Wilson directly.

To our amazement, he said straightaway that 'we' had tried it once before, but had not succeeded and Wilson was now suspicious of any such approaches. When we asked why he was so important, Giovanni sniffed that he was the best known Shroud researcher (laughingly adding 'so far') in the UK, if not in the West, and that he is considerably less pro-authenticity than his public stance would have people believe. We were frankly sceptical.

He went on to say that, as he had clearly failed to get to Ian Wilson either directly (whatever that might mean) or through Lynn, he had decided to choose us to promote what he called 'the truth' about the Shroud. Put like that, it was hardly complimentary and the whole scenario was, we were beginning to feel, distinctly unsavoury. Rather sharply we told him that if we were to take his Leonardo story further, we would do so with open minds and we would not agree at any stage to act simply as a mouthpiece for him and whoever he might represent.

At this first sign of real anger, the whole tone of the conversation changed. Giovanni visibly relaxed, and began to ask us what we thought about *The Holy Blood and the Holy Grail* in terms that suggested he knew something that the authors of that book did not. He asked us what we thought of the evidence for the existence of the Priory of Sion, and when we said rather politely that it seemed intriguing but hardly conclusive, he laughed.

The conversation then moved to secret societies in general and we expressed our view that conspiracy theories might be fun, but that way madness lies. Giovanni shrugged and murmured that such opinions were odd coming from us, considering just how many members of such organisations we actually knew. As we sat stunned, he listed several of our acquaintances by name, giving their rank in groups such as alchemical movements, the Templars, the Freemasons and the Priory itself. It was particularly chilling to hear him name a publishing consultant and a publishing director whom Lynn had worked with closely as respectively a fellow member and a master alchemist. Although by this time we were in a state of shocked denial, what was truly chilling about these apparently wild statements was the ease with which we later discovered at least some of them to be true. For example, it transpired that the director not only writes under a pseudonym on the subject of alchemy but he also lives near Rennes-le-Château – and shortly after this Lynn found herself working with him again. While we were unable to establish that the consultant was a member of the Priory, we did confirm that he belonged to an esoteric order.

Giovanni said that he had arranged to meet us because as far

as he was personally concerned, 'things were hotting up' and he
deemed it prudent to go back to Italy. Although he refused to
elaborate, he seemed to be implying his contact with us had
made his departure rather urgent. Almost as an aside, he asked us
to destroy his letters, in case they could be traced back to him.
An expressive silence followed this statement. We agreed, but to
our shame did not actually get rid of the Giovanni file until certain circumstances hinted heavily that such a course of action
might be wise . . .

As he gathered up his crumpled raincoat, he said over-casually,
'This is not a game, you know, for children. You will find your-
selves the subject of unwelcome attention and not just from
those who worship Leonardo's face without knowing it.'

He turned to go, and with perfect dramatic timing, he said,
'Why are our Grand Masters always known as John? Leonardo
was, of course, a Giovanni. This is no small point, but it is the
key. Just think about it.'

When we had sat there in silence for a few more minutes and
discovered that we had not turned back into pumpkins, we
finally began to unwind. We simply did not know what to make
of Giovanni or his obsession with secret societies.

Sinister Events

In the following weeks and months we had just begun to come
around to the idea that Giovanni was a sad case, even though our
independent research had already confirmed many of his apparently wilder statements. Then events, some of them already
disturbing, began to form a pattern.

There had already been one worrying incident which may
have had some connection with something that was a sign of
'unwelcome attention', although we had tried to push it, and its
implications, to the back of our minds. In June 1990, Ian Wilson

and Lynn were still seeing each other, until there was a sudden – and final – silence. A friend telephoned him to ask why he was no longer in touch with her. He replied mysteriously that he had 'come into some information'. Of course this may have been some gossip about Lynn that had no bearing on anything other than her character, but in the light of what was to come – the attempts to discredit our work – it was certainly provocative. We later gathered that this was an anonymous letter which seemed, as far as we could tell, to link Lynn with some satanic subculture. Such was the impact of this missive that Wilson later wrote to Clive warning him in the strongest terms that 'if you have any personal regard for Christian values you are doing yourself no favours by following the path on which Lynn is leading you . . . playing around with the "Leonardo" theory is a mere minor gambit of hers in a game that is much more sinister.' Despite our repeated insistence that he tell us what Lynn was accused of, he steadfastly refused to say 'for legal reasons'.[11] We have been told that he then telephoned at least one leading British Shroudie to hint that she was involved in satanic occult practices.[12]

Shortly after our meeting with Giovanni, in March 1991, by which time our research was already quite advanced, Lynn was walking around Hampstead Village in north London with her friend Peter. They were looking in art galleries and window-shopping, and therefore wandering all over the place quite randomly. At first they thought they were imagining it, but there did appear to be a man following them. Whenever they turned round there he was, abruptly looking in shop windows; when they crossed the road, so did he. Whenever they stayed for any length of time inside a shop or gallery he kept looking in at them, presumably checking to see if they were still there, or whether they might have left by another door. The peculiar thing was that he was so bad at it, far too obvious. In the end they turned round to face him and stared: he disappeared into a pizza restaurant rapidly. But when they walked past and looked

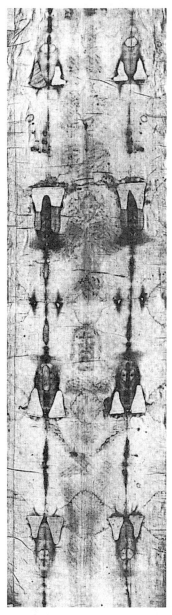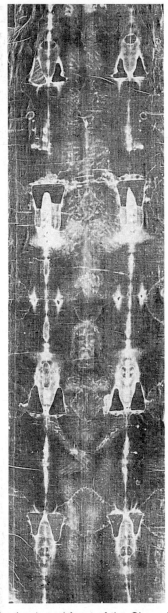

The Turin Shroud as it appears to the naked eye. The image is that of a crucified male body, 'hinged' at the head.

The back and front of the Shroud in photographic negative, revealing a startling clarity of detail. This in itself has been taken as proof of miraculous origin.

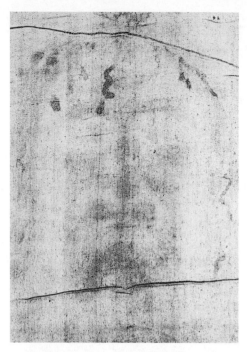

The face of the man on the Shroud as seen to the naked eye.

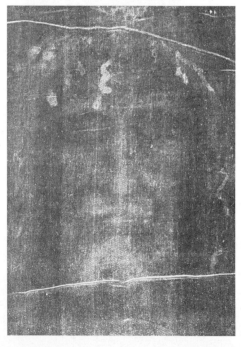

The face of the man on the Shroud as seen in photographic negative.

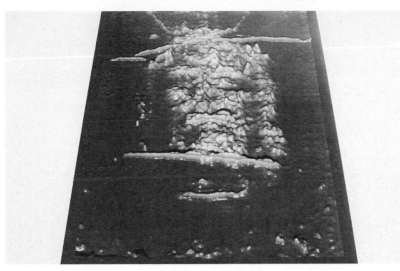

Andy Haveland-Robinson's computer wizardry produced this image of the Shroud head for us. Displaying areas of different brightness as different heights it reveals that not only does the head appear to be totally separate from the body, but also that there is an almost complete absence of the much-vaunted 3-D information.

Another of Andy's computer-enhanced images, using a more extreme scale, also does not contain the 3-D information claimed by other researchers, and shows the abrupt termination of the head image at the neck in starker detail, with a clear space between head and body.

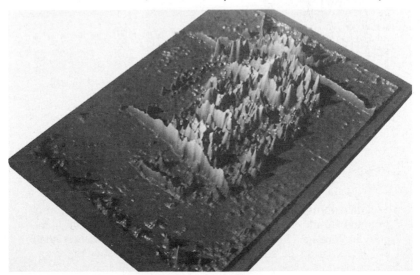

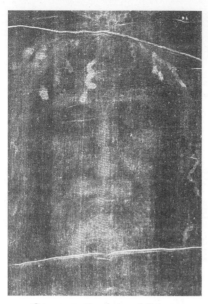
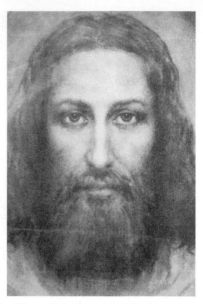

Compare the face of the man on the Shroud, both in negative and in Ariel Aggemian's 1935 portrait taken from the cloth, with that of Leonardo's as in the three best-known portraits reproduced below. The similarities are striking.

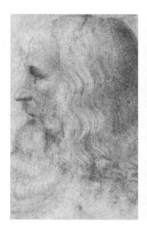
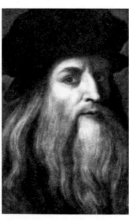
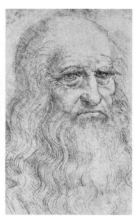

The profile portrait from the Royal Library at Windsor.

The posthumous portrait held at the Uffizi Gallery, Florence.

The self-portrait (c.1514), in the Biblioteca Reale, Turin.

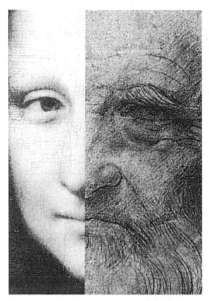

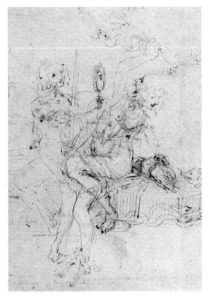

In the 1980s both Lillian Schwartz of Bell Laboratories and Dr Digby Quested of London's Maudsley Hospital demonstrated that the *Mona Lisa* is a self-portrait of its creator. Leonardo may have become the 'most beautiful woman in the world' but did he also become the very image of the son of God?

Leonardo's sketch *Witch using a Magic Mirror* (detail from 'Allegory of the political state of Milan') shows a female face on the front of the head and a male face (very like his own) on the back. This classic occult symbol provides an intriguing link between Leonardo and the alchemical underground.

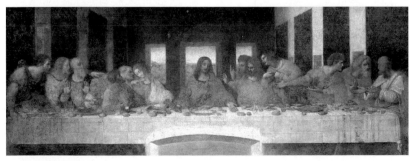

In his *Last Supper* Leonardo painted himself as the disciple on the second from the right: note how he is turned away from Jesus. We discover that the 'young man' on Jesus' right is joined to him by a giant spread-eagled 'M' shape. Is this meant to be seen as the Magdalene? Where is the all-important wine, symbol of the sacramentals blood?

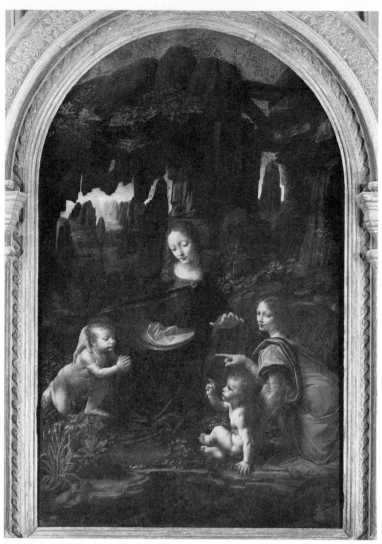

One of Leonardo's most admired religious paintings. *The Virgin of the Rocks* (Louvre version) is, in fact, a profoundly – even shockingly – heretical work. Although it appears that the infant Jesus is blessing the child John the Baptist, the children are with the wrong guardians: Jesus should be with his mother and John with his traditional protector, the archangel Uriel. However, if the children are with their *right* guardians, Jesus is in the submissive position, being blessed by John. This is, we discovered, entirely in keeping with Leonardo's passionate Johannite beliefs: he upheld the Baptist as the true Christ, while secretly despising Jesus.

Leonardo's famous Cartoon (preliminary work) for *The Virgin and Child with St Anne*, contains further evidence of the artist's Johannitism. Among other details is St Anne thrusting her forefinger into the air, in the 'John gesture'. We discovered that, in Leonardo's works, this always refers to John the Baptist and here may mean 'Remember John'. In any case, many experts agree that St Anne is, in fact, meant to be St Elizabeth, the Baptist's mother.

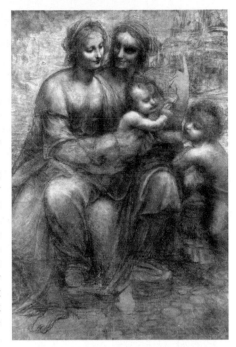

In *St Anne with Virgin and Child* – the final version of the Cartoon – the infant John has been replaced by a lamb. Although Jesus is often represented as 'the Lamb of God', John the Baptist is symbolised as a lamb by Johannites. Note, too, how roughly Jesus handles it – hooking his leg over its frail neck and pulling at its ears. The composition ensures that it looks as if the lamb's head is severed.

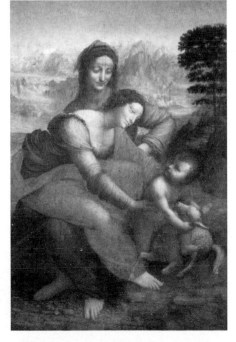

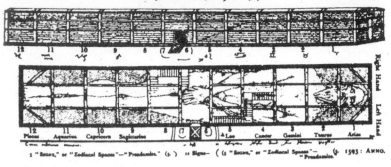

The 'Rosicrucian Ark of Noah', dating from 1593, shows a Shroud-like figure with astrological associations.

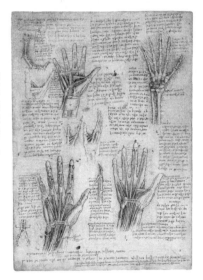

Leonardo's studies of the hand. His anatomical research provided him with opportunities to experiment with the techniques of crucifixion.

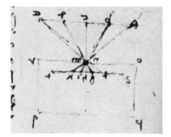

Leonardo's camera obscura (*left*), and his 'Model of Sight' (*below*). Does the secret of the Turin Shroud lie in his obsession with optics, lenses and light?

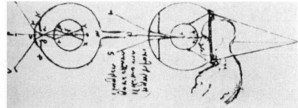

in, he was sitting by the window peering over his newspaper: seeing them stare, he looked away. To this day Lynn can describe him perfectly.

We both had a similar experience in a wine bar off Great Portland Street in central London, where we used to meet regularly for lunch, to discuss our research. A different man sat in the shadows behind us and was quite clearly listening to what we were saying to such an extent that we made pointed references to it and very obviously changed the subject. It was all so blatant, but being typically British we found it impossible to challenge this man. When we left he followed us, and when we parted he followed Lynn, even to the extent of trailing her round every department of Marks and Spencer in Oxford Street, where she went quite deliberately. She only lost him when she was the last one to be allowed on a full bus, leaving him standing in the queue. Lynn watched to see if he jumped in a taxi to 'follow that bus', but he shrugged and disappeared into the crowd. Whoever was behind it, they wanted us to know that they were on our trail.

There have been many occasions when we felt as if we were being followed, but they were less clear-cut than the episodes we have just described. Shortly after that Lynn had telephone calls from several people she had dealings with, checking to see if she had suddenly moved house. Apparently their letters to her had been returned, with 'not known at this address' scribbled on them. Checking with the local sorting office Lynn discovered that they had received two letters which had been addressed to her with 'gone away' written on them, had concluded that she had moved, and had returned all her mail subsequently. She never got to the bottom of this, but it was a somewhat chilling experience.

There were several similar incidents, none of them adding up to anything very much in themselves. But then, one Saturday in July 1992, came the most dramatic of them all. Because of the nature of a writer's lifestyle, Lynn is almost always at home. However, on this particular day, we were visiting the church of Notre-Dame de France off Leicester Square with our friends Craig Oakley and Tony Pritchett. While we were out, there was an attempted break-in at Lynn's flat, the only one in her then nine years' residence. Curiously, the would-be burglar made his attempt in full view of a busy road in bright sunlight on a Saturday afternoon, perhaps simply because this was the only time he found that Lynn was out. The next-door gardener had chased him away, and the police were called, who promptly became suspicious about the apparent bizarreness of this very public crime. They asked if Lynn had any enemies because there are many more secluded premises in her road which are easier to break into. To smash your way into her flat you have to cross a garden that can be clearly seen from the main road and there is only one entrance with no means of a quick getaway. It seemed as if she had been singled out personally.

It was after this that Lynn destroyed the Giovanni letters, with more than a little sense of relief.

Perhaps the most worrying of these incidents took place at the Rome Symposium of the international Shroud community in June 1993. Although – for obvious reasons – we were not there ourselves, a few days after it finished Clive received a letter from the wife of one of the BSTS officers, crowing that 'all your tricks have backfired', and accusing him of mounting some kind of campaign against Ian Wilson. We had learned to take this particular correspondent less than seriously, but after making some enquiries among others who had attended we were able to confirm that, shortly before the symposium, letters had been sent to various leading lights in the international Shroud community making allegations about Ian Wilson – and apparently signed by Clive. Despite our efforts, we were unable to obtain copies of the letters, and never discovered the exact nature of the allegations.

Clive had sent no such letters, and we had not the slightest knowledge of them before the symposium. However, the intention of the forger was obvious – and successful. The Shroudies closed ranks around Ian Wilson and we became effectively *personae non gratae*. Several previously cordial correspondences stopped abruptly. The serious side of this was the effect it had on our research, as access to much of the more obscure literature was made more difficult. This, presumably, was the intention of the forger, besides discrediting us in the eyes of the Shroudies.

Taken individually, none of these incidents is particularly significant. After all, strange things do happen in big cities these days, and we were well aware that we could be accused of being paranoid. However, taken together, these events seemed to point to some kind of concerted effort to harass and intimidate us, and also to discredit us and our work in Shroudie circles.

It might be thought that these were the actions of some of the more fanatical Shroudies, but this sort of energetic campaign is hardly their style (waspish exchanges of letters being as far as they generally go), and several of the earlier incidents took place before we were known to them.

Interestingly, we were not the only sindonologists to experience odd, if not sinister, goings on. Holger Kersten in *The Jesus Conspiracy* reveals that the BSTS are quite used to such attentions. He describes how on a visit to London in January 1989, when he was trying to find evidence against the carbon dating, he was warned by the then Secretary to be careful in his investigations as he might find himself hanging under Blackfriars Bridge, like 'God's banker' Roberto Calvi. She stressed that the BSTS had had a disturbing experience when overtures were made by a neo-Templar organisation in 1979. Ian Wilson had tried to investigate them, and managed to gain an informant, only to back off when this woman completely and mysteriously disappeared.[13] We remembered Giovanni's words about how they had tried to influence Ian Wilson – perhaps this episode was what he meant.

We became aware ourselves of the modern-day Templars'

interest when we were approached by one of the BSTS founder members, who not only claimed one of the grander Habsburg titles, but also announced to us that he was an active Templar. After showing a marked interest in us and our work (which was not very advanced at that stage) he abruptly dropped us and has not been seen at any BSTS meeting since.

The Templars were not the only candidates for this strange little campaign against us. If Giovanni were really part of a schismatic group of the Priory of Sion or whoever is behind them, and if he had passed on to us some of their secrets, then we might well have found ourselves under such scrutiny. As we were to discover (see Chapter 6) the Turin Shroud has always been an object of great fascination to the Priory, and perhaps the closer one gets to the reason why, the less they like it.

It may be that it is not the Priory that we need to be wary of. There are, after all, other vested interests in maintaining the mystery of the Shroud. However, we have come to realise that, once the true message of that image is understood, there will be considerably more at stake than a few academic reputations. Even discovering the identity and purpose of the Shroud's creator is, we have discovered, tantamount to opening Pandora's box, because within the mystery of that cloth lies another, infinitely greater secret.

5

'Faust's Italian Brother'

'Leonardo formed . . . a doctrine so heretical that he depended no more on . . . any religion . . .'

Lives of the Artists, by Giorgio Vasari, 1550
(this sentence was removed from subsequent editions)

Conspiracies, real or imagined, may seem beguiling, even a little romantic, but we soon realised that they really served as little more than a distraction. There we were, a commonsensical systems analyst and a hard-headed journalist who were concerned with investigating the Shroud, and our research into it soon became the focus of our lives.

We could hardly overlook the apparent lead given to us not only by Giovanni but also by young Abigail and several visitors to the exhibition at Bath: namely that the Shroud had been created by Leonardo da Vinci and that he used himself, at least in part, as the model. Since those early days there have been many dismissive comments about our mysterious source of information. Shroudies have called all our work 'worthless' just because we have admitted we acted on a tip-off. Yet no-one ever berates the police, for example, for doing the same if they solve a case as a result. The effect of the tip-off is to make them search for admissible evidence. We think this analogy is particularly apposite here.

Unlike many other Shroudies, we were not sceptical about

the carbon dating (while admitting that it can sometimes be inaccurate) and believed it to be just as valid as any other scientific research into the Shroud, including STURP's work in the 1970s. The carbon dating results told us the period of history we should be concentrating on, and immediately we realised that not only did this timespan include the heyday of faked relics, but it could also cover the lifetime of Leonardo da Vinci.

Of course the core period pinpointed by the carbon dating – 1260–1390 – is some time before Leonardo's day (1452–1519). But Teddy Hall said he would accept a date as late as 1500, when Leonardo was 48. In any case, that hoaxer of all people would have realised that to fake a purportedly ancient relic, you do not use brand new cloth. He may well have used a piece of old linen. It is ironic that Shroudies who challenged our work have actually used the carbon dating against us – claiming that it puts the forgery well outside Leonardo's lifespan! Sometimes their logical convolutions are frankly incredible.

The Leonardo scenario certainly made a lot of sense to us, although there did appear to be one problem with chronology. As we have seen, most of the historical literature traces the Shroud back to the 1350s, and Leonardo was not born until 1452. However, the history of the Shroud's early days before it achieved renown as a relic is remarkably hazy and theories that the Lirey Shroud was replaced by a new and better model are not unknown. We were to find that there is persuasive evidence such a substitution did indeed take place (see Chapter 6).

It would have been obtuse and ungrateful of us to disregard all the helpful comments that had come our way about Leonardo's part in faking the Shroud, and so it was natural for us to begin by researching this extraordinary and enigmatic individual.

The Perfect Candidate

Leonardo is the perfect, perhaps the only candidate for creator of the Shroud. Pierre Barbet attempted to demonstrate the improbability of the image being the work of man by summing up the attributes which would be required of the perpetrator in these words: 'If this be the work of a forger, he must have been a supergenius as an anatomist, a physiologist and an artist, a genius of such unexcelled quality that he must have been made to order.'[1]

Citing Leonardo as author of the Shroud has long proved irresistible to the more open-minded sindonologists as it is obvious that if it is a forgery, someone of genius must have been behind it. The forger had to have been someone with spectacular gifts, and whose method in this case was unique and so advanced that it still refuses to yield its secrets to art experts and scientists. He had to be an innovator, someone who thought beyond all obvious and conventional methodology, and also a real hands-on researcher, who had actually tested the method of crucifixion, for example. For the same reason, this faker had to have a working knowledge of anatomy. Leonardo, as Peter Brent and David Rolfe put it in their book *The Silent Witness*, was 'the only man with the blend of artistic ability, technical ingenuity and psychological insight who might plausibly have forged so powerful an icon.'[2]

Of course to most believers the idea that the Shroud was created by human hands is nonsense. Yet Leonardo's name does come up time after time in the literature. Ian Wilson has mused that the creator of the Shroud must have been 'an obscure Leonardo of his time'.[3] Noel Currer-Briggs has declared that the putative artist's 'knowledge of human anatomy rivals that of Leonardo da Vinci . . .[4] The big question here is: is it possible that someone of such genius could have remained unknown to history?

Sometimes Leonardo's name is invoked by the pro-authenticity lobby but only to damn him with faint praise. Recently, German researcher Holger Kersten wrote: 'Even a genius commanding skills and talents greater than those of a Leonardo da Vinci would clearly have been incapable of such a masterly feat.'[5]

The regularity with which Leonardo's name is mentioned in this context is a sure indicator that these writers realise that not only is he the best candidate for the forgery – he is virtually the *only* candidate. In fact, once one realises that there are good reasons for believing that the Lirey Shroud is not the same as today's Turin Shroud, the identity of the latter's creator becomes almost self-evident. Add to that the remarkable similarity between Leonardo's own face and that of the man on the Shroud and coincidence begins to stretch too far.

Leonardo has been proposed by others as the genius behind the Shroud. The earliest was Noemi Gabrielli, a member of the Archbishop of Turin's secret commission of 1969–73 (see Chapter 1), and formerly director of Piedmont's art galleries.[6] To be strictly accurate, she thought that an artist of Leonardo's school was responsible, as she detected a similarity in the shading of the face of the man on the Shroud to a technique invented by Leonardo and used by his pupils, and even went so far as to draw a parallel with the face of the Redeemer in Leonardo's *Last Supper*. As to method, she suggested that, rather than being painted or drawn directly on to the Shroud, the figure was the result of a block print, first painted in clay and yellow ochre on a separate piece of cloth, which was then pressed against the Shroud with a padded block, a technique used in the early days of printing. Her ideas were given short shrift by the believers, who brushed them aside without bothering to try to analyse their merit, often with extremely patronising comments and thinly veiled slights on her competence and even her mental health. However, although we are broadly sympathetic about the abusive treatment she received from the believers, her suggestion could not account for the characteristics of the image as later isolated by STURP.

Gabrielli, like others before her, had failed to notice the resemblance between the Maestro and the man on the Shroud. To our knowledge, the first to do so was Anthony Harris in his 1988 book, *The Sacred Virgin and the Holy Whore*. His theory that it was an ingenious self-portrait is just a small part of that book, which is an investigation into the underground church of Mary Magdalene that flourished in France. The fact that he made the connection that had been literally staring researchers in the face is to his credit, but unfortunately he fails to explain just how Leonardo committed this dangerous and blasphemous act. He believes that the image was created using red chalk – a technique of which Leonardo was master – or possibly powdered pigment à la Walter McCrone, neither of which work. And, unconvincingly, he argues that Leonardo drew himself while looking in a mirror, balancing on tiptoes to create the effect of a stretched-out body.[7]

Finally, we learned that, by a remarkable coincidence, an Italian research group, Project Luce, had arrived at a very similar conclusion to ours at the very time that we were researching the subject. In March 1993, *Oggi* magazine carried an interview with the founder and president of the group, Maria Consolata Corti, under the headline 'Outcry! The man on the Holy Shroud is Leonardo!' Corti and her co-researchers had noted the uncanny similarities between Leonardo and Shroudman, and their work had convinced them that the image was indeed a self-portrait. They believe that he had been commissioned for the work by the Turkish Sultan of Constantinople, Bajezid, although they offer very little evidence to support this idea. Neither have they any answers about just how he might have done it. They speculate that the image was created using blood, sweat and other bodily fluids, but are unable to say exactly how they were applied. Corti also notes that Leonardo experimented with the camera obscura – of which much more later – and muses that the image may have been 'the first experiment in photographic negative', in the sense that he attempted to create such an effect by painting.

This is an odd example of the well-known phenomenon wherein a similar idea surfaces in two completely unconnected places at once. The *Oggi* article appeared just three days before a similar piece on our work in the London *Evening Standard*. The timing – and the fact that both pieces carried photographs of, respectively, Maria Corti and Lynn Picknett, holding enlargements of the face of Shroudman/Leonardo – raised the paranoia level among Shroudies, particularly the French CIELT, who took it as evidence of some form of conspiracy, apparently on the grounds that both of these exponents were women!

Inside the Mind of a Genius

In searching for the identity of the forger we were looking for someone capable of devising a technique so advanced and unparalleled that the twenty-first century has yet to unravel it. This unknown genius must have had a great knowledge of anatomy, and an obsession with perfection that went beyond the mere need to satisfy the uncritical public of his day.

Leonardo's advanced ideas and inventions – flying machines, armoured cars, diving suits and contact lenses to name but a few – are too well known to need us to elaborate further. Curiously, however, Leonardo's bicycle, one of his most far-sighted inventions, is relatively little known.[8]

Fifty years after the Maestro's death, the sculptor Pompeo Leoni, horrified by the way Leonardo's manuscripts and papers had been allowed to be scattered, bought all that were left and did what he could to recover the rest, ordering and cataloguing what he collected. Loose sheets were glued into an album, which is now known as the *Codex Atlanticus*. The reverse sides of these sheets were therefore hidden for almost 400 years. In the 1960s the sheets were carefully unglued to see what was on the back. One of them revealed crude (in both senses of the word) drawings by one of Leonardo's young pupils, including some obscene sketches aimed at his young servant Salai (and presumably Leonardo himself), an unflattering sketch of the boy – and, in one corner, by the same hand, a bicycle. Clearly this was drawn from life.

Some scholars were so flabbergasted by the overtly modern design of the instrument that they refused to accept it, declaring it a modern addition put in as a joke (despite the known history of the *Codex*), until some historical detective work showed that it really did date from Leonardo's day. The proof is that the chain mechanism appears in one of his notebooks (the *Codex Madrid*), dating from the same period, around 1493. The pupil must have copied one of Leonardo's inventions. The design is almost identical to that of modern bicycles, with two equal-sized wheels and pedals linked to a chain to drive the rear wheel. The most astonishing thing of all is the way it anticipates in one go all the major steps in the evolution of the bicycle.

The first modern bike was invented in 1817 and was propelled by the feet of the rider, something like a scooter. It developed over time: pedals were added, although they were used to turn the wheel directly – one turn of the pedals made one revolution of the wheel, hence the enormous front wheels of the penny farthing. They were slow, and riding one was very hard work. Eventually, shortly before 1900, the chain and gear mechanism was added, enabling the wheel to be turned several times for one turn of the pedals, as on today's bicycles. This slow evolution, involving many factories, entrepreneurs and inventors, took no less than eighty years, yet Leonardo got there in one leap, 400 years before. Arguably, the concept of travelling by bicycle was more original than that of flight.

Leonardo was also a pioneering anatomist, being one of the first to dissect corpses in an attempt to discover how the human body worked. His perfectionism is summed up by one writer: 'Leonardo would spend hours, days or even weeks studying the muscle of an animal appearing in the background of a painting so that it could be drawn perfectly.'[9]

Had Leonardo been commissioned to paint a crucifixion there is no doubt that he would have researched the anatomy of the physical position and the dire physiological changes that result from this particular mode of execution. He would have discovered, among other things, the proper position for the nails to be hammered in at the wrists and ankles, And significantly, although he never painted a crucifixion there are indications in his notebooks that he had actually studied its anatomical requirements. A note that has long puzzled the biographers, dating from 1489 or 1490, refers to a specimen that Leonardo had borrowed: '. . . the bone that Gian Giacomo de Bellinzona pierced and from which he easily extracted the nail . . .'[10]

It seemed quite plausible to us that The Shroud image was in some way a self-portrait: not only had Giovanni said as much, but the recent computer work on the *Mona Lisa* had shown that Leonardo was not averse to using his own image in works that were allegedly depictions of quite other people. Besides, despite the wilful blindness of BSTS officers, it *does* obviously look like him, as our vox pop and Luigi Mattei had shown. It had been hinted that he also had used some kind of basic photographic technique to create this dark masterpiece for posterity. Plus, we had been told that he had been motivated by a profound distaste for the Church, arising partly from his secret magical and alchemical activities, and partly from his own anti-Christian nature. Somehow we had to provide persuasive evidence for all that. We had to show, as in classic crime detection, that Leonardo had the 'means, motive and opportunity' to create the ultimate fake relic.

A Magical Mindset

For a start, there was no accepted evidence that Leonardo was involved with magic, alchemy or any underground organisation. He did not appear, on the surface, to be enthusiastic about such matters as divination, which are normally (although often erroneously) linked with the whole subject of magic. Yet his name was included in the *Dossiers secrets* of the Priory of Sion as one of their Grand Masters, and although evidence for the authenticity of those documents themselves is by no means concrete, it did at least hint that Leonardo was known in 'heretical' circles to be one of their number. We also came across a nineteenth-century Rosicrucian poster depicting Leonardo as 'the Keeper of the Grail', Joseph of Arimathea. Again, this was proof of nothing except perhaps a familiarity with his reputation as an occultist in esoteric circles. It has also been reported that historian the late Dame Frances Yates (1899–1981) described Leonardo as being of a 'Rosicrucian frame of mind'[11] – somewhat courageously for an academic.

The Rosicrucian movement, which was closely associated with alchemy and the development of Freemasonry, did not become known as such until 1614, when documents began to circulate from Germany that told of a secret brotherhood of Magi.[12] It was claimed that the order had descended from one Christian Rosenkreutz who had lived until the age of 106 and been buried in an extraordinary tomb in 1484. Rosicrucians, it was said, were alchemists and magicians, Cabalists and Hermeticists. Modern commentators claim that there never was a Christian Rosenkreutz and that the whole early pedigree was an invention, perhaps a metaphor. The Rosicrucians are thought by some to be the immediate precursors of modern Freemasons.[13]

'Rosenkreutz' means 'Rosy cross', a powerful alchemical symbol that owes little to Christianity,[14] and one that is not unknown in the symbology of the Priory of Sion.[15] And with its roots in alchemy, there is no reason why it should not have been known in Leonardo's day. Presumably the Rosicrucians themselves had a precursor – which may or may not have been the Knights Templar – and this other order or organisation must have been known to Hermeticists and esotericists when Leonardo was alive.

Yet perhaps this is not quite what Frances Yates meant. To have had a 'Rosicrucian frame of mind' obviously hints at 'heresy', at a wide range of esoteric knowledge and a questioning, daring, intellect. This then, was Leonardo in a nutshell.

Significantly, the works of the Rosicrucians reveal that they attached some importance to the Shroud image. In a book of theirs dating from 1593 there is a diagram labelled 'Ark of Noah'[16] (see illustration), which shows a naked, bearded figure superimposed on a plan of the Ark, which is divided into compartments with astrological associations. The figure is very similar to the Shroud image.

Less immediately obvious is the figure that recurs in the complex diagrams of the great English Rosicrucian (and Grand Master of the Priory, if we are to believe the *Dossiers secrets*) Robert Fludd (1547–1640). Taken to represent Adam, the primal man, the figure lies on his back, with his knees raised and hands crossed over the loins. This position is exactly the same as that reconstructed by artist Isabel Piczek (see Chapter 7).

Frances Yates was also to muse in her *Giordano Bruno and the Hermetic Tradition*: 'Might it not have been within the outlook of a Magus that a personality like Leonardo was able to co-ordinate his mathematical and mechanical studies with his work as an artist?'[17]

Given Leonardo's cast of mind and his place and time in history, it would have been very odd if he were not interested in esoteric and alchemical experiments. As we shall see, to the informed and questing thinker of his time and place there was no problem with being both scientist and magical adept, with on the one hand denying Jesus as God and on the other invoking archangels and ancient archetypes. There was no discrepancy in them being cynical about established religion and also throwing themselves heart, mind and soul into ceremonies that were designed to bring them into profound and challenging contact with the terrifying world of the 'Abyss' – what may be seen now as the innermost and uncharted reaches of the unconscious mind.

One problem that many people today have in linking Leonardo with magic is the notion that the Renaissance was essentially a 'scientific' revolution, where hocus-pocus and ritual had no place. In fact, this is completely wrong.

The early Italian Renaissance was an explosion of art, science and culture that effectively obliterated the intellectual darkness and crippling timidity of the Middle Ages. New techniques were developed in art and architecture, new discoveries made, new ideas sought and eagerly discussed.

A great many would-be freethinkers had been frozen in their tracks by the implacable and forbidding power of the Church, like rabbits caught in the headlamps of onrushing vehicles, only to collude in their own death through the terror of moving on. In Leonardo's time it was not unusual for anyone who dared to study beyond the confines of the Church's corpus of knowledge to find themselves guests of the Inquisition.

What lay behind this explosion of thought and enquiry was nothing less than a sudden and dramatic change in man's concept of himself and his place in the world – yet the causes of this abrupt shift have not been satisfactorily explained by standard authorities. The invention of the printing press was an important factor in the dissemination of new ideas: it was not, however, in itself a cause. Traditionally, the origins of the Renaissance have been traced back to the collapse of the Byzantine Empire – due to the military might of the Turks in 1453 – which resulted in an influx of classical works into Europe: however, this is a simplistic view.

Frances Yates has shown in her books that the major influence in the intellectual flowering of the Renaissance was an upsurge of interest in ideas that are now termed 'occult'.

To us, the very idea seems incongruous, at least at first glance. We tend to think of the Renaissance as the start of the age of science – Leonardo himself is spoken of as 'the first scientist', which is, to the modern mind, the very antithesis of magic and the occult. But to a very large extent this attitude is the result of the way our culture has developed. To understand the Renaissance we must first abandon our tendency to compartmentalise knowledge, and to sneer at those compartments that lie outside our own understanding.

The very essence of the typical Renaissance mind was that nothing was compartmentalised: everything was part of one great store of knowledge. Today we regard science and the arts as two separate, irreconcilable activities, and our education system is shaped by that idea, but in Leonardo's time that was far from true. Artists were philosophers, poets, engineers, musicians, scientists – and occultists. In fact, mechanics was then regarded as a branch of magic: both pursuits were concerned with understanding and harnessing the laws of nature.[18]

It was only later, in the second half of the sixteenth century, that there came a schism among the various branches of knowledge, one that has become an unbridgeable gulf. The new freedom of thought had led to the questioning of previously unchallenged dogmas of the Church, which culminated in the Reformation (many of the important figures in Renaissance occultism, such as Henry Cornelius Agrippa [1486–1535] were closely allied to the early Reform movement).[19] The Catholic Church fought back with the Counter Reformation, enlisting the aid of the Inquisition and loyal Catholic monarchs, such as those in Spain, and Europe was engulfed in a whirlwind of war and violence that drove the occultists underground. To survive, men of learning had to disown their occult roots. Even so, the distinction remained one of appearance only for many years afterwards. Isaac Newton (1642–1727) devoted more of his life to alchemical pursuits than to the study of optics and gravity or the invention of the infinitesimal calculus. Gottfried Wilhelm Leibniz (1646–1716), the German mathematician and philosopher, was a Rosicrucian who saw this mathematical wonder as only the first step in a system that would eventually be applied to spiritual, as well as mundane affairs. Even the arch-rationalist René Descartes (1596–1650) flirted with Rosicrucianism.[20]

Yates argues persuasively that the debt owed by modern scientific thought to the occult has been undervalued. To take just one of her examples: we are often told that one of the great triumphs of science over superstition was the discovery that the Earth is not the centre of the solar system but orbits the sun. However, when Nicolaus Copernicus (1473–1543) advanced his heliocentric theory, it first gained ground among the Hermetic philosophers, since it agreed with one of their fundamental principles, which stated that the Sun holds the ultimate magical power. Copernicus himself quotes the major Hermetic work, the *Asclepius*, in the introduction to his thesis, and he found his staunchest defender in Giordano Bruno, the greatest of the sixteenth-century Hermeticists. Yates questions whether or not the heliocentric theory would have received the same acceptance without its enthusiastic endorsement by the occultists.[21]

She sees the elusive 'secret' of the origins of the Renaissance in an awakening of interest in occult ideas and what they taught about man's nature. Rather than ascribing it to the death throes of the Byzantine Empire, she sees the impetus as stemming from nearer home in the increasing persecution of the Spanish Jews.[22] They had long been the guardians of various mystical and magical systems, the most important of which was the Cabala, an immensely complex esoteric tradition that claimed to represent the secret laws of the Universe. Under intense pressure they began to migrate, taking their ideas with them. Matters came to a head in the fateful year of 1492 when all Jews were forcibly expelled from Spain, which had the immediate effect of making the Cabala, at least, known to a new, Christian audience. In fact, it was a Christianised version of the Cabala that became the cornerstone of the new and dynamic occultism.

Two other major factors came into play at this point: Neoplatonism and Hermeticism, both of which were undergoing a period of renewal. Neoplatonism was a development of the classical philosophy of Plato, which most historians see as an essentially rationalist, protoscientific philosophy. It was not so: it taught that man is a partly divine being trapped in an imperfect world, who can, theoretically, potentiate his godhood through the mastery of occult laws.

Hermeticism is the philosophy based on works said to have been penned by the great Egyptian magus Hermes Trismegistus, the *Asclepius* and the *Corpus Hermeticum*. The former had been known in Europe during the Middle Ages, but the latter only became known when rediscovered and translated into Latin by a Florentine, Marsilio Ficino (1433–1499), in the middle of the fifteenth century. Then, in 1486, another Italian, Pico della Mirandola (1463–1494) published a treatise on the Cabala. He had been taught by Spanish Jews, including a mysterious figure called Flavius Mithradates, who is now known to have altered Cabalist texts to make them more acceptable to Christians. Put together, the three systems – Neoplatonism, Hermeticism and the Cabala – were to transform the spirit of the age.

Throughout the Middle Ages, the Church, sole dispenser of truth, had taught that man is a weak, miserable creature, born in original sin and dependent solely upon God's mercy to keep him alive and – if he is lucky – save him from the fires of Hell. The medieval heaven was defined, not by the presence of pleasure, but by the absence of pain. Against such a background, there was nothing to inspire anyone to broaden their outlook, no point in developing a healthy, enquiring mind. But the Hermetic philosophy elevated the soul of man, teaching that each individual is a potential god. It said that everyone could actuate this personal divinity if only they could recover the secret knowledge that had been handed down throughout history, from adept to adept.

Suddenly anything seemed possible: the shackles fell off. The world became a fascinating place to be investigated fearlessly and, within the limits of the laws of nature, mastered. The glories of the Renaissance were nothing less than a surge of collective self-confidence due to the occult idea of man as Divine being, coming into the world – as the eighteenth-century English poet William Wordsworth was later to write – 'trailing clouds of glory'.

Occult ideas had of course been known before this time: alchemists in particular had a well-developed underground network. But suddenly these ideas were seized upon by enthusiastic young students who saw in them an end to the intellectual sterility of the age, and the beginnings of a return to the exciting freedom of the classical world.

It was in Italy that the new Hermetic philosophy took shape, and it was also here that the Renaissance began. This was because, ironically, the Pope's authority was weaker here than anywhere else. The Italian states saw him as a political rival, and made sure they kept the Church's power to a minimum for that reason. From Italy the new age spread throughout Europe until the Church realised it had been too lax, and tried to bludgeon the world back into the Middle Ages. But wherever the new spirit went it flowered in paintings, architecture and literature, although its roots were firmly in the new occult philosophy, to use Frances Yates's term. She has traced a direct line of transmission and development from mid-fifteenth-century Italy, through the works of the German magician Agrippa, the great Hermetic prophet Giordano Bruno and the Elizabethan magus Dr John Dee at the end of the sixteenth century, to the origins of the Rosicrucian movement in the early seventeenth century, and beyond.

The occult philosophy underscores all the manifestations of the Renaissance and should never be divorced from them, for it is in occult thinking that their often obscure symbolism lies. One of the key tools of Hermetic magic is the talisman – Ficino was obsessed by it. Although often taken to be synonymous with an amulet or charm, a talisman is in fact much more. It was supposed to attract certain kinds of magical power to it, which it then channelled. Many Renaissance paintings and sculptures can be seen as talismans – *Primavera* by Botticelli (1444–1510), for instance, is a talisman for Venus.[23] A century later, in Amsterdam, Rembrandt (1606–1669) was incorporating Cabalist elements into his paintings.[24]

Significantly, in the light of our research, it was in Florence that the three strands of Neoplatonism, Hermeticism and Cabalism came together most forcibly and most creatively. And the catalyst for this explosive intellectual transmutation was none other than Lorenzo de Medici (1450–1492), ruler of Florence and foremost patron of Andrea del Verrocchio (1436–1488) – who, as we shall see, was a prime mover in Leonardo's formative years.[25]

So eager was this court to establish Florence as a centre of culture and scholarship, that Lorenzo's grandfather, Cosimo, had sent agents throughout the Mediterranean seeking lost manuscripts. The greatest prize they brought back was the *Corpus Hermeticum*, which Cosimo rushed to translate. So great was the honour accorded this work that Marsilio Ficino was told to drop his translation of the complete works of Plato and concentrate on translating this instead.

Ficino also wrote or translated many of the classic works of Renaissance occultism, such as the *Orphica*, a collection of hymns to pagan gods, and *De triplica vita*, his treatise on astral magic and talismans, and was Lorenzo's tutor and mentor, later becoming the tutor of Lorenzo's children. Pico della Mirandola, champion of the Christian Cabala, wrote his famous treatise in Florence after Lorenzo offered him protection from the Inquisition. And, astonishing for his day, Lorenzo's Florence tolerated Jews: indeed, he often interceded personally to stop their persecution in other Italian states, making Florence an ideal haven for those fleeing the attentions of the Spanish Inquisitor General Torquemada.

We should not be surprised to discover that Lorenzo was also actively interested in the occult. According to historian Dr Judith Hook: 'His writings show a considerable familiarity with the Latin poets . . . a mastery of Hermetic literature, contemporary medical and architectural theory, and an interest in magic and astrology . . .'[26]

Florence was obsessed with groups and societies – guilds, committees, councils, religious cliques and so on. There was a network of secret religious organisations (although no-one today knows their *raisons d'être*), called the Companies of Night. A society especially associated with the Medicis was the Confraternity of the Magi, the nucleus of the Neoplatonic philosophers. Lorenzo, like his father and grandfather, was its president. Ostensibly orthodox, it nevertheless became more like a modern Masonic Lodge under Lorenzo, and those aspiring to influence were eager to be admitted to the 'rank of the Magi'.[27]

This, then, was the Florence to which Leonardo would become passionately attached, a centre of fervent occult discussion. It is inconceivable that Leonardo, who was interested in everything, would have ignored these new and exciting possibilities.

The Darker Shadows

It was a world, however, that should not have been immediately welcoming to one such as Leonardo. By rights, he should have been subjected to the thumbscrews, the rack and the flaming pyre dozens of times over for his 'heresies'. Yet even apart from his radical beliefs we must also look at his other habits that should easily have qualified him for the loving attentions of the Inquisition.

Leonardo was left-handed; he was a strict vegetarian; he dissected dead bodies; he sought the company of alchemists and necromancers; he worked on a Sunday and only attended Mass when at court. The last two can be deemed obvious sins at a time when outward piety was all, but what of the others?

At that time, being left-handed was deemed to be evil, yet Leonardo, although technically ambidextrous, flaunted his left-handedness. He even wrote in 'mirror writing' in far from secret documents – devilish writing from the hand of the Devil.

He was also vegetarian.[28] To modern Westerners the idea that one's diet could be deemed heretical may seem surprising. Yet in many religions, such as Orthodox Judaism, Islam and Mormon Christianity, obedience to rigid dietary regimes is still mandatory, and any lapses are punishable.

The Church lays great emphasis on man's dominion over the animal kingdom, as given him by God in the Book of Genesis. However, it goes further: if God gave us the beasts as ours, to do what we like with, then to eschew them in any way must be blasphemy. In Leonardo's day vegetarianism was referred to as 'the Devil's banquet', and to avoid eating meat (except on Fridays of course) was a sure way to be convicted of heresy. But the question remains: how did he get away with it?

For most of his professional life, Leonardo had a special dispensation to dissect cadavers for purposes of anatomical research, something that normally carried the death penalty. Yet not only did he work long hours among stinking corpses, his hands wrist-deep in intestines (although he invented a way of keeping his fingernails clean)[29], but he also frequently boasted – even, astonishingly, while in conversation with priests – about how many men, women and children he had cut up. It was only towards the end of his life, around 1513, when Pope Leo X took an active dislike to his anatomical researches, that they ceased. Leonardo's charmed life was threatened, and it was around that time that he left for France, where he would eventually die.

While it is not generally known or accepted among standard authorities that Leonardo himself was an alchemist or a necromancer, there are several references to his frequent association with those who were known to be dabblers in these so-called 'black arts'. For example, the only surviving sculpture in which he had a hand was mainly the work of Giovan Francesco Rustici, whom Serge Bramly, in his book *Leonardo: the Artist and the Man*, somewhat airily dismisses as 'an amateur alchemist and occasional necromancer'.[30] The work, depicting John the Baptist (who is raising one forefinger skywards), still stands in the Baptistry in Florence, the patron saint of which was also John the Baptist. Giorgio Vasari, the sixteenth-century art historian, says in his *Lives of the Artists*, that while Leonardo and Rustici worked on this figure no-one was allowed anywhere near them. Although there could have been many possible explanations for this desire for solitude, whatever they were up to, Leonardo and his friend Rustici did not want to be disturbed.

Necromancy was a very black art that required the use of corpses for divinatory purposes. Roughly a generation after Leonardo, Queen Elizabeth I's astrologer, the polymath Dr John Dee, was known to practise it with terrifying results. It was a widespread practice among knowledge-hungry Renaissance men: certainly if Leonardo himself did not belong to that bizarre and unsavoury fraternity then he had absolutely no qualms about mixing with those who did. And he would, of course, have been an excellent source of raw material for them, having had such regular and unchallenged access to corpses for his anatomical researches.

While never for one moment considering Leonardo as either a necromancer or an alchemist, the cautious Serge Bramly writes: 'Leonardo no longer dared even to indicate clearly the ingredients of the alloys he had developed: he used code, or else borrowed the vocabulary of the alchemist, referring to Jupiter, Venus or Mercury, describing a metal as having "to be returned to its mother's breast" when he meant it had to be returned to the fire . . . But worse was to come: in order to discredit Leonardo at the Vatican, Giovanni [the Maestro's mirror-maker assistant] accused him of practising necromancy: from then on Leonardo was forbidden to carry out the anatomical work he had been doing at the San Spirito hospital.'[31]

It seems strange that someone who did not 'dare' to commit details of his work to paper still 'dared' to use blatantly alchemical imagery: surely such language was considerably more dangerous than letting lesser brains puzzle over his work? And then there is the point that, when the Pope was faced with an accusation against Leonardo of heresy in the form of necromancy all he did was ban further anatomical research. Rumours have always abounded about Leonardo's secret work: he has been called 'Faust's Italian brother',[32] and Serge Bramly remarks 'there was the whiff of sulphur about Leonardo'.[33]

It was a cynical age and a power-hungry place. Perhaps it would not have mattered to his patrons, even to the Vatican, if he stank to high heaven of sulphur, as long as he had something – some knowledge or some technique – that others did not, something that was uniquely useful in his time and place. In one of his notebooks he wrote: 'To dare to be the first, to make the dream a reality . . .': one can almost hear the tone of longing, of the passionate desire to be the ultimate innovator. But what made him the extraordinary man that he was? What drove him, what induced the restless energy, the power to create?

The Boy From Vinci

Leonardo was born at 10.30 p.m. on Saturday, 15 April 1452 in Anciano, a village near the small town of Vinci in Tuscany. His grandfather, Antonio, eagerly noted down the exact time of the boy's birth: he may have wanted it for a horoscope to be drawn up.

His father was a notary, Ser Piero da Vinci, who had an important business in Florence. His mother was the mysterious Caterina (sometimes Chateria), a local woman who never married his father. Very little is known about her: local tradition has it that she brought the little boy up for the first five years of his life, then she married Attabriga di Piero del Vacca (possibly a soldier) and moved to Campo Zeppi, about a mile (1.6km) from Vinci. They were to have three daughters and a son. She may have been the Caterina who was eventually to be the adult Leonardo's housekeeper, ending her days with him, but even this is debatable. This is all that scholars acknowledge about the shadowy woman who brought the tormented genius, Leonardo da Vinci, into the world.

However, there are traditions that do not belong to the historical mainstream. Giovanni laid great store by Caterina, whom he sometimes referred to as 'the Cathar woman'[34] (Leonardo's vegetarianism may have been inspired by the Cathar tradition) and at other times hinted that she was herself no small fry in the underground movement of heretical belief and magic. Perhaps she was a 'witch' – a local wise woman with healing powers – or perhaps her abilities were more marked, more disturbing, more likely to influence the mind of a tiny boy with a magical world of enormous potential already burgeoning inside his head.

For just a few months Leonardo was the sole apple of his father's eye, then Ser Piero married Albiera, the first of his four wives. She was to die childless (in 1464), as was his second wife – but his last two wives between them were to present him with no fewer than twelve legitimate sons and daughters. Although it is likely that Piero's lusty nature resulted in several illegitimate offspring, Leonardo was the only one he officially acknowledged; his illegitimacy was to cause the adult Leonardo enormous grief and rage, perhaps being the single most important factor in what may be termed his inner torment in his later life.

Also living in the house near Vinci were Antonio, Leonardo's paternal grandfather, and his uncle, the amiable wastrel Francesco, sixteen years older than the boy. After Caterina's departure, the only women in the household were stepmothers, mothers of his father's legitimate children.

So the young Leonardo sought out the world of his mind, a world where anything is possible. There is evidence that young Uncle Francesco spent time with him, perhaps being almost the only playmate who could quite stomach the endless questions, the ceaseless mental activity, the frenetic energy. Perhaps, like most other geniuses, Leonardo was essentially lonely, isolated from other children by the inner powers that drove him, intimidating to those not so well equipped as he was to explore his inner space.

His bastardy prevented him from entering the law, the family's profession, so the thirteen-year-old Leonardo was apprenticed to Andrea del Verrocchio, an artist in nearby Florence. At that time, artists were regarded as little more than craftsmen, and their studios were seen as rough-and-ready workshops. Apprentices – botteghe – were expected to master many artistic and mechanical techniques, often making their own materials. They lived 'over the shop' and rarely had time to venture into the outside world.

Verrocchio was fascinated by mathematics, music and – more controversially – by magic and alchemy.[35] Leonardo was a quiet and studious worker, whose talents were evident from the first day. By the time a gilded copper ball, worked on partly by Leonardo and weighing over two tons, was placed atop the spire of Florence cathedral in 1471, the boy had become Verrocchio's second in command.

At this time Leonardo met the geographer Paolo Toscanelli ('Maestro Pagolo'), who later charted Columbus's great voyage, and from whom he learnt much about machinery. Another major influence from this time was Leon Battista Alberti (1404–1472), a polymath who experimented with the camera obscura. Like

Leonardo, Alberti had almost superhuman physical strength; perhaps it was he who taught the apprentice the secrets of mind-over-matter, of martial-art-like control that appeared to lie behind the feats of both of them.[36] The adult Leonardo, for example, frequently straightened horseshoes as a party trick, and once casually lifted a heavy locked door off its hinges – with, we are told, virtually no discernible exertion.[37]

Another early contact was the artist Botticelli (Sandro Filipepi), who was seven years older than Leonardo and, if we are to believe the Priory of Sion's *Dossiers secrets*, eventually became Grand Master of that organisation (and whose esoteric interests are said to have found expression in his designing a Tarot pack).[38] It was upon Botticelli's death in 1510 that Leonardo is said to have taken over at the helm of the Priory.

Florence at that time was a wealthy city state controlled by businessmen and ruled by the banking family of Medici. Verrocchio's workshop was kept busy making statues, decorations and portraits to add to their status. Leonardo was to write many years later 'The Medici created me and destroyed me',[39] although exactly what he was referring to in the latter part of that sentence is not known. Certainly contact with the Medicis was something of a mixed blessing in 1476, when the twenty-four-year-old artist was arrested on an anonymous accusation and charged with 'heresy', together with a group of other young men. This is generally taken to mean that the charge was sodomy; they were all released very rapidly, almost certainly owing to the fact that one of the accused was related to the Medicis. This may have got Leonardo off, but had this bad company got him arrested in the first place? And if the charge had not been sodomy, then just what was the heresy of which they stood charged? The punishment for both sodomy and heresy was the same in the law at that time anyway: death by burning.

Rumours of Leonardo's homosexuality were to follow him throughout his long life, and beyond. Apart from that brief and uncertain court case, and the fact he never married, there is little direct evidence for Leonardo being gay. His notebooks occasionally recorded his contempt for the sex act and it may be that his emotional life, so carefully subliminated in his work, never took on a physical expression. Or, as some commentators have suggested, his brush with the law over a sodomy charge effectively terrified him so much that he was never even tempted again.

However, salacious rumours continued to dog his name, even posthumously, and the recent discovery[40] of some pornographic doodles by his apprentices certainly reinforces the idea that he and homosexuality were not unacquainted. It is also true that his relationships with women were superficial and distant, and his comments on heterosexual relations frequently sneering and dismissive. Serge Bramly points to the Maestro's strange drawing in section of a couple engaged in sex; while the man – with a curiously abundant mane of hair – is drawn in great detail, the woman is a mere sketch. Bramly also points out, however, that the man's penis, entering into her vagina, seems to have met another penis.[41]

Over the years many commentators have cited the *Mona Lisa* as an example of Leonardo's tormented sexuality; there have always been rumours that it was, in fact, an ingenious self-portrait. Then in recent years two researchers – Lillian Schwartz of Bell Laboratories in the USA[42] and Dr Digby Quested of London's Maudsley Hospital[43] – have both demonstrated that this is indeed the case. Unlikely as this may seem, both these investigators have managed to show, using sophisticated computer imaging techniques, that the female face is the mirror image of the Maestro himself, certainly when matched to his self-portrait as an old man which is now in Turin. All the major lines of the face – lips, tip of nose, eyebrows, eyes – match perfectly in both pictures.

Many people have seized on the *Mona Lisa* as an expression of Leonardo's female side, his tortured anima that was so assiduously kept locked away from public view. But it certainly shows his propensity for subtly building his own image into the greatest of his works. Also, much has been made of Leonardo's pornography: sketches showing 'hermaphrodites in a state of sexual excitement', which have recently been returned to the Queen's collection at Windsor after many years. (They were stolen during Queen Victoria's reign: it is said she was glad they had gone!) It is only too easy to ascribe Leonardo's apparent obsession with hermaphrodites to a perverse, perhaps even perverted, sexual craving, and to his fascination for dual gender, as expressed in his most famous self-portrait, the *Mona Lisa*.

Secret of the Great Work

There was another reason for a Florentine of that era to be obsessed with sexual ambiguity, with the idea of intertwining one gender with the other. The hermaphrodite is a pure alchemical symbol, representing the perfect balance achieved in the Great Work, and the perfect being, in which the alchemist himself is transformed and transmuted spiritually – and, as many believe, physically as well. It was a 'consummation devoutly to be wished' and had little, if anything, to do with sexuality as we understand it today. The Great Work was an explosion of the potential into the actual, where the mystical quest takes on concrete form. According to the alchemists' axiom, 'as above, so below', this process was believed to make spirit into matter and transmute one sort of matter into another. It made a man into a god.[44]

In the scientific and technological twenty-first century an alchemist is viewed as a poor deluded fool, and all his practices, aspirations and beliefs being just so much mumbo jumbo that we can eschew with arrogance and confidence. And, to a large extent, when we first came to research it, that was also our stance. But we soon realised that alchemy may be apparently bizarre and laughable – the most serious alchemists deliberately fostered that image to keep unwanted investigations at bay[45] – but it is also extraordinarily powerful. It exerts a potent appeal to a person who wants to fulfil their physical, intellectual and spiritual potential and rise way above their fellows in understanding of the universe and their part in it. Alchemy is an often apparently bizarre fusion of philosophy, cosmology, astrology, physics, chemistry and even a form of genetic engineering. As Neil Powell, a modern authority on alchemy, says:

> The greatest alchemists were skilled in many fields. The scope of knowledge in those days was small enough that a person might hope to master all there was to know about subjects as diverse as medicine and religion, philosophy and alchemy, logic and magic. The seeker of knowledge would see nothing incompatible in the different fields of study. Magic would not conflict with medicine, or philosophy with religion. Knowledge was thought of as a unity, and all the different branches were different aspects of this unity. They all led to a greater understanding of the Universe.[46]

We came across the following rich storehouse of meaning to 'those with eyes to see', which helps to underscore the appeal of alchemy to a seeker such as Leonardo.

In the early years of the twentieth century the occult underground of Paris was agog when one 'Fulcanelli' published his book *The Mystery of the Cathedrals*, a work purporting to show that the great Gothic cathedrals of Europe, in particular Chartres, were codes in stone that contained ancient alchemical and magical knowledge. For example, one alchemical symbol that is widely acknowledged by modern scholars is that of an old bearded man, the back of whose head shows a young woman looking into a mirror. A statue with this image graces the interior of Nantes cathedral, as does a bearded king with the body of a woman that depicts the Queen of Sheba in the porch at Chartres.

One day in early 1993, Lynn was sorting out slides for a talk on Leonardo and the Shroud and found herself staring at one slide in particular, one with which she had thought herself very familiar. However, we had both failed to make a major connection.

The slide was of a sketch by Leonardo entitled 'Witch using a Magic Mirror' (see illustration).[47] We had regularly used it to illustrate Leonardo's secret fascination with magic, mirrors and dual gender, but had completely missed the point. We had realised long ago that although it apparently showed a young woman looking into a mirror, if you look carefully you will see that the back of her head is actually an old man's face – Leonardo's own. It is nothing less than the same symbol as that of the alchemical statue at Nantes. We must have drawn hundreds of people's attention to points of interest in that sketch in previous years, but we never realised that all that time we had been using what amounted to clear evidence for Leonardo's involvement with alchemy.

We also discovered, as mentioned above, that he used alchemical symbols in his notebooks, a dangerous practice indeed. This almost seems like an aberration, for they appear only briefly among the dozens of extant notes.

Leonardo would be unlikely to write at length anything that praised alchemy for obvious reasons of discretion. It is not enough to say that his notebooks were not intended for public consumption: he was famous in his lifetime and knew the value of all his scribbles. Besides, his young servant Salai was a notorious thief – who knew where his Maestro's valuable notebooks might end up? They could easily have fallen into the wrong hands during his lifetime.

The second important factor when considering Leonardo's writings on alchemy is to note their precise tone and content. As we have already seen, serious alchemists were primarily concerned with spiritual transformation, not with turning base metal into gold as is commonly believed. According to the occult scholar Grillot de Givry it is important to distinguish the true alchemist from 'the scrambling throng of the uninitiate, who have utterly failed to penetrate the secret of the true doctrine and continue working on anomalous materials which will never bring them to the desired result. These are the false alchemists, who are called Puffers.'[48]

It is clear that Leonardo's writings are directed at the Puffers. For example he asks them 'why do you not go to the mines where Nature produces such gold, and there become her disciple? She will in faith cure you of your folly, showing you that nothing which you use in your furnace will be among any of the things which she uses in order to produce this gold.' However, his attitude is not entirely hostile, for he also says that the alchemists 'deserve unmeasured praise for the usefulness of the things invented for the use of men'.[49]

Serious alchemists would agree with him. The contempt they felt – and still feel – for Puffers is on a par with many scientists' feelings towards those who still believe that the Shroud is really that of Jesus.

On the whole it is true that modern alchemists – there are alchemical institutes in both France and the USA – are just as keen on anonymity as their historical counterparts. This may seem odd, for surely the time is long gone when they would face the flaming pyre for their beliefs and practices. Some think that anonymity has simply become so ingrained in the psyche of alchemists that it is by now a tradition, but there is more to it than that. Put simply, alchemy is for initiates only, just as is any occult knowledge. Secrets must remain secrets. Or, as Neil Powell writes: 'Alchemists delighted in shrouding their writings with mystery and obscurity because they were always afraid the information would fall into the hands of the wrong people. Perhaps they enjoyed the secrecy for its own sake.'[50]

Alchemy still has elaborate and often impenetrable codes, employing fantastic imagery, but essentially it is a tough-minded system aimed at totally transforming not only the substances with which the alchemist works, but also the alchemist himself. Alchemists have a saying: 'There is no God but God in Man', not only a deeply dangerous axiom to bandy about in the days of the Inquisition, but also the perfect sentiment for one such as Leonardo.

We have come to believe that one of the most profound *raisons d'être* of the Priory of Sion is alchemy. Nicholas Flamel is listed as one of their earliest Grand Masters, and January 17 – given by him as the date on which he achieved the Great Work in 1392[51] – is a day held sacred by them. Also on the list are Sir Isaac Newton, Robert Boyle (1627-1691) and Robert Fludd, all known to have been passionate alchemists. (Interestingly, Newton, like Leonardo, is now known as an arch-rationalist, but in his day there was nothing illogical about being an alchemist: all knowledge was valid.)

Alchemy is not a hobby like stamp collecting or growing orchids; it is a complete system for understanding both Man and the world which he inhabits. Leonardo's 'Witch using a Magic Mirror' shows that he was familiar with alchemical imagery.

The Real da Vinci Code

In our quest to provide Leonardo with the means, motive and opportunity to create the Turin Shroud, we were to show that alchemy provided him with the means. Perhaps, however, his means and motive were inseparably linked. Alchemy may not only have provided the technical know-how for a bold and ingenious fake – one that, after all, could not be detected as a hoax in his lifetime – but it would also have put him in touch with a massive underground network of like-minded heretics.

We looked at Leonardo's work and immediately found that he is generally taken to be the young man turning almost violently away from the 'Holy Family' in his unfinished *Adoration of the Magi*.[52] Some have ingenuously suggested that this is because he did not feel worthy to face them. But given his secret background, it is much more likely to represent a complete aversion to the accepted Bible story.

It is also hardly a cosy, spiritual hymn to the Christian religion. The scene is set before a carob tree – symbol of John the Baptist – and the Magi may be seen bringing frankincense and myrrh to the baby Jesus, but there is no gold, for gold is not only a symbol of kingship, but also the alchemical symbol for the highest truth and perfection. As Leonardo wrote, gold is the 'most excellent of Nature's products, true son of the sun'.[53] While those who appear to be worshipping the elevated roots of the carob tree seem perfectly normal, those who apparently come to worship Jesus and his mother are hideous, gaunt, walking skeletons like the cadavers with whom Leonardo spent long candlelit nights with a scalpel in his hand. They claw and paw at the air around the insipid Virgin and child, while one man's hand appears to cut across the throat of a bystander in the manner of the Freemason's oath: to be reminded of it so graphically is to be called a traitor and to face execution. It is a gesture that is to be repeated in Leonardo's *Last Supper*, a controversial twenty-year restoration of which was completed in 1999.

The only remaining part of the original church of Santa Maria delle Grazie at Milan, this fresco, the *Last Supper* has come to be seen as the artist's expression of his Christian piety. It is in fact quite the reverse.

Many art historians agree that Leonardo painted himself as Saint Thaddeus, second from the observer's right. Certainly the model was a tall man: he is bent nearly double in order to meet the gaze of the last disciple at the table. In so doing, he is turned completely away from the centre figure, that of Jesus. Even though the fresco is badly aged, it is still possible to make out this character's features: shoulder-length hair parted in the centre, beard and moustache, long, knobbly nose with its idiosyncratic tip; just like the man on the Shroud.

It is strange that one of the most famous paintings in the world should be so little known, and certainly so little understood – but then that is probably just as well, for many who once loved it may now come to be repelled by it. The point of the Biblical Last Supper was, as all churchgoers learn, for Jesus to instigate the sacrament of wine and bread, saying 'this is my blood that is shed for you . . . this is my body . . .' Yet apart from a token drop on Leonardo's table, there is no wine. Certainly there is nothing Grail-like, no great – or indeed small – cup set out in front of the Redeemer, and you have to look very hard indeed to find the little that there is (except in copies, where the artist has corrected Leonardo's 'oversight'). Is Leonardo saying to those with eyes to see, that Jesus did not die on the cross, that he did not shed his blood for us?

Look at the figure of Jesus with his red robe and blue cloak and look to his right where there is what appears at first glance to be a young man leaning away. This is generally taken to be John the Beloved – but in that case, should he not be leaning against Jesus' 'bosom' as in the Bible? Look yet more closely. This character is wearing the mirror image of Jesus' clothing: in this case a blue robe and red cloak, but otherwise the garments are identical. As much as Jesus is large and very male, this character is elfin, and distinctly female. The hands are tiny and a dark smudge on the upper chest surely indicates breasts. As we realised in the early 1990s, this is no John the Beloved: this is Mary Magdalene. And a hand cuts across her throat, in that chilling Freemasonic gesture indicating a dire warning. This is the one figure that no self-respecting true heretic could possibly leave out of such a scene. It would have been unthinkable to do so. And the femininity of this character is even more blatant in the copy of this work, which mysteriously remains bricked up in London's Burlington House.

More significant by far, however, is our discovery of clear Johannite symbolism in many of Leonardo's allegedly pious Christian paintings. Even to us, who by then had become used to the idea of his heresy, the extent to which he managed to imbue his works with astonishing anti-Christian – and specifically anti-Holy Family – subliminal suggestions was almost literally shocking. And not only is John the Baptist himself a central figure in many of his creations, but symbolic references to him are also scattered throughout even some of his most revered 'sacred' works.

The last painting he ever did was his extremely disturbing *St John the Baptist* – painted for himself, not for any commission. (An extraordinary thing for a so-called atheist.) Neither was this intended to be the object of pious Christian meditation as he breathed his last. To Leonardo, the Baptist was not the forerunner of Christ – the humble herald, who knelt at his feet submissively. To the artist, as to most Johannites, John *was* Christ. And interestingly, Leonardo's only surviving sculpture is also of John the Baptist (now above the entrance to the Baptistry in Florence), which, as we have seen, was created together with Rustici, an alchemist and necromancer. But there is considerably more evidence of Leonardo's profound reverence for the Baptist and the deep distaste he felt for Jesus and the Virgin Mary.

The clearest expression of this is his famous *Virgin of the Rocks* (dating from the 1480s), of which there are two versions, one in the Louvre in Paris and the other in London's National Gallery. The more heretical by far is in Paris. (Although we describe this in greater detail in *The Templar Revelation,* its curious, even outrageous heresy is also very relevant here.) Commissioned by a religious fraternity, the theme of the painting is the Christian legend of a meeting in Egypt between the infant Jesus and the young John the Baptist, in which Jesus bestows on John the authority with which he was to baptise him in later years. (In itself this is interesting: the legend was invented to overcome the theological problem of why the sinless Son of God submitted himself to John's authority.) According to this legend, it was during the flight into Egypt that Mary and Joseph encountered the infant John, then in the care of the archangel Uriel. It is the moment when the two children and their guardians meet that Leonardo captures in his painting. It appears to show the Virgin Mary with her arm around the baby John, kneeling in submission to Jesus, who is apparently in the care of Uriel. Clearly, however, the two children are with the wrong adults: surely Jesus should be with his mother and John, according to tradition, with his protector, the archangel Uriel. But what if the children are with the *right* adults? *Then it is Jesus who is kneeling in submission to John.*

There are many other visual clues worked into the scene that confirm this heretical and shocking interpretation, and also underscore Leonardo's extreme personal distaste for the Holy Family. (This includes one quite astounding, and very schoolboyish feature – literally the biggest thing in the painting, which is formed from the rocks above the Virgin. This apparently pious painting depicts two fine testicles and an enormous phallus rising from her head to the skyline, topped with a little spurt of weeds . . .)

Also scattered liberally throughout Leonardo's works is what we rapidly came to call the 'John gesture' – the upraised forefinger of the right hand, which always, without fail, is either actually made by John himself or in some way refers to him (at least in Leonardo's art). A prime example is the famous cartoon of *The Virgin and Child with St Anne* in London's National Gallery, in which 'St Anne' is virtually thrusting the John gesture into the Virgin's beautiful but oblivious face above the young John the Baptist's head. In fact, many art experts believe that 'St Anne' is actually Elizabeth, John's mother, which is confirmed by the fact that her son is leaning against her, and that she is making the distinctive John gesture. The cartoon of 1501 was the preliminary sketch for *St Anne with the Virgin and Child* (painted some time between 1501 and 1507), which also shows Mary perching rather uncomfortably on the older woman's lap. Yet in the final version, there is a major difference: the child John has been replaced by the figure of a lamb, with which Jesus is playing. In fact, closer inspection reveals that he is treating the lamb extremely roughly – almost *wrestling* with it. The position of his right arm and leg, which is hooked over its fragile-looking neck, creates the illusion that the lamb's head is severed, or even that Jesus is actually trying to pull it off . . . What is particularly interesting about this is that the symbol of the Lamb of God, not representing Jesus, but John the Baptist, was also used by the Knights Templar, specifically in the Languedoc.

When Leonardo wrote 'Miserable mortals, open your eyes' he may have had in mind the symbolism with which he imbued all his work, some of which, as we have seen, is remarkably easy to grasp once it is perceived.

We began to realise that the curious heresy of Johannitism ran through our Shroud investigation like a golden thread. First, we were contacted by Giovanni, apparently a high-ranking member of what turned out to be a Johannite-Templarist group, then we discovered that Leonardo – contrary to both popular imagination and academic certainty – also imbues his work with so much Johannite symbolism that it is hard to avoid the conclusion that he, too, was a member of that intriguing brotherhood. And, as we will see, his secret beliefs were intimately connected with his faking of the ultimate Christian relic.

Of course, Leonardo was not alone in his heretical beliefs, nor was he a lone conspirator against the established Church. Indeed, tracing the history of the Shroud was to reveal an astonishing network of conspirators, who created an aura of mystery and secrecy around the relic, for their own purposes.

6

The Shroud Conspiracy

'... history is an alloy of reality and lies. The reality of history becomes a lie. The unreality of the fable becomes truth.'

Jean Cocteau[1]

If Leonardo da Vinci had indeed created the Turin Shroud in 1492, one thing was certain: a Shroud that was supposedly the same one had existed since the middle of the previous century, so Leonardo's version must have been a substitute. Of course this raises two major questions. First, was there any evidence to show that the Shroud that was displayed before 1492 was in any significant way different from the one that was exhibited afterwards? Clearly, if records showed that they were identical then Giovanni's information was wrong. Secondly, was there any evidence from around 1492 of the substitution actually taking place, or at least of some skulduggery occurring in connection with the Shroud at that time?

Mistaken Identity

To look for answers to our first question we worked our way through the Shroud literature for information on pre-1492 copies and descriptions of that alleged relic. In fact, there is virtually nothing there. There were no copies or depictions of the Shroud before the sixteenth century, testimony to the cloth's low status before honours began to be conferred on it towards the end of the 1400s. Other writers have realised that this almost total lack of information at least hints at the possibility of a switch having been made at some point. For example, in 1978 Magnus Magnusson asked: 'Has sufficient attention been given to the possibility that the forgery is much later [than the fourteenth century]?'[2]

Some commentators have considered the possibility that, as was rumoured at the time, the original Shroud was destroyed in the 1532 fire. Others counter this by referring to the copy in the church of St Gommaire in the Belgian town of Lierre. The circumstances in which this copy were made are unknown, but it bears the date 1516, sixteen years before the fire. The image is shown much as it is today and, most specifically, the 'poker marks' are present. However, it is not a particularly good copy. The blood flows in particular are inaccurate, and some features appear that are not visible on the Shroud, such as toes. It appears to be painted from memory rather than from the Shroud itself.

The Lierre version is the earliest painted or drawn copy. Some Shroudies cite the pilgrim's badge that was found in the Seine in 1855 as an earlier copy. As we have seen, the medal has not been conclusively dated, but because it shows the coats of arms of the de Charny and de Vergy families it is assumed that it was made at the time of the first expositions at Lirey in 1357 or 1358, way back in the time of the first Geoffrey de Charny or his widow, Jeanne de Vergy.

These assumptions, however, may be wrong. There is nothing in the design or function of the medal itself that specifically reinforces this attempt at dating it. Such things were made and sold as souvenirs throughout the Middle Ages and well into the sixteenth century, and were it not for the coats of arms there would be no way of telling, even vaguely, what period it came from. In fact, it was not realised until 1960 that the medal showed the Lirey Shroud – before that it had been thought that it depicted its rival from Besançon. This was made in the mid-sixteenth century and destroyed during the French Revolution, but it is known to have been a painting. Surviving copies show it to have been copied from the Turin Shroud, which was then at Chambéry. The vital difference between the two Shroud images is that the Besançon version showed only the front of Jesus – so the medallion found in the Seine, which shows both sides of the image, could not have been a copy of that one.[3]

The presence of the two coats of arms does not necessarily prove that the medal was struck at the time of the very first expositions at Lirey, since both Geoffrey de Charny's son, Geoffrey II, and his granddaughter Margaret were entitled to use them, being descended from both families. There is every likelihood that the medal had been made to commemorate a much later exposition: the coats of arms merely added the gravitas of the best possible pedigree. At this stage it is hard to tell. But, assuming that the medal does date from the fourteenth- or early fifteenth-century exhibitions, what does this tell us about the Shroud? Does it help to establish that this Shroud was the same one as today's?

The main problem is that the medallion – a sort of badge usually worn on the pilgrim's hat – is far too small for a proper comparison to be made, being 'little bigger than a large postage stamp'.[4] As these things were mass-produced to make a quick profit, accuracy was not of paramount importance. There is no question of being able to use the image on the medal to compare it to the fine detail on the Shroud, although it does show the same general characteristics – the double image with the hands crossed modestly over the loins – but further than that one cannot go. And being metal, it tells us nothing about the colour of the image. Amazingly, however, the cloth is depicted as being herringbone weave, but then a clever substitute would obviously be made on the same kind of cloth. Perhaps it would even be imprinted on the same piece, with the original image removed.

Some commentators[5] have suggested that the boldness of the medallion image indicates that the cloth it copies portrayed a more definite-looking Shroudman than the one we know today. Does the medallion show a different image altogether, or has today's Turin Shroud faded since the medal was made? It is much more likely that there was simply no point in creating anything other than a well-defined medal. Who would want one that you could hardly make out?

There is one feature, however, that is clearly visible on the medal that is not present on the Turin Shroud – a curious thick twisted band, like a rope, across the width of the cloth at the small of the figure's back. What this represents is anybody's guess. Also, one feature is missing – the prominent footprint on the dorsal image – but perhaps we should remember that this was hardly a work of precision.

Unfortunately, pre-1500 documents are little help either. Most of those that mention the Shroud are concerned with the various disputes in which the relic was embroiled, and do not bother to describe it. The earliest one, the D'Arcis Memorandum, does mention that the cloth shows a front and a back image, but gives no further detail. This is hardly proof one way or the other, as any halfway decent replacement would have the double image as well.

Evidence that suggests that the Shroud has altered in appearance over the centuries comes from the records of Cornelius Zantiflet, a Benedictine monk. He witnessed the expositions by Margaret de Charny at Liège in Belgium in 1449, when a commission set up by the local bishop concluded that it was a painting. Zantiflet does not describe any details of the Shroud he saw, but, while agreeing with the findings of the Bishop's commission, he does compliment it as being 'admirably depicted'.[6] We must remember that we can only appreciate the full glory of the image in photographic negative: in his day what is today's Turin Shroud would have seemed pale and lacklustre to the naked eye. By no stretch of the imagination could it have been called 'an admirable depiction' of the crucified Jesus.

Zantiflet, like Bishop d'Arcis fifty years before, was also in no doubt that he had seen a painted image. In fact, everybody who expressed an opinion about 'the' Shroud before the second half of the fifteenth century states that it was a painting. Even so, there is no real evidence one way or the other to show whether the Shroud that was exhibited after 1492 was – or was not – identical to the one that was shown before. Certainly there is nothing to demolish the idea of a substitution, and there is enough doubt to have allowed several leading researchers to speculate about such a switch.

So uncertain is 'the' Shroud's pre-1500 history that Ian Wilson, in 1994, after years of championing the 'orthodox' version of its early whereabouts, still felt able to ask: 'Was it possible that instead of ever being owned by the de Charnys, the true Shroud had been in Cyprus and has been brought into the Savoy family by a Cypriot princess?'[7] This refers to a northern Cypriot legend that the Shroud had been kept at a monastery at Lapithos until it was given to the Savoys – the princess being presumably Anne de Lusignan, of Cyprus' ruling house. Wilson took this rumour seriously enough to allow a Dutch television company to finance his trip there: unfortunately the monastery is a barracks these days and they took exception to his knocking at their gate. There were a tense few moments as he and his wife looked down the barrel of a gun, before being unceremoniously turned away.

Some years earlier, in his 1986 book *The Evidence of the Shroud*, Wilson had acknowledged the possibility of a substitution in Leonardo's lifetime. When discussing Noemi Gabrielli's suggestion that Leonardo or one of his school was responsible for the Shroud, he writes: 'The theory does of course demand

that someone from the Savoy family must secretly have commissioned Leonardo for the task, but this is by no means unthinkable
in the notoriously unscrupulous times of the Renaissance.'[8]
While he personally rejected the idea, it was impossible for him
to produce solid evidence to refute it.

The Superior Substitute

This brings us neatly to the second of our two major questions,
namely: is there any positive evidence of a substitution around
the crucial year of 1492? Obviously, when dealing with a conspiracy that would involve people at the highest level, it would be
unlikely that any direct documentary evidence would survive –
certainly not in the public domain – even if any had existed at
the time. But it should be possible to find suggestions of such a
plot in the highways and byways of history, in the provocative
links between the major players in this drama and in the patterns
of the events they shaped.

Of all times, the early 1490s was the most likely for the
Shrouds to be switched. Between the supposed transfer of the
relic from Margaret de Charny in 1453 and a display by Duchess
Bianca of Savoy at Vercelli on Good Friday 1494, there are no
verifiable records of any major displays – a gap of just over forty
years.[9] Some suggest that it was not displayed because in 1471 work
began on rebuilding the Savoys' church at Chambéry specifically
to house the Shroud, and this was not finished until 1502 (when
the relic was installed there with great pomp). But the fact remains
that the Shroud was exhibited elsewhere in 1494, so this can
hardly have been the reason for the delay.

We referred above to the 'supposed' transfer of 1453 because
it is by no means certain that the Shroud was given to the Savoys
at that time, despite the frequent assertions of the believers. The
date is inferred from the gift of a castle and lands to Margaret de

Charny in that year in exchange for 'valuable services'. It is usually understood that this includes handing over the Shroud, but it ignores the fact that Margaret's family were related to the House of Savoy and that her late husband had served it in various capacities throughout his lifetime. In fact, four years later the canons of Lirey were still involved in legal proceedings against Margaret for the return of the Shroud, which they claimed as their own property – and in 1459, her half-brother was negotiating between her and the canons over the question of compensation. This is an extremely odd – not to mention futile – thing to have done if she no longer actually owned the Shroud! In fact, the first documented evidence of the Savoys' ownership comes a full five years afterwards, in 1464 when Louis of Savoy paid the required compensation (fifty gold francs). So the Shroud could have come into his hands at any time up until that point.

The year 1464 is significant because it was then that the first serious claims of its authenticity were made by churchmen. Before then it had attracted little interest and a fair amount of actual hostility. The new claims were made by a Franciscan, Francesco della Rovere, who subsequently rose to become Pope Sixtus IV, in his treatise *On The Blood of Christ*,[10] although there is no evidence that he ever actually saw the Shroud for himself. In his treatise the relic is mentioned only briefly, but since its supposed authenticity supports his theological arguments it is given his wholehearted approval. However, his role in changing the fortunes of the Shroud did yield some highly provocative clues. A conspiracy was beginning to emerge.

At this time the papacy – never a stranger to intrigue, corruption and outright decadence – was going through one of its most colourful periods. Several factions, grouped around rich and influential families, were engaged in plots and counter-plots to gain or keep control of this most powerful position. Sixtus – the builder of the Sistine Chapel, which is named after him – was of one such family, the della Roveres, and even by fifteenth-century standards he still manages to emerge as one of the most corrupt, ruthless and ambitious popes ever to have held office. The insti- gator of several wars within Italy, he has been said to have 'embodied the utmost concentration of human wickedness'.[11] He had several illegitimate sons ('papal nephews' as they were officially known), one quite probably by his own sister, and introduced a number of novel ways of raising funds for the Holy Office, including licensing the brothels of Rome. It was Sixtus who instituted the Spanish Inquisition and appointed the dreaded Torquemada as its Grand Inquisitor – altogether not what one would hope to expect from the first champion of the Holy Shroud.

When Sixtus died in 1484 there was the usual undignified scuffle over the succession. The della Roveres managed to retain control, but it was deemed expedient to do so through a puppet rather than a member of the family. Sixtus' nephew (a genuine nephew, apparently) masterminded the election of Giovanni Battista Cibò as Pope Innocent VIII. He was one of the weakest and most ineffectual of all the fifteenth-century popes (British writer Colin Wilson sums him up as a 'belligerent nonentity'[12]), but he still managed to keep a string of mistresses in the Vatican and introduce one major innovation: he was the first pope to acknowledge his bastards publicly, a precedent followed by his successors. Another of his acts was to have such long-ranging effects, on both the everyday life and the psychological and spiritual health of millions, that its echoes are still felt to this day: he endorsed the *Malleus Maleficarum* (*Hammer of the Witches*), the infamous textbook of witch-hunting by Heinrich Kramer and Jakob Sprenger. A terribly dull read, it was nevertheless to spread the ultimate superstitious paranoia throughout Europe and was to cost the lives of thousands, perhaps even millions of innocent people – mainly women – before sanity reasserted itself.

Innocent was Pope in 1492 (dying in August of that year) and, according to Giovanni's information, he was the authority behind

Leonardo's Shroud forgery. On his deathbed, Innocent was attended by physicians who attempted to prolong his life by the direct transfusion of blood from three youths, who all died as a result. After his death, the della Rovere faction was outbribed and lost control of the papacy to the Borgias, in the person of the notorious Alexander VI (Rodrigo Borgia, who reigned as Pope 1492–1503), father of Lucrezia and Cesare (who employed Leonardo as military engineer between 1502 and 1503). During this time no further honours were granted to the Shroud, even though the rebuilding of Chambéry church was finished and the relic had already been installed there.

After the incumbency of Alexander's successor, Pius III, who was Pope during 1503, the della Roveres made a comeback. Giuliano della Rovere became Pope Julius II until his death in 1513. Within a few months of taking office in 1506 he began to promote the Shroud, granting the church at Chambéry the title Sainte Chapelle – a rare privilege, as this had only been given once before to St Louis's famous chapel of relics in Paris – and assigning the Shroud its own feast day (4 May). A clear pattern emerges: when the della Roveres were in power, the Shroud's cause was advanced, and when they are not in control, it received little papal attention.

We also found that there were close ties between Innocent VIII and Lorenzo de Medici who (even though Leonardo was by then working at the Sforza court in Milan) was still the Maestro's patron. (Artists were regarded as diplomatic 'gifts' from one ruler to another, but were still subject to their original masters, which sometimes gave rise to acrimonious disputes as cities demanded 'their' celebrities back.) Lorenzo worked hard to build diplomatic bonds with Innocent, even marrying his favourite daughter, Maddelena, to the Pope's dissolute and unpleasant bastard son, Franceschetto Cibò.

Leonardo's patrons in later life had dynastic connections with the House of Savoy. During his troubled period in Rome around

1515, when Lorenzo de Medici's son was Pope Leo X, Leonardo's protector and patron was another of Lorenzo's sons, Giuliano (who was, incidentally, obsessed with alchemy). This young man married a daughter of the Duke of Savoy. Leonardo's last patron, Francis I of France, was the son of Louise of Savoy, marrying one of his daughters to Duke Emmanuel Philibert, who took the Shroud to Turin.

Giovanni said that Leonardo faked the Shroud in 1492: so this is precisely the right time, being just two years before the Shroud emerged from its forty-year period of obscurity. Moreover, Leonardo himself was in exactly the right place at the right time. The Duchy of Milan shared a long border with Savoy, and Vercelli – the place where the Shroud was 'returned' to public gaze in 1494 – was virtually on the border of the two duchies. It is about 40 miles (65 km) from the city of Milan where Leonardo was working at the time.

We know that at some time in the late 1480s or early 1490s (the exact year is not known) he took a trip to Savoy. His visit is mentioned in his notebooks dating from the last years of the 1490s, in which he reminisces about a waterfall and lake that he saw there.[13] The reason for his trip is not recorded. The lake in question, however, is near Geneva, less than 50 miles (80km) from Chambéry, capital of Savoy, where the Shroud was – it is believed – then kept.

A final, but very significant piece of evidence lies in the fate of Leonardo's notebooks. Several people have asked us why, if he was such a compulsive note-maker, did he fail to jot down references to the Shroud? Apart from the necessity for the utmost secrecy, it is quite possible that he might well have jotted down some aspects of his preliminary research – for example, the photographic method and his relevant anatomical experiments. A third of all his notebooks have, however, been lost over time, but the fate of some of them is known.

Leonardo left all of them to his faithful companion, Francesco

Melzi, who kept them carefully. But they began to be dispersed under Melzi's son, who did not prize them so highly. In the 1570s just one of the notebooks was bought by an agent acting for none other than the Duke of Savoy, Charles Emmanuel. The book disappeared into the Savoys' library, and since then nothing has been heard of it.[14] Why should that family have been so keen to own that particular book – and then be so careless as to lose it? David Sox, among others, has suggested that the extensive archives of the House of Savoy might include some guilty secret about the Shroud. Umberto II, the last Savoy to own it, seems to have believed it to be authentic, but his estranged wife, Maria José, thought the opposite. She lived in Geneva, and used the Savoys' archives to write a history of the family. It has never been published, but according to those who have read the manuscript the Shroud receives a single mention in a footnote, where it is dismissed as a forgery. As Sox writes: 'One cannot help but wonder what led her to this conclusion.'[15] Perhaps Leonardo's 'lost' notebook had something to do with her unequivocal pronouncement about the Shroud. In considering these circumstances even Ian Wilson admits, 'While there are no known documents suggesting the Savoys had secret dealings with Leonardo, the idea is by no means impossible'.[16]

In on the Secret

There were two other events that took place during Leonardo's lifetime which provide circumstantial evidence to show that at least some key people knew about his role in faking the Shroud. The great German artist Albrecht Dürer (1471–1528) travelled to Italy in the late 1490s and in the first decade of the 1500s to learn the technique of the Italian masters. Described by Kenneth Clark as 'the artist most like Leonardo', Dürer was a great admirer of the Maestro and consciously emulated him – some of his works are direct copies of those of his hero.

It is highly significant that Dürer went out of his way to see the Turin Shroud making a long and detailed study of it.[17] In the light of our discoveries about Leonardo and the Shroud, it is also interesting that in 1500 Dürer should have done something that, certainly in his day, would have been an unthinkable blasphemy – he painted himself as Jesus.

This picture is often taken to be an imaginary portrait of Christ, and was featured as such on the cover of an SPCK book in 1993. For the same reason it was also used to dress the set of Castle Dracula in Francis Ford Coppola's 1992 film *Bram Stoker's Dracula*, although it was very subtly altered to include physical characteristics of actor Gary Oldman as he looked in the lead role.

Another of Leonardo's great admirers was the French king, Francis I, with whom the Maestro stayed in the years immediately before his death. Just six months after Leonardo arrived at his court, Francis made a trip to Chambéry to see the Shroud.

The Templar Connection

Having established to our satisfaction that there is at least circumstantial evidence of a conspiracy to substitute Leonardo's Shroud for the cloth originally acquired by the Savoys, it seemed logical to try to trace the conspiracy back to its inception. Did the Savoys of the fifteenth century begin to panic that the relic they owned was no longer convincing to the public of the increasingly discerning Renaissance? Was the Lirey cloth just another fraud to trick gullible pilgrims? To answer these questions, we had to look more closely at the characters involved in the Lirey affair, namely the first recorded owner of the relic, Geoffrey de Charny the elder, his son Geoffrey and granddaughter Margaret and their respective spouses.

Like many conspiracy stories of that era, it appeared to begin with the Knights Templar: in this case with Geoffrey's supposed link with them. Ian Wilson had, as we have seen, invoked the Templars to provide a link between the Mandylion's disappearance from Constantinople in 1204 and its supposed reappearance as the Lirey Shroud in the late 1350s. He based this idea on the fact that Geoffrey was linked to one of the highest ranking Templars executed in 1314 – his uncle, also called Geoffrey de Charny.[18]

However, there is more to this than merely the fact of their blood ties. Geoffrey of Lirey was a prime mover in establishing a new chivalric order that was a clear attempt to revive the Templars. Since their overthrow there had been many such new orders that sought to maintain their ideals (and pass on their secrets). Some, such as the Knights of Christ in Portugal and the Order of Montesa in Spain, consisted of Templar survivors regrouping under new titles. Others, such as England's Order of the Garter, were established to ensure that at least their ceremonies survived. In one form or another, the Order of the Temple maintained a potent hold on the hearts and minds of those who yearned for high ideals: it was not going to sink into the mists of history without a struggle.

At around the same time that he founded the church of Notre-Dame de Lirey, Geoffrey created a new order, whose ideals, rule and ceremonies were clearly based on the Templar model: the Order of the Star, founded in January 1352.[19] It was not to survive long – Geoffrey and most of the other founding knights died at the battle of Poitiers four-and-a-half years later. (A purely ceremonial version was revived almost immediately, but did not last beyond the seventeenth century.)

So Geoffrey de Charny, first recorded owner of what is supposed to have been the Turin Shroud, clearly had Templar sympathies, if only because of his family ties. But it still requires a huge leap to deduce from all this that the Shroud had originally belonged to the Templars, or that they originally came to own it after the sack of Constantinople. The major drawback here is that the Templars were not actually present at that event. Wilson and other enthusiasts, notably Noel Currer-Briggs, have to make some quite wild assumptions to account for the Templars – allegedly – coming to own the Shroud.

It strikes us as odd that the core of their argument is their identification of the Shroud with Baphomet, a demonic idol in the shape of a man's head that the Templars confessed to worshipping. It was supposed reverence for this head that was enough to have them executed for heresy. Wilson, however, believes that Baphomet was really the Shroud folded – as in its alleged incarnations as the Mandylion – so that only the head showed.[20] The allegations of devil worship were, he suggests, simply their enemies' deliberate attempts to discredit them. But this theory does not hold up. Wilson claims that the secret of the Mandylion (that it was in fact the Shroud) was discovered while it was in Constantinople. But if it was known to be a full-length image, why did the Templars fold it up again and worship just the face? Either its true dimensions were unknown, in which case it could hardly have been Robert de Clari's *sydoine*, or they were known, in which case it could not have been the Templar idol.

When the Templars were interrogated they made it clear that whatever else Baphomet was or was not, it was certainly a three-dimensional object; probably some kind of severed head, not a flat image.[21] Their confessions included a variety of descriptions of this thing: that it was the head of a bearded man being the most common, or a skull, or a head-shaped reliquary. Isolated references were made to it as a painting, but only ever as being on 'a beam or wall', never on cloth. A few referred to the head as that of a cat, or a multiple image made up of two or three cats.

Out of all those descriptions there is nothing at all that is remi-
niscent of what we know as the Turin Shroud.

There being few, if any, other candidates to provide the necessary missing link for the Shroud's early history, we believe that
the Templar connection is manipulated, distorted and forced by
those who have come to rely upon it. Noel Currer-Briggs, for
example, notes one Knight's confession that described the idol as
being 'a head with four feet'.[22] He suggests that this is in fact a
good description of the Shroud, if you imagine it being hung
over a rod at the middle and falling so that the legs of both front
and back images can be seen: hence the 'four feet'. But why
were the body and hands not described? And, once again, if they
had the Shroud why did not one of the Knights, especially in the
persuasive grip of atrocious torture, actually say so? Why, indeed,
was there any necessity to display it in such a perverse fashion?
Why not just hang it up full length so it could be appreciated
properly? And we have tried, but failed, to find any similarities
between the Shroud image and even the largest cat!

In *The Jesus Conspiracy*, Elmar Gruber points out in particular
the selectivity of Ian Wilson's descriptions of the idol head taken
from Templar confessions, demonstrating that Wilson omits parts
of the full texts that do not fit the Shroud comparison.[23]

Currer-Briggs disagrees with Wilson about the Shroud having
been the Mandylion, while accepting that the cloth had reached
Constantinople by an unexplained route. He maintains that it
had always been known to be a full-length image, which makes
the Templar worship of it as a head only all the more mystifying.

Equally mystifying to us is the amount of space given in
Shroud literature to a wooden panel bearing the painted image
of a man's head that was found hidden in the ceiling of a cottage
at Templecombe, Devon, in the 1940s.[24] Since, as its name
suggests, Templecombe was a Templar holding, and because the
painting bears a very slight resemblance to the Shroud face – it
depicts a bearded man with long hair – it is taken as evidence for

the 'idol head' theory, on the assumption that it must have been copied from the Shroud by the Templars. There is, however, absolutely no evidence that the painting ever belonged to them. Why it was hidden in that fashion is anyone's guess, but it could hardly have been put there by the Templars as the cottage was only built centuries after they had been dispossessed of their property in that area. Also the image is extraordinarily unlike the Shroud face: its eyes are wide open and its mouth is gaping. There are no traces of blood, which would have been an essential part of the image had it been copied from the Shroud, and it is a natural colour, without the brownish stain-like quality of the alleged relic. In our view, this is the best 'evidence' that Currer-Briggs, Wilson and others can offer to back up their theory that the Templars were once custodians of the Shroud.

However, perhaps one should not dismiss the connection between the de Charnys of Lirey and the Templars too hastily. Taken with other evidence the connection is highly suggestive of some kind of historical conspiracy involving the people who owned the Shroud in the fourteenth and fifteenth centuries. Our own research has revealed that there were dark secrets that drew together those whose interests would be best served by Shroud forgeries.

BSTS member Currer-Briggs, a distinguished genealogist who worked for *Debrett's* and *Burke's Peerage*, accidentally pointed us in the right direction in his book *The Shroud and the Grail* (1987), which he had researched because of his fascination with the idea that there may be some connection between the Shroud and the Grail romances of the late twelfth and early thirteenth centuries. He thinks that the Shroud is literally the Holy Grail (or rather, the Grail was the reliquary in which the Shroud was kept).[25] He developed his argument in *Shroud Mafia* (1995), although after the carbon dating – and reading our book – he no longer believed the Shroud is genuine.

He notes that the Grail romances arose at the time when Western Europeans were beginning to re-establish links with the Byzantine Empire. News of Constantinople's treasures had become a talking point. He also points out that the first Grail stories do not actually describe the relic: it could have been any-thing. In the most persistent legends it was the cup that had been used by Jesus at the Last Supper and which contained his blood, or in some versions, his sweat, and which was later taken by Joseph of Arimathea to Europe. Currer-Briggs believes that the early Grail romances were actually describing the Shroud, which 'contained' the blood and sweat that had soaked into it. Later writers assumed that it must have been a cup or some such sim-ilar vessel – and so, he suggests, a great myth was born. There is, however, no evidence that the cloth was in existence at the time the early Grail legends were being written. As a genealogist, Currer-Briggs is on a much firmer footing when he attempts to show links between the French Crusaders involved in the sack of Constantinople and the later Shroud story; events that hint at the real purpose behind the foundation of what he calls the 'Shroud Mafia' (a term that seems, to us, perhaps more appropriate in describing the relic's most recent enthusiasts; see Chapter 9).

The families involved all hail from France, mostly from the regions of Burgundy and Champagne, and, as might be expected, they include the de Charnys. The family is also known as Mont-Saint-Jean, after a village close to Charny. Also involved in the 'Shroud Mafia' of this date were the de Vergys, into which Geoffrey married, and two closely linked families from Champagne, the Joinvilles and the Briennes.

In the early thirteenth century the House of Brienne bore the title of King of Jerusalem, which, according to the Priory of Sion, indicated that they were of the Merovingian bloodline, and which eventually came down to Anne de Lusignan, wife of Louis, Duke of Savoy. Besides the Savoys, Currer-Briggs also lists in his 'Shroud Mafia' the families of de la Roche, Courtenay, Montferrat and d'Anjou.

Currer-Briggs made several interesting discoveries, the first being that the two families that have owned the (or a) Shroud, the de Charnys and Savoys, besides the la Roche and Vergy houses, into which the de Charnys married, had close links before, during and after the time when the Lirey Shroud appeared. The most significant link was the fact that the de Charnys were related to the House of Savoy, to whom the Shroud was passed. (Making it all the more likely that Margaret de Charny did not, as believed, actually sell the relic to the Savoys. She may simply have given it to them, to 'keep it in the family'.)

The extent of the intermarriage among these families was remarkable, even for those times. Margaret de Charny and both her husbands were directly descended from Guillaume de Vergy (her great-grandfather). Both she and her second husband, Humbert de la Roche-Villersexel, were direct descendants of Otto de la Roche (of whom more later). Her first husband, Jean de Beauffrémont, had maternal grandparents who were both direct descendants of Jean de Joinville, another significant player in this complex and subterranean game.

In those days it was common to reinforce dynastic links through marriage, but with these families the connections were repeated to an unusual extent – which points to a common purpose and, presumably, aims.

Secondly, the same families all had close connections with the leadership of the Templars, especially during the final dramatic years of the Order's official existence. For example, not only was Geoffrey de Charny the nephew of the Preceptor or overseer of Normandy, but was also second cousin to Jacques de Molay's predecessor as Grand Master, Guillaume de Beaujeu, who was one of the Mont-Saint-Jean family. (Actually, there was a short-lived Grand Master between the two.) The Templar Geoffrey de Charny was officially received into the Order by Amaury de la Roche, Templar Master of France, who came from the same family as Margaret de Charny's second husband.[26]

As the home of the Order, the Champagne and Burgundy

regions had always welcomed the Templars, but even so the close ties between these families and the Order's leadership are still remarkable.

Both Geoffrey de Charny and his wife, Jeanne de Vergy, had grandfathers who were seneschals (roughly the equivalent of an English sheriff), of Champagne and Burgundy respectively. His grandfather was Jean de Joinville, who is best known as the author of the *Life of Saint Louis*, a work that extolled the piety of his friend and patron, Louis IX, the polar opposite of Philip IV, who had instigated the vicious Templar purge. Jean was seneschal of Champagne, while Jeanne's grandfather, Jean de Vergy, was seneschal of the Duchy of Burgundy.

It was the seneschals who, two weeks before the Templar arrests, received Philip's secret orders to round up all the Templars within their districts. Of all the Templars in France, it was those in Burgundy who most successfully evaded capture, including the Commander of the Paris Temple, Gérard de Villiers, the only senior member to escape. He was a kinsman of both the seneschals mentioned above. Apart from him, only sixteen French knights escaped, two because they were out of the country at the time. And, writes Currer-Briggs: 'Of the remainder, most were Burgundians and kinsmen of each other or of the de Charny, de Joinville and de Vergy families'.[27]

Finally, a century before the demise of the Templars, and a century and a half before the appearance of the Lirey Shroud, the same families had also held key positions in the Fourth Crusade, in which the *sydoine* disappeared.

The leader of the Crusade was Boniface, Marquis de Montferrat, whose House was closely connected to that of Savoy through frequent intermarriage. In time, the Montferrat title was absorbed by the House of Savoy and became one of the minor titles of the dukedom (as did the title of Lord of Mont St Jean). One of Boniface's closest confederates was Otto de la Roche, ancestor of Margaret de Charny and of her second husband.

Obviously there is a need for caution here, for virtually every French noble in Geoffrey de Charny's day would have had ancestors who had taken part in the predominantly French Fourth Crusade. But as Currer-Briggs points out: '. . . the de Charnys and the Savoys who owned the authentic [*sic*] Shroud in the fourteenth and fifteenth centuries were not only related to each other, but shared common ancestors in three, if not four, of the principal men and women who had the handling of it in 1204. One is bound to ask, therefore, if there were a long-standing Mafia-like conspiracy to obtain it by fair means or foul . . .?'[28]

This led Currer-Briggs to the following theoretical reconstruction: the 'Shroud Mafia' group of families, believing that they had some claim to the relic and knowing it was among the treasures in Constantinople, conspired to capture it and bring it back to Europe where it could be secretly kept by them. Over the next seventy years it was transferred among the families, including those who were Templars and Templar sympathisers, where it became an object of worship. It was saved from the Templar Treasury in Paris by Gérard de Villiers, who had been warned of the impending arrests by his kinsmen in Burgundy, and eventually, after the decimation of the Order, it passed into the safe-keeping of Geoffrey de Charny and his widow, Jeanne de Vergy, who instituted the public expositions. Even after this it was kept 'in the family' when the last of the de Charnys, Margaret, married Humbert de la Roche-Villersexel and eventually passed the Shroud on to the Savoys.

These connections may seem persuasive, but there are difficulties. First, the carbon dating and the historical evidence discussed in Chapter 2 indicate that the Shroud did not exist at the time of the Fourth Crusade (1204). Secondly, it would mean that the Crusade had been deliberately engineered for the specific purpose of obtaining the Shroud. This is extremely unlikely, as the Crusader attack on the city only came about after a series of complex and unpredictable events. There was certainly some kind of hidden agenda for the Crusaders, but it was not one that involved the Shroud. The Crusaders had agreed, in return for support for their mission to the Holy Land, to help the deposed Emperor Isaac II regain Constantinople. They hoped that, in return for help in regaining his Empire, the Emperor would bring the Eastern Orthodox Church over to Rome, thus healing Christianity's then greatest schism. When he was killed, however, the only way their objective could be achieved was by installing a European – one of the Crusaders Baldwin of Flanders – as ruler. It all made perfect sense: it was simple politics.[29]

It was only after Baldwin was installed that the Shroud was taken by Boniface de Montferrat, according to Currer-Briggs. He suggests that it was through Mary-Margaret of Hungary, widow of Boniface, that the Shroud returned to Europe.

There was no reason for the 'Shroud Mafia' families even to think they had any claim to the Shroud. Currer-Briggs's suggestion that they were so inspired by the Grail story that they sought a Quest of their own is unconvincing, to say the least. Then there is the problem of why, if they had the Shroud, they were so keen to keep it secret for years, then suddenly display it for no apparent reason. None of it fits. Something else was their prime motivation, something much deeper – and some would say darker.

The Grail Families

Two books, Michael Baigent and Richard Leigh's *The Temple and the Lodge* (1989) and John J. Robinson's *Born in Blood* (1990), have made a strong case for the Templars surviving the official dissolution of their Order, and that they still exist to this day. Both books claim that it was the Templars who were the early Freemasons. Apart from this, it is a matter of fact that, outside

France, many Templars simply transferred their allegiance to other orders. Some, such as the Portuguese Knights of Christ, were created specifically as a haven for the fugitive Templars, while others, such as the Teutonic Knights of Germany, were already in existence but welcomed former Templars with open arms. If, as claimed, the Shroud had been such a sacred object to the Templars, why did they not simply give it to one of these orders instead of handing it over to Geoffrey de Charny?

The genealogical links discovered by Currer-Briggs seem to indicate that the 'Shroud Mafia' were up to something, but certainly before Lirey it could hardly have been anything connected with the Shroud. However, if one takes into account other, considerably more controversial evidence, then a highly provocative pattern does indeed begin to take shape.

Whatever the Templars got up to later on, there was definitely something mysterious about their origins. The official story of the Order's foundation, accepted unquestioningly by historians, makes little sense, and several writers have suggested that this story was a cover for other activities.

The official version[30] states that in or around 1118, after the recovery of Jerusalem by the First Crusade, nine French knights, led by Hugues de Payens and Godfrey de St Omer, travelled there and pledged themselves to keep the pilgrims' routes safe. For several years they seem neither to have done anything nor to have gained any new members, before returning in triumph to Europe in 1127. Shortly afterwards at the Council of Troyes, the Order was officially recognised with Hugues de Payens as its first Grand Master, and given its own Rule, which was – significantly – drawn up by St Bernard of Clairvaux. From this date it underwent the enormous expansion that led to it becoming, in a remarkably short time, one of the wealthiest and most influential institutions of the Middle Ages.

This story is patently nonsense. How could just nine knights police all the highways and byways of Palestine? There was, anyway, another military organisation doing precisely that, the Knights Hospitallers of St John. And the Templars' cover story dates from at least fifty years after the events it describes, whereas the names of Hugues de Payens and his eight companions are conspicuous by their absence from contemporary chronicles, which otherwise eagerly recorded every event in the Holy Land at this time.

So what were those nine knights really up to? British writer Graham Hancock has argued convincingly that they were engaged in a search for the Ark of the Covenant, which they believed to be buried under the Temple Mount in Jerusalem.[31] Baigent, Leigh and Lincoln came to a similar conclusion, but believe them to have discovered some kind of document relating to the Priory of Sion mystery. But there is evidence that the Knights of Christ (as the Templars were known before the Council of Troyes) existed four, perhaps even ten years before 1118.[32] There are equally clear signs of conspiracy concerning the Council and its official recognition of the Order.

Baigent, Leigh and Lincoln uncovered evidence of a conspiracy that involved a number of families from Champagne. This, they claim, was behind the founding of the Templars. The prime mover in these events was Hugues, Count of Champagne, who was instrumental in founding the Order, and who eventually joined the Templars himself. Some historians believe that he was related to Hugues de Payens – the records are sketchy – but he certainly was his feudal lord.

The Templars and the Cistercian Orders – one military, the other spiritual – grew and expanded together. The Cistercian Order was founded in 1098 and St Bernard became its third leader, but it was not a significant movement at its start. One of the original nine knights was André de Montbard, who was St Bernard's uncle. It was Hugues of Champagne who donated the site of Clairvaux to Bernard, where he built his abbey and from whence he expanded his 'empire'. He became the official 'sponsor' of the Templars, and it was his influence that ensured papal recognition at the Council of Troyes, this being the capital of Hugues' land. It was here that the Templar Rule was drawn up by Bernard, based on that of the Cistercians, and it was from here that they were granted their livery of white mantle, later to be emblazoned with the distinctive red cross pattée (an equal-armed cross with the arms tapering towards the centre). It was a disciple of Bernard, Pope Innocent II (formerly a monk at Clairvaux), who freed the Templars from all allegiance to anyone except the Pope himself.

Following the Priory of Sion's *Dossiers secrets*, Baigent, Leigh and Lincoln argue that the Order of Sion was founded in the 1090s by Godefroy de Bouillon, one of the leaders of the First Crusade that had recaptured Jerusalem. They write that it was this Order that lay behind Hugues of Champagne and the founding of the Templars. They record that: 'In 1104 the Count of Champagne had met in conclave with certain high-ranking nobles, at least one of whom had just returned from Jerusalem . . . Also present was the liege lord of André de Montbard.'[33]

Immediately after this conclave Hugues of Champagne travelled to the Holy Land, where he remained until 1108. He returned there briefly in 1114, then went back to Champagne and donated the Clairvaux site to St Bernard. Four years later – according to the official story – his vassal and possible relation, Hugues de Payens, with André de Montbard and seven companions, set out on their mission and formed the embryonic Knights Templar. Later Hugues of Champagne himself joined the new Order.

It was the conclave of 1104 that had set the train of events in motion, and, as the authors of *The Holy Blood and the Holy Grail* note, 'Among those present at this conclave were representatives of certain families – Brienne, Joinville and Chaumont – who . . . figured significantly in our story'.[34]

The *Dossiers secrets*' central claim is that the great secret protected by the Priory of Sion – the reason for its formation and continued existence – is that the Merovingian dynasty, believed by historians to have come to an abrupt end when it was usurped by the Carolingians in the eighth century, survived, and that it represents the true and sacred kingship of France. (To this Baigent, Leigh and Lincoln added the hypothesis that the Merovingians owed their sacredness to their descent from Jesus and Mary Magdalene, though this was something that the Priory was quick to repudiate. Despite this, the notion that the Priory exists to protect Jesus' descendants has taken hold, most famously in *The Da Vinci Code*.)

The *Dossiers secrets*' genealogical tables, which link the Merovingian survivors to various other European noble families, were followed up by Baigent, Leigh and Lincoln, who found independent evidence that these families had indeed been involved in many shadowy events and developments, particularly through their connections with the Templars and the legends of the Holy Grail.

However, there is an apparent paradox. Our own investigation into the *Dossiers secrets*, set out in *The Sion Revelation*, shows that many of their central claims simply fail to stand up. This particularly applies to what is supposedly the most important thing as far as the Priory is concerned, the survival of the descendants of the Merovingian king Dagobert II and the descent of certain key historical figures, such as Godefroy de Bouillon, from that dynasty. On the other hand, the *Dossiers* do contain much abstruse and obscure historical information that does check out – that is what makes them so compelling. This contradiction between the falsity of the Priory's major claims and the accuracy of much of its more arcane information led us to the conclusion that the material disseminated publicly was *misinformation* designed to throw researchers off the scent. Like all the best misinformation, it contains nuggets of truth.

But if we dismiss the Merovingian connection of the families named in the *Dossiers secrets*, how can we accept the findings of Baigent, Leigh and Lincoln about those same families? In fact, the paradox is only superficial, and fits with the misinformation hypothesis. While Baigent, Leigh and Lincoln may have been inspired by the *Dossiers secrets* to investigate these families and individuals, the information they uncovered – the families' connection with the formation and later history of the Templars, and their relationship to the Grail romances – is genuine enough; in fact, these connections are not spelled out at all in the *Dossiers*. Making the connections may have convinced Baigent, Leigh and Lincoln to take the central claim seriously – that what united these families was their Merovingian origins – but in the misinformation scenario that was precisely the point. Nevertheless, the authors' discoveries and conclusions about those families are valid, even if the documents that pointed them in that direction turn out to be largely fabrications.

Currer-Briggs's linking of these same families with conspiracies connected with the Templars and the Grail – even though he started from a completely different place and confined himself entirely to conventional historical and genealogical sources and ignored material such as the *Dossiers secrets* – reinforces the accuracy of the *Holy Blood* authors' conclusions. Obviously, it follows that whoever created the *Dossiers* was aware of the families' activities and secrets, even though they grafted the fictitious 'Merovingian bloodline' material onto the facts. But it also shows that the families were involved in many projects, and were working to a long-term programme, not simply, as Currer-Briggs suggested, to acquire and keep one holy relic. His Shroud Mafia may well have been involved with the relic, but to them it was only one of their many interconnected and very long-term ambitions.

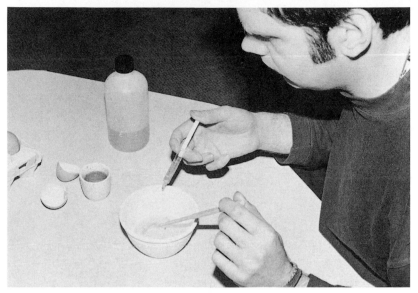

Step by step, how we replicated the Shroud image. First, Keith Prince makes up the light-sensitive mixture (egg-white and chromium salt solution). It is left for a couple of hours to bind.

A coating of the mixture is applied to the cloth, which is left to dry.

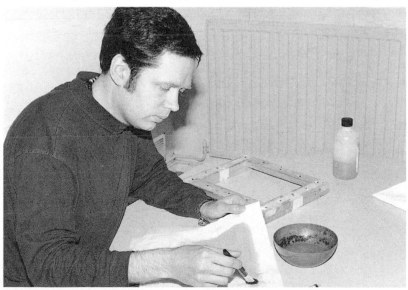

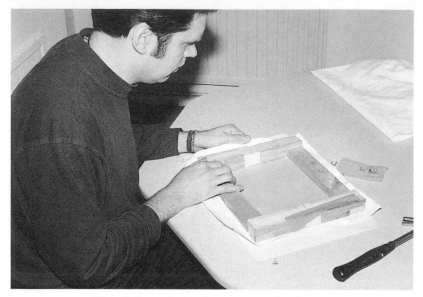

The cloth is stretched over a wooden frame.

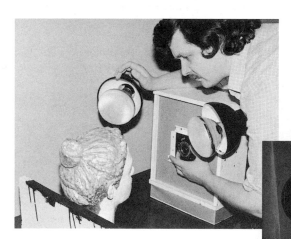

Clive Prince positions the model in front of the camera obscura.

The UV lamps are turned on and the exposure left for a minimum of twelve hours. The hot Italian sun would have sufficed for Leonardo.

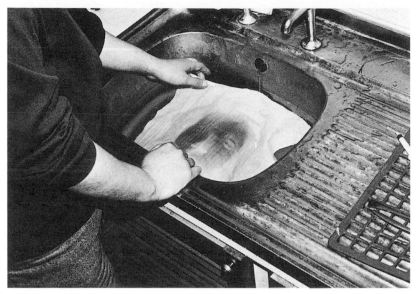

When the frame is removed from the camera, the image parts have hardened and are insoluble in water, whereas the rest is still soluble. Washing in cold water removes the mixture from the unexposed parts, leaving only the image.

Lynn Picknett heats the cloth: the mixture acts like invisible ink, scorching the underlying fabric. A second wash of hot water and detergent removes all trace of the mixture, leaving only the scorched image.

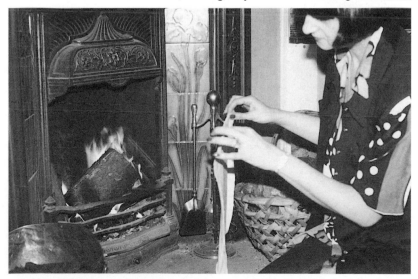

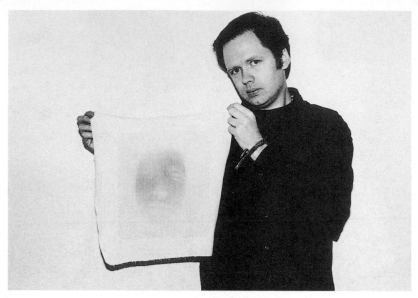

Keith Prince displays the end result.

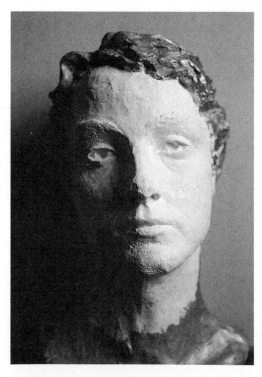

The plaster bust we used in our experiments.

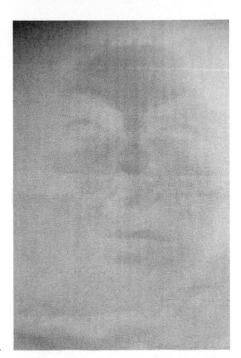

The positive image of the bust.

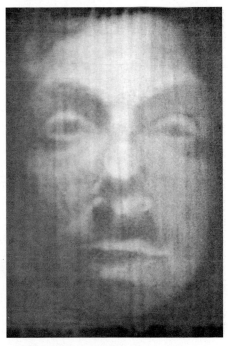

The negative image. Note how much more lifelike it looks, just like the Shroud image seen in negative.

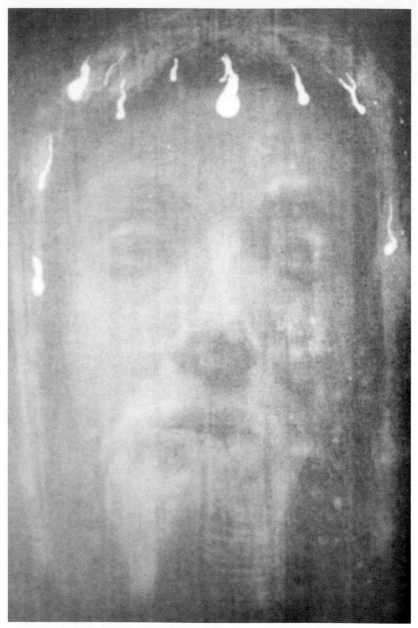
Negative image of the bust with retouched hair and blood.

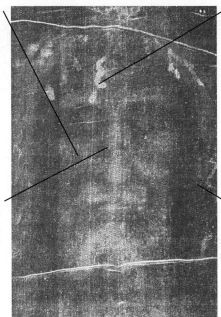

Unnatural thinness of face, due to lensing effect (eyes at the edge of the image and no ears)

Foreshortening of forehead

Light circle surrounded by unexposed area, caused by lens

Hair follows incorrect hairline, showing signs of 'retouching', i.e. being added by brush

Features of the head image revealing use of lens.

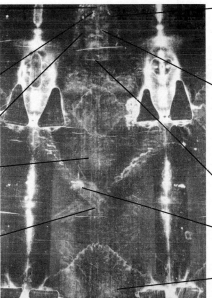

Head (of front image) too small for body

Hair hangs down despite body supposedly being prone

Hairline too low

Composed expression strange for person tortured to death

Ears invisible

Blood still flowing, wrong for a corpse

Neck appears severed

Hands crossed modestly over genitals, possibly suggesting intention to display

Hand impossibly long

Height of man: 6ft 8in at front but 6ft 10in at back

Anomalies of the Shroud image.

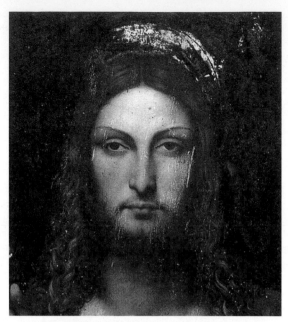

Above: Leonardo's *Salvator Mundi* (*c.*1513). Seen in 'split screen' with (*below left*) Shroudman and (*below right*) Aggemian's portrait, it is obvious they are exact matches – proving that Leonardo had an intimate knowledge of the Shroud. But is this also da Vinci's 'confession' to faking Catholicism's holiest relic?

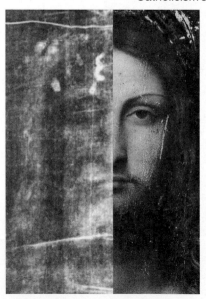
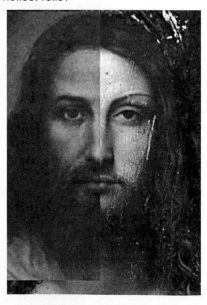

Yet more of a pattern, an intertwining of families, began to emerge. Guillaume de Champlitte, part of the 'clique' surrounding Boniface de Montferrat during the Fourth Crusade – and married into the Mont-Saint-Jean de Charny family – was descended from Hugues, Count of Champagne, prime mover in the establishment of the Templars. When he finally joined them himself, Hugues handed his lands and titles over to his nephew, Theobald. Guillaume de Champlitte was Theobald's great-grandson.[35] Moreover, the leader of the Fourth Crusade was originally to have been the then Count of Champagne, a later Theobald and a closer relative of Hugues. However, this Theobald died while the Crusade was in its planning stages, and Boniface de Montferrat replaced him.

We have seen that this Boniface married Mary-Margaret, widow of the former Emperor of Constantinople. It was a short marriage, as he was killed in 1207 in Greece. Within three months she married her third husband, Nicholas de St Omer, who was from the same family as one of the original nine Knights Templar, Godfrey de St Omer, who was second in importance to Hugues de Payens himself.[36] Mary-Margaret made another unfortunate choice as Nicholas died in 1212.

While looking back at the founding Templars we should also note that a Joinville – André, uncle of Jean de Joinville – became Templar Preceptor of Payens, a prestigious post, being connected to the lands given by the first Grand Master of the Order.[37]

Currer-Briggs notes that his Shroud Mafia are all 'families descended from or linked with Fulk of Anjou' who died in 1143.[38] This Fulk (or Fulques) was so closely associated with the early Templars that, according to *The Holy Blood and the Holy Grail*, he 'became, so to speak, an "honorary" or "part-time" Templar'.[39] His father had been Templar number ten, joining the order in 1120. By marrying the niece of Godefroy de Bouillon, Fulk also became King of Jerusalem in 1131. One of his grandchildren, Princess Sybilla of Jerusalem, married twice, first to one of Boniface of Montferrat's brothers and then to Guy de Lusignan – from whom was descended Anne de Lusignan, who by marrying Louis of Savoy brought the title of Jerusalem to the House of Savoy.

This title brings us back, yet again, to the Priory of Sion. We have seen that they claimed to exist in order to restore the Merovingian bloodline to a position of power. While we understand this to be a smoke-screen, it is clear that they want people to *believe* in the importance of that bloodline. By the time Anne de Lusignan married the Duke of Savoy, the title of King of Jerusalem was meaningless, if still prestigious. Yet the Priory are proud of the genealogies they have drawn up that link the Lusignan family with the bloodline as far back as the mid-tenth century – but why?

The Shroud Mafia group seem particularly anxious to keep the title of King of Jerusalem among them. Fulk's son Amalric of Jerusalem, who died in 1174, had two daughters (by different wives) but no male heirs, so he left it to the Pope, the Holy Roman Emperor and the Kings of France and England to decide which one of them should succeed him. The daughters were Isabella and Sybilla, who had earlier both married the brothers of Boniface de Montferrat, thereby ensuring that the title was kept in the family. But one brother, William, had died and his widow, Sybilla, married Guy de Lusignan. While the succession was being debated, Conrad de Montferrat, husband of Isabella, was murdered. Within two days a marriage was arranged for her with Henry, Count of Champagne, and within eight days they were married. While the speed of events might suggest that Henry himself was behind the murder, an equally plausible explanation might be that this was simply crisis management – Henry could well have been acting swiftly to prevent the title from slipping away from the conspirators in case of a decision being made in Isabella's favour. Henry was a descendant of Hugues de Champagne, the man behind the founding of the Templars, and

also second cousin to Guillaume de Champlitte. In fact, the decision was finally made in favour of Sybilla, thus giving the title
to Guy de Lusignan, but when Henry died Isabella married
Guy's brother, Amalric de Lusignan, who inherited the title on
Guy's death.

The title to Jerusalem was one of the most fraught successions
in history, which may seem very strange as there was no land to
go with it. It was often bequeathed outside the direct line of
descent, so eventually there were two lines claiming to be the
rightful heirs. At one stage it was with the House of Brienne, but
its claim was lost in 1264 to the House of Lusignan when the
Pope decided (improperly, according to the rules of succession)
in their favour. Another rival claim derived from the marriage of
the Holy Roman Emperor (of the Hohenstaufen family) into
that of Brienne, but in 1268 the last of this line died out and the
Lusignans became – for the time being – undisputed heirs.
Another claim, that of René d'Anjou, came from the time when
an ancestor, Charles, bought the title from yet another rival
claimant.

It was directly as a result of René's influence that Cosimo de
Medici sent agents out to look for ancient texts (see Chapter 5),
which resulted in the revival of Neoplatonic and Hermetic
thought, which in turn played such an important part in
Leonardo's life. And René's viceroy in Naples was one Arano
Cibò, father of Pope Innocent VIII, the pope who, according
to Giovanni, had commissioned Leonardo's Shroud forgery.[40]

There is also a potent geographical link between the Shroud
and the preoccupations of the Priory of Sion. Throughout *The
Holy Blood and the Holy Grail* the story continually returns to
the area surrounding the enigmatic village of Rennes-le-Château
in the Languedoc, the centre of the mystery. Arguably Rhedae to
the Visigoths, that area was subsequently known as the Razès. It
was also the centre of the Cathar faith, the so-called 'Albigensian
Heresy'. After the loss of the Holy Land the Templars attempted to

create their own state in this very same area, and the ruins of many Templar castles can still be seen around Rennes-le-Château. So it struck us as something more than a mere coincidence that, according to documents preserved in the French National Archive,[41] Geoffrey de Charny (of Lirey Shroud fame), though living in the north of France, held lands in precisely this region, covering Toulouse and Carcassonne – and including the 'holy place' of Rennes-le-Château itself.

A Calculated Enterprise

Our research has convinced us that Currer-Briggs's Shroud Mafia and the network of families that Baigent, Leigh and Lincoln connected with plots centred on such evocative subjects as the Templars and the Grail were one and the same.

This means that these families were involved in a much wider-ranging conspiracy than simply stealing and gloating over a lucrative relic, and one that went much further back in time even than the Fourth Crusade, back to the founding of the Templars themselves. Currer-Briggs was essentially right about the existence of a conspiracy, but he was mistaken in thinking that because of the involvement of these people with the Shroud, the relic was their only concern.

When seen in this light, as a calculated enterprise that stretched over centuries, a pattern can be discerned in the actions of the de Charny and Savoy families. In fact, they made three attempts to foist a fake Shroud on Christendom. First, at Lirey in the late 1350s, which was foiled not so much by the intrusion of the Bishop of Poitiers but by the death of Geoffrey de Charny himself and the uncertainty caused by the war with England. Secondly, there was the attempt by his son, Geoffrey de Charny the younger in 1389, which was stalled by the scepticism of Bishop Pierre d'Arcis. (The obvious behind-the-scenes activity surrounding these expositions has caused Ian Wilson to remark: 'there is something more to the affair than meets the eye'.) And last – but emphatically not least – was the third attempt in 1492 in the shape of Leonardo's Turin Shroud.

7

Getting the Measure of Shroudman

'Why is his head too small?'

Abigail Nevill

Having delved and delved again into the historical background of
the Turin Shroud, we then posed ourselves another question. Was
there anything about the image itself that effectively gave away
the fact that it was 'made by hands', and which even suggested
whose hands had made it? Was it possible to prove that the face
of the man on the Shroud was, in fact, that of its creator,
Leonardo da Vinci? Most open-minded people we had asked for
their opinions had said it looked like him, but we wondered if
there was any way of comparing Leonardo's face and the Shroud
objectively, perhaps using the kind of techniques the police use
to determine someone's identity.

We decided to examine the Shroud closely. We believe that it
is composed of three images – the face, the body from the neck
down at the front, and all of the back. Was it possible to prove
that this was the case? And could we show conclusively that it is
a photographic image? We already knew that the face was a bad
fit, which supports the idea that the whole image is a composite,
and this was an obvious place to start, but we hoped that something in the actual image would yield clues.

Clearly we needed expert help from someone with a background in image analysis, and who had the equipment with which we could examine the image on the Shroud in minute detail and under different conditions. The best way to achieve this was by using computerised image enhancement; with the image converted into digital form it could easily be manipulated so it would give up at least some of its secrets.

Making the Face Fit

One expert who offered us help at an early stage of our research was Mark Bennett, a Canadian living in the UK whom we had known for some time. The editor of the futuristic magazine *Black Ice*, he was eager to discuss the whole subject of Leonardo and his relationship with the Shroud (of which he was more than a little persuaded), and he found us the video of the now-rare 1970s Italian television series *Leonardo*, which proved useful in many ways. Mark also produced some interesting digital enhancements of the Shroud image for us, before the pressures of editing an independent magazine took over his time.

Steve Pear, a friend with a great deal of knowledge of the rapidly expanding cyber-culture, put out an appeal on the Internet asking for help from computer graphics experts who might be interested in our work. Within a day, one of the best in the field was intrigued enough to reply. Andy Haveland-Robinson, then a north London desktop publisher and consultant in 2-D and 3-D computer graphics, rapidly became an integral part of our project, devoting many long hours to our work with great insight and inspiration.

Today's revolution in information technology is, perhaps, something akin to the great leaps forward in knowledge during the Renaissance. Our new technology has finally managed to bring scientific and creative minds together: computer graphics and animation techniques have created new art forms that effectively remove the barriers between logic and imagination – just as Renaissance thinkers saw no distinction between science and magic. And just as the Renaissance was supported by a revolution in communication, the spread of printing, our Renaissance is underpinned by the growth of communication networks, enabling millions of people and archives the world over to be reached instantaneously from our own homes.

If this is indeed a new Renaissance, then Andy Haveland-Robinson is a good example of a new Renaissance man. Apart from his successful desktop publishing business, he also designs computer animations for pop videos, and has a wide range of other interests, such as music. Our first meeting with him in summer 1993, when he demonstrated some of his amazing computer animations, left us spellbound and convinced that we had found the person we needed. We have to say, however, that Andy always remained strictly objective, and was by no means a total convert, although he would say, after many hours of scrutinising the Shroud image, 'I think Leonardo was involved in this somewhere'.

We had hoped that there would be some way of using computer imaging to establish beyond doubt that the face of the man on the Shroud was Leonardo's own, by matching up the image with portraits of the Maestro – in the same way that Lillian Schwartz had shown that the *Mona Lisa* is Leonardo's self-portrait.[1] However, this was not possible. There is simply not enough information about Leonardo's appearance to make hard-and-fast comparisons. All likely techniques, whether computer-based or forensic, need certain basic reference points and some way of calculating the scale of different images in order to compare them. Surviving portraits of Leonardo do not provide this information.

In fact, the best equipment for measuring the similarity between two pictures is the human eye and brain. A computer, unless given extremely precise data, can never hope to match them.

The pictures have to be pinpoint-accurate. Comparisons often involve tiny measurements – such as the distance between the inner corners of the eye, something that does not change with age or fluctuations in weight – and even minute errors in the picture will throw the comparison out. Obviously all representations of Leonardo are painted or drawn, so there is never any guarantee of accuracy, especially in the fine detail.

The only portrait that we could be sure was accurate enough was his only surviving self-portrait (disregarding the pictures in which he painted himself as a character, such as *The Adoration of the Magi* and *The Last Supper*), a drawing in red chalk. He did this when he was in his sixties, but looking considerably older and more than ever like an Old Testament prophet. It now hangs in Turin, in the Royal Library. (It is a source of some amusement to us that Serge Bramly's biography of Leonardo opens with the words: 'Not far from the Turin Cathedral, which houses the famous but now disputed Shroud, there is, in the Biblioteca Reale, the least contested self-portrait of Leonardo da Vinci.' Bramly goes on to draw parallels between the reverence with which both images are kept – 'Like the Shroud, this self-portrait is rarely exhibited in public: ravaged by time, it is stored away from the harmful effects of air and light.'[2])

We know that this portrait is accurate because it was used successfully by Lillian Schwartz to match up with the *Mona Lisa*. However, it dates from many years after his creation of the Shroud, and although there is still a resemblance to Shroudman, it is not precise enough for our purposes. The cheeks are sunken with age and the mouth has changed, probably because he had lost several teeth over the years. But the biggest problem of all is that the angle of the face is different from that of Shroudman: here Leonardo half turns to the viewer.

There is only a handful of portraits of Leonardo that date from his lifetime. Later pictures, such as the engraving in Vasari's *Lives of the Artists* (first published in 1550), although based on earlier portraits, are not at all reliable. The second well-known depiction shows Leonardo nearer to the right age, but in complete profile, making comparison with the Shroud impossible. This is now in the Royal Library in Windsor (with a copy in the Ambrosiana Library in Milan), and was probably painted by a pupil, possibly Francesco Melzi. Raphael painted Leonardo as Plato in *The School of Athens* but, although the two artists had met, it could not have been painted from life as Leonardo was living in France at the time. A painting in the Uffizi Gallery, which has perhaps the most striking resemblance to the face of the man on the Shroud, was long thought to be a self-portrait, but was shown in the 1930s to be a seventeenth-century work. It was certainly based on a lost self-portrait, but it is invalid for purposes of comparison.

What we needed was a portrait of Leonardo at the age of forty, looking straight out at the observer. If there had been lots of surviving portraits, even from several different angles, we could have combined them to make a three-dimensional model that could have been rotated to face the screen. Sadly and frustratingly, we could not even begin to do this.

The few existing portraits show many signs of inaccuracy. The Windsor portrait is widely believed to have been altered in order to flatter the Maestro: his nose – in life a splendid example of nasal domination – has dwindled to less alarming proportions, thanks to the instant plastic surgery of a crafty paintbrush. It is even possible that the Turin self-portrait has been altered over the years.[3]

With Andy we looked at all the possible candidates in case there really was some way of making an objective comparison. We even considered the possibility of using the *Mona Lisa*, but in the end we had to accept that we simply could not do it. As Andy put it: 'The tolerance with people's features is quite small and with different angles of view of Leonardo and lack of scale information the result would be inconclusive. Without a full-frontal picture of his face, it can't be done.'

The Severed Head

With that avenue closed to us, we turned instead to a study of the image itself, looking for tell-tale discrepancies that might support our theory or throw some light on Leonardo's method. To us, the single most important anomaly is the 'severed head' effect. As Abigail Nevill had pointed out so shrewdly, the head is 'on wrong' and is too small for the body. Not only is it in the wrong position in relation to the body, but there is also a clear gap between the end of the neck and the beginning of the chest – the head appears almost to be floating in a sea of darkness. The space itself might – assuming the Shroud's authenticity – be explained by the lie of the cloth, but the unnatural positioning of the head cannot, nor can the fact that the neck ends so abruptly in a transverse line, neatly squared off. Some photographs even show a sharp white line (in the negative) at the base of the neck, but this could be a fold in the cloth, as it does not appear in all pictures. However, even without this the head appears very clearly to be cut off at the base of the neck, even in the infrared and ultraviolet photographs taken by STURP and in the '3-D' pictures produced by John Jackson and Eric Jumper. Andy's computer-enhanced images also reveal this anomaly quite dramatically, showing the image falling away completely at the neck-line, with not the faintest trace of an image beneath it until the upper chest. At the very start of our research, we had asked two Shroud experts, Ian Wilson and Ian Dickinson – both believers – how they accounted for the 'severed head' effect, and got two diametrically opposed answers. Wilson[4] said he could not see anything wrong with the position of the head at all, while Dickinson[5] said there was an anomaly, but that he could explain it. (When he first met one of us, at the exhibition at Bath, he said, 'I've been over this image with a fine-tooth comb and there is something very peculiar about it: the head appears to be dislocated.') He says that the cloth was folded under the chin when the image had been created. When the Shroud was straightened out, the fold made the head appear as if it had been displaced upwards and caused the neck image to be abruptly terminated by a horizontal line. However, we had already noted the complete absence of any similar distortion due to folding and draping anywhere else on the image: if Dickinson was right we should be able to see other such anomalies elsewhere on the cloth, particularly on the face. They are not there.

The odd positioning and squaring off of the head cannot be explained by any of the other theories of how the image was formed. However it makes perfect sense if the image is a composite – that is, Leonardo's own face and someone else's body. The line under the neck is the cut-off point. This would also explain the small size of the head.

We needed to measure the differences in size between the body and head objectively, which meant looking closely at the physique of the man on the Shroud. What we finally came up with – by applying the 'Emperor's new clothes' approach we had learned from young Abigail – was very unexpected.

To the naked eye, the head is too small for the body. But could we demonstrate this anomaly? We set out to compare the ratio of head to body.

With Clive's brother Keith – who as a trained artist is familiar with the proportions of the human figure – we made some crucial calculations. The usual ratio between head and total height is 1:8 (that is, the head goes into the total height eight times). This is an average, with individual variations ranging from about 1:7.5 and, very rarely, going as low as 1:8.5. The smaller ratio tends to happen in people of smaller build – the shorter you are, the larger your head is in comparison with your body.

To find out the head/body ratio of the Shroudman, we obviously needed to know his height, something which has proved to be a vexed question for Shroudies. In part this is due to the faintness of the image and the way it appears to fade into the background at the edges, making precise measurement difficult. There is also disagreement about the way the body is positioned, which is important in that attempts to work out the height need to allow for any foreshortening due to the positioning of the limbs. Those who believe that the image was formed by direct contact with a body also have to take into account any distortion caused by the way the cloth was draped. (Although, as we have seen, the cloth must have been laid flat.) A great setback here is the way the shoulders were obliterated by the 1532 fire: this was especially frustrating for us, as it would have been much easier to judge how badly positioned the head is if the shoulders were visible.

By far the most extensive work on the position of the man on the Shroud has been done by Isabel Piczek, a leading American religious artist who is very much in demand for her striking murals, which grace many churches and cathedrals in the United States. She approached the problem as a professional artist trained in depicting the human figure and very experienced with the problems of foreshortening. Although a believer in the Shroud's authenticity, and therefore given to over-enthusiastic acceptance of some of the odder theories around (her own is that the image was the result of 'time reversal'), her work here is convincing and well-argued, and does indeed present the most acceptable reconstruction.

Piczek looked at the way the limbs are foreshortened and the varying intensity of the image – for example the way the backs of the knees are less clear than the calves and the buttocks – and found that the whole image is absolutely consistent with the attitude of crucifixion. She assumes this is because rigor mortis had set in by the time the body was placed in the Shroud. There is however, no reason why an anatomically aware artist could not have depicted the body in this way to reinforce the identification with Jesus, or why Leonardo could not have arranged his model in such a position. This explains why we can see the footprint, since the knees are drawn up so that the feet are placed flat on the cloth – perhaps with one foot slightly over the other because of the way the body had been nailed – which is borne out by the foreshortening of the legs on both front and back images.

Piczek's work also confirms that there is no distortion due to the cloth being draped over and around the body, which agrees with our conclusion that the cloth had to have been flat when the image was created. But something else, something that was to prove much more significant, also emerged from her work.

During a visit to London in November 1992, she presented her findings to a meeting of the BSTS, which we attended with some friends. Her talk showed convincingly that her reconstruction fitted the body as we see it on the Shroud, and included slides of her work showing how models had demonstrated her theories. It was only during question time that one fact she had failed to mention came to light, in reply to a question from our colleague Tony Pritchett. He asked what conclusions she had reached about the positioning of the head, something that she had conspicuously avoided mentioning. Piczek replied that she had had problems in determining how the head had been placed, since she was unable to find a model who could get their head into the same position as Shroudman while maintaining the correct position of the rest of their body. In fact, she said *'the head appeared separated'*. This was, to us, impressive confirmation by an expert of Abigail's innocent observation in Bath. Put simply: the head just does not fit.

It is also clear just by looking at the image that the face is brighter (in negative) and much sharper than the rest of the image – that is, the rest of the front and the whole of the back.

This is also apparent from the '3-D' pictures created by the VP-8 Image Analyzer, in which the face stands out more clearly than the rest of the image. Although, as we shall see shortly, we have grave doubts about the validity of all the claims made for that particular series of tests, this does not affect the fact that the Image Analyzer found the face to be more intense than the rest of the image. This cannot be explained (as some have tried) by saying that the face is more angular. If the intensity of the image is due to its proximity to the body, then those parts that were supposedly touching the cloth – the tip of the nose, the chest, the backs of the hands, the knees – should all be equally intense. But instead we find that the face as a whole is much more clearly defined, another indication that it was created separately and, perhaps, with more care.

A Tall Story

Still trying to puzzle out the head/body ratio, and the need to discover Shroudman's true height, we soon realised that Isabel Piczek's work was the best basis on which to work. One might think that measuring his height would be a simple matter, even allowing for a few inches at either end, but not so. When we came to look at the literature for clues, we simply could not believe our eyes.

The most common height given for Shroudman is about 5ft 11in (180cm), although this is always hedged around with some qualifications about the problems of making a precise measurement given the vagaries of the image. In fact, estimates of the man's height have varied so enormously as to be farcical.

Giulio Ricci, a staunch (some would say fanatical) believer, calculated that the man was only 5ft 4in (162.5cm), allowing for the distortion caused by the (non-existent) draping and, curiously, the 'expansion of the cloth' over time.[6] As a believer, he had obviously calculated that this expansion had taken place over a period of 2000 years – an assumption that is hardly scientific. At the other extreme, Lorenzo Ferri (a professor at the University of Rome) and anatomist Luigi Gedda independently arrived at an estimate of 6ft 2in (188cm).[7] Such wide discrepancies prompted us to do our own sums.

The problem is that, as the real thing is locked away, we always see the Shroud image in miniature. If it were on permanent display, perhaps one of the Shroud's most telling anomalies would be more widely known and questioned.

We realised that we first had to know the actual length of the image as it appears on the cloth, from the top of the head to the tips of the toes. From that (making allowances for the foreshortening found by Isabel Piczek) we should be able to arrive at a reasonably good estimate of the man's height. Absolute precision is impossible, but we should be able to get a good enough estimate for our purposes. As we believe the head of the front image to have been created separately, it would be particularly interesting to see if the front image is exactly the same height as the back. We bought a photograph of the entire Shroud from the Holy Shroud Guild of New York, measured it and, knowing the dimensions of the Shroud itself, scaled up our results accordingly.

Our calculations put the height of the man on the Shroud – at the front – at 6ft 8in (203cm). Not surprisingly, we blinked and repeated our calculations several times. But we were not mistaken: the front image is indeed around the 6ft 8in mark. So what is the height of Shroudman at the back? Curiouser and curiouser – he is 6ft 10in (208cm)! Strangely enough, if you look sufficiently closely at the Shroud literature you will find these calculations in there somewhere, but they are hardly picked out in banner headlines.

Not only is the image absurdly, impossibly big, but the image – supposedly of the same man and made at the same time – is two inches (5cm) taller at the back than the front! (The tips of the toes are missing from the front Shroud image, as the cloth stops slightly short, but this would not make a whole two inches difference.)

Believers have never made much of the overall length of the body, although they all know it. If they mention it at all they argue that the drape of the cloth over the body's contours would distort the measurements, making the image appear much taller than the actual body. But from the work of Isabel Piczek, herself a believer, as well as the evidence of our own eyes, we know that there is simply no such distortion. The cloth could only produce the foreshortened – but otherwise entirely natural – image if it were flat.

A possible explanation is that the crucifixion position shown by Piczek's work (with the knees drawn up and the feet flat on the floor) extends the image by the length of the feet, adding several inches onto the height. Ricci, for example, argues that measurements should be taken only as far as the heels. This is true, but then we also have to allow for the length lost by the raising of the knees, which foreshortens the image and makes the legs appear too short. In order to discover just how much difference the raising of the knees does make to the overall length of the human body as seen from directly in front, Keith and Clive measured themselves lying completely flat with knees raised to the level found by Isabel Piczek, while keeping their feet flat on the floor. By doing this they found the optimum position for such raising of the knees. With the feet placed flat the knees are drawn up much too far and the image would be ridiculously foreshortened, but it is possible to reach a good compromise with the backs of the knees about 10 inches from the ground.

In fact, the overall length of the body – from the top of the head to the heels when lying flat and to the tip of the toes with the knees raised – hardly changes at all. The extra length given by the feet is exactly offset by the foreshortening caused by drawing the knees up. Of course individuals will always vary, but even at the most generous estimate the figure could only be extended by at most 2 inches (5cm) through this explanation.

Although we had discounted Ian Dickinson's idea that the head appears to be displaced upwards by the folding of the cloth under the chin, we decided to check to see if it could account for the extra height. But no – the back image actually confirms our measurement and goes even further, being 2 inches longer than the front.

Now we understood the real reason for all the endless discussion about draping, folds and expansion of the cloth. It was flim-flammery to obscure an unpalatable fact, one that edges the Shroud into farce. Surely, if Jesus had been a giant, wouldn't it have been mentioned in the New Testament? But its pages are as innocent of such a fact as they are about a miraculously imprinted Shroud.

In his 1998 book, Ian Wilson complains that we arrive at these 'astonishing' figures 'without giving any clear reason'.[8] In fact, we gave the best reason of all – *we measured the images on the Shroud*. There is absolutely no question about it: but, as usual the believers tie themselves in knots trying to come up with some explanation, no matter how ridiculous, to explain away the astonishing anomalies of the Shroud image. Although Shroudies – if pressed – do admit that the *image* is 6ft 8in, since this is clearly absurd they try to think up reasons why it is bigger than the man himself. They invoke such variables as the way the cloth was (allegedly) draped over the body or the 'fact' that the cloth somehow expanded over the centuries. Clearly the extraordinary height worries them – as indeed it should, because to most objective people it would prove that this is obviously a fake.

Wilson also dismisses our measurements because we are 'non-professionals' instead citing those given by 'medical specialists' such as Dr Pierre Barbet and Dr David Willis. We fail to see how medical training bestows a superior ability to hold a ruler.

Admittedly, at the time of the first edition of this book we had only measured Shroudman from photographs, and therefore we could, perhaps, have been mistaken. But in 1998 we were given a splendid opportunity – better than almost any modern Shroud researcher – to double-check our findings. Having moved from the Royal Photographic Society at Bath, Amanda Nevill had now become the Chief Executive of The National Museum of Photography, Film and Television at Bradford, and wasted no time in involving Lynn as consultant for a photographic exhibition called 'The Unexplained'. Once again, the full-length transparency of the Shroud (a perfect replica of the original) was to be the main exhibit but this time in much grander and more spacious circumstances, having a whole, huge room to itself. Moreover, the 'Shroud' was displayed in a particularly visitor-friendly manner, on a massive back-lit lightbox, at virtually floor-level surrounded by plenty of space. This meant that, unlike the expositions of the real thing, visitors could take their time and look at the Shroud from all angles and a variety of distances. And what a difference that makes . . .

At the opening of the exhibition and several times afterwards, we involved the visitors in a simple experiment. We invited them to lie down on the floor, mimicking Shroudman's posture and aligning their heads as closely as possible with the top of his head. Seeing as none of our volunteers were 6ft 8in, not even the tallest man matched the height of Shroudman, or even came close. (Clive, who is exactly six feet [1.8m] tall, found there were several inches to spare.) And even before we asked them to take part in our experiment, when told that there was 'something odd with the height' they, without exception, suddenly realised he was impossibly tall. It is no exaggeration to say that many people who came into the exhibition with no strong views either way about the authenticity of the Shroud went out of it convinced it is a fake. (And, as we will see, the ridiculous height is not the only visually obvious anomaly.)

This anomaly is hardly a problem for those who believe that the image is painted – or for us, who suggest it is in fact projected. When projecting images from life (as we were to discover) it is very easy to make them a little too small or a little too big. Moving the object that is being projected just an inch or two towards the focusing mechanism results in a disproportionately enlarged image. And the reason why there is a discrepancy between the front and back images is because the head does not actually belong to the body.

From Rodney Hoare's *A Piece of Cloth* we learned another seldom-mentioned fact – that the back of the head is slightly wider than the front.[9] Of course, Hoare has a ready explanation. The head must have been on some kind of a pillow, he says, placed under the Shroud and around the sides of the head. Hence the back of the head appears to be wider. But there is none of the distortion one might expect to find in such a case.

Now that we had an estimate of Shroudman's height, we could work out the head/body ratio. Measuring the head and comparing it to the estimated height gave a ratio of 1:8.7 for the front image, well outside the normal range. Knowing exactly where to take the measurement, given the faintness of the image's outline, is difficult, but we had built in a generous margin of error. Comparing the size of the image of the head at the front with the height we had calculated for the whole of the back image – again erring on the side of caution – produced a minimum ratio of 1:9, possibly as much as 1:9.4. So we had proved that the head really is too small for the body. Laboriously we had finally confirmed Abigail's insight. And, as Isabel Piczek had confirmed that the rest of the body is in good proportion, it supports our theory that the head is a completely separate image. This fact also makes it seem unlikely that the Shroud is painted, as the image as a whole is quite brilliant, and what good artist in his right mind would get the head so wrong?

The Biggest Cover-up in History

Our work on the physique of the man on the Shroud had made us aware of other discrepancies and anomalies, some of which were to prove very important when we came to replicate Leonardo's method, others which deserve a passing mention.

We had observed quite early in our studies something that has been commented on by sceptics but largely ignored by believers: the convenient placing of the hands, crossed over the genitals. It seems an unusual way to lay out a corpse, and preserving the man's modesty seems to indicate that the cloth was intended for display with the hands arranged in order to avoid offending the sensibilities of the faithful. Perhaps, however, the position of the hands was also chosen to avoid another dilemma. As it was supposed to be Jesus, accuracy would demand that he would be circumcised (as medieval and Renaissance Christians knew only too well, there being several Holy Foreskins doing the rounds in their day), yet as Peter de Rosa points out in the prologue to his *Vicars of Christ*, Christians would not have been comfortable with this reminder of the Jewishness of their Lord. So the artistic convention grew up of depicting the crucified Jesus with a loincloth, which de Rosa calls 'the biggest cover-up in history'.[10] We are particularly amused to note that many copies of the Turin Shroud add a loincloth.

It is also impossible to place the hands of a corpse in such a position without either tying them together or supporting the elbows. Predictably, believers have argued that there were supports, in the form of bundles of cloth under the elbows. (If all the pillows and bundles of cloth that are cited to explain away anomalies had actually been used, not to mention the accompanying blocks of spices, the entombment of Jesus must have presented one of the oddest spectacles in history – more like the first day of the sales in Harrods' linen department than the entombment of Christ.)

If, on the other hand, the image was faked, it would have been easy to keep the hands in the required position while also keeping the means of doing so invisible. The easiest way would be to tie the thumbs together.

There is also the matter of the hairline and the hair. If the man had been lying down, as is generally believed, the hair would not frame the face as it does, but would fall back away from the face. The hairline itself is completely unnatural, and there is a curious blank strip between the sides of the face and the hair. Then there is the bizarre fact that Shroudman has no ears. The face is too narrow: the outside corners of his eyes are virtually at the edge of his face. This man has neither ears nor temples.

But the oddest aspect of the face is the size of the forehead. Any artist will tell you that as a rule the eyes are just about the centre of the face, midway between chin and crown. (The centre line is, in fact, just below the eyes.) However, on the Shroud image the eyes are much too high because the forehead appears to be foreshortened. We began by thinking that it must have been due to the way Leonardo overlaid the image of his face, but it was only later – as we will describe in the next chapter – that the full significance of the size of the forehead became apparent.

A New Dimension

By far the most often quoted of the oddities about the Shroud is the '3-D information' it allegedly contains. This means that there is a precise relationship between the intensity of the image (darkness as seen by the naked eye, brightness as seen in negative) and the distance of the body from the cloth. That relationship can be used to construct a three-dimensional picture of the man on the Shroud by showing the lighter areas as higher, as in a contour map. This was demonstrated most graphically by the VP-8 Image Analyzer pictures in the mid-1970s.

The 3-D information contained in the Shroud was, we were led to believe, an odd and extremely unusual property of the Shroud image. Neither paintings nor photographs, unless they are taken under very specific conditions, behave in such a way. Other image-creation theories cannot account for it, except, perhaps, the 'nuclear flash' theory championed by John Jackson, which (as we have seen) can be easily dismissed on several grounds, some of them pure common sense.

The 3-D information is different for the face and the body. If the Image Analyzer is adjusted to show the face in natural relief, the body (front and back) hardly stands out at all. If the body image is adjusted in this way, the features of the face stand out far too prominently. This supports our idea that the two images were created separately.

We realised, however, that if it were a photographic image it would be unlikely to exhibit the '3-D effect'. The Image Analyzer works with light and shade, assuming that darker areas are further away than the light areas, and that there is a direct relationship between the intensity of the image and the distance. Normal photographs are invariably lit more on one side than the other, so that the two sides of a face, though equally distant from the camera, are of different brightnesses. Only when the light source is shining from the same direction as the camera will you get a 3-D effect. A spotlight mounted above a camera might do the trick, but it is still unlikely because the difference in the amount of light reflected would probably be too subtle, the variations too small to make a reliable attempt to work out the distance from camera to object. A rough estimate would be possible, but not the precision of the VP-8 images.

Initially we had speculated that there might be a way of lighting the scene to cause a 3-D effect accidentally, which might then give us some clues about how it had been lit. The effect could have been a coincidental by-product of the exposure times. The sun would have moved during an exposure time that must have been several hours long, so the two sides of the face would have been lit at different times, whereas the high points – the nose and brows – would have been illuminated constantly, exposing them more fully.

We asked Andy to look into ways of reproducing the VP-8 pictures using modern software. Using the Holy Shroud Guild's photographs of the full image and close-ups of the face, he scanned the images, converting the pictures into pixels, each being assigned a value according to its brightness. The resulting data was stored in digital form, which meant it could be used by many different programs to manipulate it in various ways. Different brightnesses could be converted into colours or displayed as a contour map. It could even be converted into sound and played as music (Andy has produced some beautiful abstract pictures by displaying sounds as shapes and colours). Individual parts of the picture could be blown up on screen to look at the most minute detail, or parts of the image could be cut out and moved to compare to other parts. For example, Andy easily managed to take half of the front image of Shroudman and match it up against that half of the rear image, showing graphically – and very effectively – that the back is indeed longer than the front.

To reproduce the 3-D pictures created by John Jackson and Eric Jumper with the Image Analyzer, Andy took the digitised data and ran it through programs that converted it into a height map. In his own words:

> The image was rendered as a height field using a public domain ray tracing package. Because of the graininess of the original image – there were speckles etc – the 3-D image would have had large spikes, which would confuse things.
>
> The spurious spikes needed to be removed and this was done using a paint-box package called Photostyler to apply a Gaussian filter to smooth out the 'noise' and leave a trend. The results were re-rendered.

This revealed a more meaningful image but the results were still disappointing if looking for 3-D 'proof'. I tried different angles of view and applied different textures to the object.

Using this technique the image could be 'tilted' so that (as with the VP-8 pictures) any intensity-distance relationship could be displayed as a three-dimensional picture. The result was – to say the least – surprising. Andy was unable to reproduce the 3-D information found by the VP-8. There was a slight three-dimensionality, but no more than one would expect from an evenly-lit photograph. Most striking was the fact that there was no appreciable difference between the brightness of the bridge of the nose and the brows, making it impossible for the image analysis software to distinguish between them in terms of height. The images, using several different scales to exaggerate any slight difference in the intensity, always showed the same result: a flat face, with nose and brows all the same height. Andy tried various methods to eliminate any errors in his findings, but found that 'the results were still inconclusive'.

We were disconcerted. We double-checked our method, but could find nothing wrong with anything we or Andy had done. Slowly the significance of what we had discovered began to dawn on us: could it really be true that the much-vaunted '3-D information', the one allegedly unique factor in the Shroud image that has puzzled believers and non-believers alike for many years, simply does not exist?

We wondered if Andy's equipment might be inferior to the VP-8, so we turned once again to the Shroud literature to trace the rise of the 3-D information as one of the Shroud's most potent selling points. It seemed to rest entirely on those twenty-year-old experiments by Jackson and Jumper. No-one apart from us seemed to have tried to replicate their work, which is especially surprising given the advances in computing power since their day.

Jackson and Jumper, because of their founding of STURP, are two of the enduring stars of the Shroud world. However, despite their scientific credentials they are and always have been firm believers in the Shroud's authenticity, even before they embarked on their detailed analyses. Although STURP is known as a scientifically based body, less attention is given to the fact that both men are on the Executive Council of the Holy Shroud Guild,[11] an organisation that was founded on the premise that the Shroud is authentic and that it has an important message for us all. Their own scientific papers, presented at the 1977 Albuquerque Conference, reveal their preconceptions – they refer to the Shroud image throughout as being that of 'Jesus' body'.[12] According to *The Jesus Conspiracy* by Kersten and Gruber, at the international symposium in Paris in 1989 'he [Jackson] declared that he could only explain the formation of the image by a miracle.'[13]

Jackson and Jumper had worked on the three-dimensionality for some time before the VP-8 was brought in, using manual techniques. They were following up a suggestion of Paul Vignon's at the start of the twentieth century. We had long realised that these experiments were open to all kinds of flaws, but, like everyone else, we were won over by the computer-enhanced pictures they produced a year later. Their initial experiments have been comprehensively attacked – especially on their protocol and the collection and analysis of data – by Joe Nickell in his *Inquest on the Shroud of Turin*. To begin with he notes that 'the whole methodology of three-dimensional reconstruction is dependent on circular reasoning, and begs the question of whether or not the Shroud ever enveloped a real human form'.[14] Jackson and Jumper started from the assumption that it had.

They had found somebody they considered to be the same build and height of the man on the Shroud – but as this person was not 6ft 8in at the front and 2 inches taller at the back we wonder just how they arrived at their conclusion – and covered him with a cloth on which they had traced the Shroud image. There is obviously something self-fulfilling about this, as for a start, they found someone who would fit their traced image. But then they had to make assumptions about the way the cloth was draped over the body, in which case they also had to find a model who fitted their assumptions. Their model was laid flat on his back, in what was then considered to be the correct position for the man in the Shroud – flat on his back with the cloth folded up at the feet. We now know from Isabel Piczek's work that this is wrong. The volunteer's knees should have been raised and his feet flat on the floor. They also made much of the fact that there was only 'one way to cover the body correctly'. But then, if they had chosen another position for the legs and feet and a volunteer of a different build, they would have discovered that there was only one possible way to cover *him*.

They then measured the distances between different parts of the model's body and the cloth, down the centre of the image only. Separately, they measured the intensity of the Shroud image down the centre line using an instrument called a microdensitometer. They plotted the two sets of figures on a graph, and claimed that the two matched up. This method allows for a great many errors. Their judgement of the height and build of the model and their assumptions about the way the cloth was draped over the body could easily have been incorrect. They took their measurements of cloth-body distance manually from photographs taken from the side (with the model covered and uncovered). And the microdensitometer readings were only valid for the middle strip of the image, so how would they know if the same effects hold true for the rest of it?

Most serious is their 'smoothing out' of the two sets of data on the graph. Although they actually show a wide scatter, perhaps due to an error in measurement, Jackson and Jumper drew a curve through the points to make an average. In his description of the results Ian Wilson writes that their graph reveals 'a perfect curve, demonstrating beyond question that there was a positive and precise relationship'.[15] Joe Nickell, however, reports that the correlation is initially 'only fair' and that the curve was added using the experimenters' own judgement: 'Any number of different curves could equally be chosen to average the data scatter and replace it with a smooth function.' Further adjustments are made, and then – most damning of all – the data is 'iteratively modified so that a more human-looking figure can be obtained'. The final result, according to Nickell, is that their method 'allows some of the Shroud-image characteristics to be superimposed on the relief of the human model. Hence the resultant "statue" is actually some blend of the shroud image and the human model.'

However, it was the VP-8 work, with which Nickell did not deal, that seemed to be more unassailable, primarily because it does not depend on plotting graphs but presents an easily understood picture. The story, as given in the believers' literature – for example, in Ian Wilson's *Evidence of the Shroud*[16] – is that one day John Jackson visited radiographer Bill Mottern at the Sandia Scientific Laboratories in Albuquerque. Mottern happened to be experimenting with the VP-8 Image Analyzer, a piece of equipment that had been developed for NASA, but which was now beginning to find wider industrial applications. He casually suggested that they put one of the slides of the Shroud that Jackson had with him into the machine. Quite spontaneously, without any special adjustments to the Analyzer, the 3-D images, now so familiar from Shroud literature, appeared on the screen. The moment has gone down in Shroud history as almost rivalling the revelation of Secondo Pia's first sight of the negative effect.

Common sense, however, suggests that there has to have been more to it than that. It is a matter of scale, of calibration. The Image Analyzer simply determines the relative intensity of different points on an image. To display it in a form recognisable to us it needs to know the distance represented by a given change in intensity, i.e. the scale. Andy demonstrated this graphically by showing us different views of the Shroud face using different distance/intensity scales. The difference between a light point and a dark point might represent, say, 6 inches (15cm), or 2 inches (5cm), or ½ inch (1cm). There is no way that any machine, no matter how sophisticated, can work this out for itself. It has to be told the scale by the operator. In fact, he can try out different scales until he finds one that suits his particular purpose. In the case of the Shroud image, you keep adjusting the scale until you get the most recognisable picture of a human body.

This in itself does not mean that the Shroud image has no 3-D information, but it does show that there must be more to the tale of the spontaneous appearance of the image without giving the Analyzer the required scale. This would be little short of a miracle in itself. In any case, Andy's results using the computer only confirm something that is obvious to the unaided eye – or should be, if we were not beguiled by the technological wizardry of the VP-8 machine. The basis of the VP-8 work is that the brighter any area of the image is, the higher it stands out on the computer-generated picture. What are the brightest parts of the Shroud face? A glance at photographs shows clearly that they are the moustache and beard. Yet in the VP-8 pictures of the face these are *lower* than the tip of the nose, which is not as bright!

Other members of STURP have been more cautious about the claims of Jackson and Jumper in relation to the 3-D information. In a report summarising STURP's work, Lawrence Schwalbe plays it down, blaming the press for misrepresenting and sensationalising the claims, and concluding that Jackson and Jumper's studies 'have not as yet suggested a particular image formation mechanism nor do they even imply that a three-dimensional object was necessary to produce the image . . .

No direct conclusions about the Shroud's authenticity can be inferred'.[17]

Without more details of the Jackson and Jumper scenario it is hard to say why Andy – using pictures and equipment at least as good as those used by Jackson – failed to see what they saw back in the 1970s. But we see no reason to doubt Andy's results. And given the criticisms levelled at Jackson and Jumper's earlier experiments with the microdensitometer, we feel that their VP-8 work must also remain open to question.

Others have made three-dimensional models of the Shroud image, but they used only the eye of the artist – there is no need of computer-enhanced images in order to see how two-dimensional pictures will look in three dimensions. To prove the point, one of the best-known models was made in the 1960s by a British fashion photographer, Leo Vala, by projecting a slide of the Shroud face onto a block of clay and fashioning the clay, estimating the depth caused by the shadows. But this technique could be used equally well on paintings – in fact, Vala made a prototype using the *Mona Lisa*.[18]

When we began our collaboration with Andy, we, like all other Shroudies, believed that the Shroud exhibits amazing, inexplicable and unique 3-D information. Though we were per-suaded that Leonardo had created the image, we could not see how he had managed to produce that particular effect and felt that attempting to replicate it would be a real stumbling block in our experimental work. Now we faced no such problem, for the much-vaunted 3-D information simply does not exist, at least to the degree that we have been led to believe by the VP-8 pictures, and not beyond that explicable by the even lighting caused by a lengthy exposure in the sun. In that sense, the '3-D information' supports rather than undermines the photo-graphic hypothesis.

What lay ahead for us was still no walkover, however. We set ourselves the task of replicating Leonardo's pioneering photographic technique, and in so doing we had to achieve what no-one else has done — we had to recreate the method used to create the image on the Turin Shroud and produce an image that bore all its hitherto unexplained characteristics. We took a deep breath, and began.

8

Positive Developments

'Every body fills the surrounding air with images of itself, and every image appears in its entirety and in all its parts. The air is full of an infinity of straight lines and rays which cut across each other without displacing each other and which reproduce on whatever they encounter the true form of their cause.'

Leonardo da Vinci[1]

Although the idea that the Shroud image was some kind of photograph went a long way towards explaining many of its most intriguing features, it was still difficult not to be sceptical. Could even a genius of Leonardo's stature have developed a photographic process some 350 years before its known invention? Even if he had the knowledge, were Renaissance materials adequate for the task? If he had invented such a process, why did he keep it a secret?

The last question is the easiest to answer. Even leaving aside his 'forbidden' magical and hermetic practices, Leonardo was obsessively secretive. Sometimes this can be ascribed to the natural caution of the innovator in an age before the advent of patent law, but sometimes far more complex reasons came into play – for example, he refused to set down details of his submarine in his notebooks, realising that if such an invention fell into the wrong hands it could result in the death of hundreds of innocent passengers.[2] In the case of photography, however, there are good reasons for believing that he regarded it as part and parcel of his magical practice.

Today we are so familiar with the whole idea of photography that it is almost impossible for us to put ourselves in the place of someone encountering it for the first time. To the average Renaissance Italian the act of capturing an image from life would have been regarded as totally magical. Try convincing the Church, which was highly suspicious of any innovation, that this was a perfectly natural process. Try convincing those whose picture you had taken that you had not also stolen something vital from them, perhaps even their very soul. Even educated men would have taken this view, and it is likely that Leonardo himself would have regarded basic photography as something magical. This is not mere speculation. It is a fact that during the Middle Ages and Renaissance experiments with optics and light were kept strictly secret, and were firmly in the province of the magical adept, the alchemist and the occultist.

Leonardo had a passion for light and optics, probably devoting more time to researching this area than any other. He had remarkably advanced ideas about the nature of light and vision.[3] In the fifteenth century the prevailing view was that the eyes see by projecting some kind of beam. Leonardo, however, understood that the eye is simply a receiver for light rays that are reflected from the surface of objects: he likened light to the ripples that spread out from a stone dropped in water. He realised that light travels in waves, and that it therefore had a speed – there are even indications that he tried to calculate it. (Remarkably, similar attempts had also been made by Roger Bacon, the highly respected English polymath, in the thirteenth century.) He dissected eyeballs and discovered that they contain a lens, understanding that they work on the same principle as what we know as a camera – a principle with which he was already familiar. He also designed devices that would reproduce the workings of the eye artificially.

The Maestro experimented extensively with lenses, particularly in order to overcome the problem of chromatic aberration – the blurring of the edges of an image that was such a drawback with all early lenses. Mirrors, which can be used to focus like a lens, were a source of endless fascination for him. He also performed some experiments investigating the behaviour of light: for example, he discovered the 'inverse square rule' – that is, the amount of light received from a source diminishes in proportion to the distance it has to travel. He invented a device, the photometer, for measuring the brightness of an object – something not rediscovered until the late eighteenth century by Count Rumford, one of the pioneer photographers.[4] Leonardo's research was precisely what would have been necessary before embarking on an attempt at photography.

Underlying all this work – with lenses, mirrors, the workings of the eye, even in his innovations in painting techniques – was his fascination with light itself. Reading through the notebooks in which he describes his quest to understand light, how it carries images, and the many ways in which reflected images can be captured, we were left in no doubt that someone with his obsessions and abilities would have at least considered the possibility that images can be caught and captured permanently. He certainly would have tried.

Evidence that Leonardo was obsessed by the thought of capturing images from life comes from the great historian of photography Josef Maria Eder. In his classic *History of Photography*, written in the 1930s, he discusses methods used by the forerunners of true photography to take images from life rather than reproducing them by painting or drawing. One simple method, known as 'nature printing', consisted of pressing painted objects, such as a leaf, onto suitably prepared paper. Interestingly, this method was invented by Leonardo and included in his writings dating from around 1490 (and which are preserved in the *Codex Atlanticus*). He recommended using paper coated with lamp-black and 'sweet oil', onto which was pressed a leaf coloured in white lead. This produced a negative image of the leaf.[5]

Leonardo was not the only one to dream that images could be captured for ever. As long ago as the first century AD the Roman poet Statius had written of the recording of people's images on silver- or gold-plated mirrors. Such ideas surfaced many times over the centuries, and could have fired Leonardo's imagination and acted as a springboard for all his most advanced inventions.

Giovanni had told us that Leonardo used photography, an idea that at first seemed completely wild, but as our research progressed it seemed increasingly likely. Others had obviously mused on the question too: a Leonardophile acquaintance once remarked to one of us, without knowing the reason for our interest in the Maestro, that if Leonardo were alive today he would be a photographer. If making photographs were possible at some level in Leonardo's day, he would have done it. Having said that, however, problems arose immediately. Surely, we thought, capturing a projected image depends on synthetic chemicals that can only be produced in post-Industrial Revolution factories and with modern lenses of high quality? Even a genius cannot create without the materials. After all, Leonardo also predicted the telephone, but in his day there was no question of actually producing a working model.

The obvious way to test this idea was to attempt to replicate a Leonardo-style 'photograph', using materials and equipment that would have been available to him, or at least within the reach of the technology of his day. If we were successful, it would go a very long way towards proving our theory, as the Shroudies frequently claim that reproducing anything like the Shroud image is impossible even using modern technology. Even *The Times* in its leader the day after the carbon dating results were announced stated: 'modern science can discredit it but cannot make its duplicate.'[6]

Just making visually satisfactory duplicates, without even attempting to replicate a likely method, has been found difficult by artists. For example, designer John Weston, who was commissioned to make two copies for use in the film *The Silent Witness*, had to experiment for several weeks before finding a satisfactory method that just used paint. Each copy took him five weeks to paint.[7]

At the start of this enterprise, over fifteen years ago, we were hampered by the fact that neither of us had anything other than the sketchiest knowledge of photography, let alone of optics and chemistry. Fortunately, we were able to call upon the talents of Keith Prince, a gifted artist who has studied photography and has an excellent working knowledge of its basic principles, with a sound grasp of physics and chemistry. In the course of our researches, we were constantly indebted to his near photographic memory, his ability to make imaginative connections, plus his skill in knocking up the most complex apparatus out of odds and ends in double-quick time.

If we were to replicate our idea of Leonardo's method for creating the Turin Shroud, we had to begin by freeing ourselves from the preconceptions of modern photography. These days we are used to the idea of complex lenses, and (at least until the advent of digital photography) film that reacts to light in hundredths of a second, creating images that need various chemical treatments – developing, fixing and printing – before they become usable. We were looking for something much simpler. It made sense, therefore, to look at the origins of photography, and see what the known pioneers had used, in the hope of finding some clues to Leonardo's method.

The Dark Chamber

Photography was the result of the coming together of two main inventions – the camera, which collects the image, and the film that records it. The first had been around for centuries in the shape of the camera obscura – literally a 'dark chamber' – or pin-hole camera. Originally it was literally a darkened room with a small hole in one wall, but later versions were portable and contained a lens for greater clarity of the image. In fact, many of the landscape painters of the seventeenth century used this device, setting up portable camera obscuras that projected images onto canvas or paper, where they were painted – almost like 'painting by numbers'. As time passed, the camera obscura was refined by adding better lenses and reducing it from the original room-size to a small box, the precursor of the modern camera. It inspired those who used it to look for a way to fix the image permanently.

The principle of the camera obscura has been known for millennia, if only as a curiosity. When light shines through a small hole into a dark chamber, pictures of things outside are projected onto the opposite wall upside down and in mirror image. Aristotle wrote of it in the fourth century BC, as did the Arab philosopher Ibn al Haitam in the eleventh century, and it is known that a description of a camera obscura was given in 1279 by an English alchemist, John Peckham.[8] But the credit for the first scientifically accurate description of such a device was for many years given to Giovanni Battista della Porta, a Neopolitan who published a description of it in 1552. He retained this claim to fame for almost 300 years, and even today some textbooks still accord him this honour. It was only towards the end of the nineteenth century that Leonardo da Vinci's long-neglected notebooks were deciphered and translated – which showed quite unequivocally that he had beaten della Porta to it by fifty years.

The *Codex Atlanticus* contains a diagram that shows the workings of the camera obscura (which Leonardo called the *oculus*

artificialis, the artificial eye), with the explanation: 'If the façade of
a building, or a place, or a landscape is illuminated by the sun and
a small hole drilled in a building facing this, which is not directly
lighted by the sun, then all objects illuminated by the sun will
send their images through this aperture and will appear, upside
down, on the wall facing the hole.'[9]

In another notebook he wrote: 'You will catch these pictures
on a piece of white paper, which is placed vertically in the room
not far from that opening . . . the paper should be very thin and
must be viewed from the back.'[10] Elsewhere he notes that thin
white cloth will do as well for the screen. (Della Porta's camera
used a linen screen.)

Returning briefly to the question of the secrecy that surrounded many of these experiments, it is instructive to take a
hard look at what happened to the early experimenters in this
field. Della Porta, for example, was a Hermeticist and alchemist –
he founded a secret group, the Academy of Secrets, which was
disbanded by the Pope, and the description of his work with projected images appears in a treatise entitled *Natural Magic*. Della
Porta makes it clear that he is consciously revealing something
secret, prefacing his description with the words: 'Now I want to
announce something about which I have kept silent until now
and which I believed that I must keep a secret.' He does not even
claim it as his own discovery, and we do not know how long
this knowledge had been kept under wraps, or from whom he
acquired it. One thing is certain: his circumspection was absolutely
justified. On giving a public demonstration of the camera obscura,
in which he projected the image of a group of actors on to
the wall of a house, he was promptly arrested and charged with
sorcery – from which he extricated himself only with the
greatest difficulty.[11]

Obviously completely unchastened by this experience, della
Porta later gave the first public moving picture show, using ani-
mated drawings.

In the 1640s a scientific Jesuit, Athanasius Kircher, invented the magic lantern (an early type of slide projector that projected pictures painted on glass). His demonstration of this device also raised suspicions that he was a sorcerer and necromancer. (Despite his calling Kircher was a devoted student of alchemy, Hermeticism and the Cabala.)

Leonardo's work with optics and the camera obscura inevitably provoked accusations of necromancy. His first known experiments into this area took place in Pavia in the late 1480s and are linked by Maurice Rowden in his biography of the artist with the beginnings of Leonardo's reputation as a sorcerer: 'In Pavia he worked on his camera obscura, to demonstrate his theory that all vision is determined by the angle at which light falls on the eye: the upside-down image thrown on the wall from the camera's pinpoint of light was a more graphic argument than words, and it was little wonder that he got the reputation of being a sorcerer and alchemist.'[12] So we have at least adequate proof that research into optics and light was an intrinsic part of Renaissance occultism, and that only a fool in those days made his work in this area public knowledge.

As we have seen, the principle of the camera – the shortened term was first used by the astronomer Johannes Kepler (1571–1630), who developed a portable camera obscura – was well known, and Leonardo was an important figure in its development.

But the camera is only half the story: photography also requires some method of permanently recording the image.

Capturing Light

In Leonardo's time it had long been known that it was theoretically possible to capture an image. Everyday observations bore this out. Many substances are affected by exposure to light: paper and cloth yellows, the colour of vegetable tissue deepens and so on. The search was on for some means of speeding up such a reaction and then fixing the image. Many of the great inventors and industrialists of the seventeenth and eighteenth centuries put their minds to this task.

In the eighteenth century, fast-reacting substances, notably silver salts, were discovered and used to make pictures – stencilled letters that would appear as if by magic on chemically treated materials. In 1802 Thomas Wedgwood, son of the famous potter Josiah, working with Sir Humphry Davy made the first successful attempt to produce an image on paper that had been treated with silver nitrate. These were silhouettes, using a camera obscura to focus the image. The great problem was that such images were not permanent, because they were created by a chemical that reacts to light, so that when the paper was removed from the camera light reacted with the area that was formerly the silhouette, and the image disappeared. The next step was to find a way of 'fixing' the image.

What is generally regarded as the first permanent photograph was taken by a Frenchman, Joseph Nicéphore Niépce (1765–1833), in Provence in 1826, using bitumen as the light-sensitive material. It was not, however, a practical method. It was Louis Daguerre (1789–1851) who in 1839 announced his success in fixing a silver iodide image using common salt. He also discovered the principle of the latent image – that is, the fact that some chemicals react to light very quickly but do not show a visible image until they are 'developed' by a further chemical treatment. By 1841 Daguerre had refined his method, chiefly through using better lenses – so that his exposure times, which originally had been about ten or fifteen minutes, went right down to around fifteen seconds. In the same year that Daguerre announced his invention, Fox Talbot (1800–1877) invented the first paper negative process. From then on many people added to the advances that led to modern photography.

However, it was the prehistory of photography that interested us – the discoveries that led up to its early days, and in particular the light-sensitive chemicals that might have been around before the Industrial Revolution. We were to find that, yet again, the pioneering photographers built on the work of the alchemists.

In an early attempt to debunk our theory, Rodney Hoare – who used to teach photography – objected that it was impossible for the Shroud image to be a photograph as it was 'inconceivable [Leonardo] could have discovered the effect of light on silver salts'.[13] This is incorrect on two counts. First, silver salts are not the only light-sensitive materials, and secondly, their action was quite definitely known before Leonardo's time. There is an enigmatic reference in Pliny the Elder's *Natural History*, written in the first century AD, that has been taken to reveal his knowledge of the darkening of silver chloride on exposure to light (and this work was very well known to Leonardo).[14] Be that as it may, it is absolutely certain that this property of silver salts was known to alchemists from at least the twelfth century, who were the first to produce and investigate many of the salts that were important in later photography.

The great eighth-century alchemist Jabir-ibn-Hayyan, commonly known as Geber, is reputed to have used silver nitrate, although the earliest known copy of *De inventione veritatis*, a work ascribed to him in which this is mentioned, dates from only the mid-1500s. Albertus Magnus (1193–1280) knew that silver nitrate turned black with exposure to light. Other alchemists who were known to have worked with silver salts are Angelo Sala and Johann Glauber in the 1600s. Robert Boyle (allegedly one of the Priory of Sion's Grand Masters) experimented with the effects of light on silver chloride. They were also familiar with the response to light of iron salts.

Another process vitally important to nineteenth-century photographers, the production of silver chloride from a solution of silver nitrate using sodium chloride, was known to alchemists from at least the early 1400s. In fact, Josef Maria Eder devotes a full chapter of his classic *History of Photography* to this work of the alchemists – which of course represents only the tip of the iceberg of what they were really up to – and states that 'it is these ideas from which sprang the science of photochemistry'.[15]

Perhaps most significant of all was the discovery that has been hailed as 'the beginning of photography'[16] – the first scientific description of the light sensitivity of silver salts, by Johann Heinrich Schulze in 1727. It is surely no surprise to discover that he made this breakthrough while trying to replicate an alchemical experiment originally made in the seventeenth century by Balduin. Schulze himself impressed his peers by making stencilled writing appear in salt sediment in bottles of water, but the image soon faded. *The Focal Encyclopaedia of Photography* (1993) reports that 'photography was eventually built on Schulze's discoveries'.[17] Eder is more emphatic: 'Schulze must be declared without doubt the inventor of photography with silver salts.'[18]

It struck us as immensely significant that the two elements that would later be brought together in photography – the means of projecting the image and the light-sensitive chemicals – had been known and investigated by alchemists for centuries.

The Experiments Begin

At this point, and without intimate knowledge of alchemy ourselves, many things had to be guesswork or intelligent assumption. We knew, though, that apart from silver salts, other materials had been known for years to be sensitive to light. The great Roman architect Vitruvius knew that cinnabar (mercuric sulphide) reacts to light, as he warns in his *De architectura* not to use it on outdoor decorations. And his works were very highly regarded by Renaissance architects, including Leonardo.

It was known even earlier that the purple dye with which Roman Imperial robes were coloured only turned this colour when exposed to light. Extracted from snails, it was yellow when first taken. But apart from the process of dyeing, nothing was done with this knowledge until the seventeenth century, when it was one of the first substances used in attempts to capture images.

Leonardo would, therefore, have been well acquainted with some chemicals that react to light. But we thought it was unlikely that he used silver salts for the Shroud, because they create a grey or black image, not a brownish one. Iron salts were a possibility, but the problem remained: how did Leonardo fix the image?

We needed to find a method that would have been within his reach, and it seemed that the obvious next step was to try it for ourselves, for only then would we learn the hard way just what his difficulties were. So throughout 1993 Clive and Keith devoted as much of their free time as they could to this task.

The first thing we did was to construct our own camera obscura. It was easily done using a wooden box, about 18 inches (45cm) square, laid on its side and with a small hole drilled in its base. With the lid removed and replaced with a paper or cloth screen – as recommended by Leonardo – and a sheet thrown over the screen end so that it could be viewed in darkness, we took it in turns to look at each other as lit by a spotlight. Even though we were used to the sophisticated images of television and cinema, there was still something oddly magical about the effect.

When the spotlight was turned full onto our faces, a pale image appeared on the screen. There was undeniably something of the ethereal, ghostly character of the Shroud image. With a very transparent screen there was an almost holographic effect, with a pale and apparently disembodied living head appearing to be actually inside the box. Although it was a simple experiment, just to get a feel for the camera obscura, there was indeed something impressive about the ability to create such an image so easily.

It was hard not to imagine Leonardo having done something similar, and with his passion for light and the representation of life, being thunderstruck at the results. But that was the easy bit. The hard part was finding a way to imprint the image onto the screen.

We knew the general characteristics of the image we were trying to create. It had to be in negative. It had to come out brown or sepia and look like a scorch mark. It had to be unacceptably faint and unremarkable to the naked eye – in other words not very impressive as compared with even early nineteenth-century experiments in photography.

The problem broke itself down into component pieces. First we needed a light source that would illuminate the object. Secondly, we needed a means of focusing the image onto the cloth. And then we needed a way of fixing the image so that it recreated the characteristics mentioned above.

The light source was easy. Although Leonardo had various techniques for creating bright lights, including one capable of mysteriously 'lighting up a room as though full of flames',[19] he would obviously have made use of the most powerful and reliable source known to him – the sun. Undoubtedly he would have supplemented it, as we did, with arrangements of mirrors to reflect yet more light onto the subject. This proved to be much more of a problem for us than it would have been for Leonardo. He had the golden light and long summer days of Renaissance Italy, whereas we had the unpredictable English summer sun to contend with. (Somehow even the best light Reading, Berkshire, could offer paled into insignificance beside that of a typical Milanese day.) It was clear that however it had been done, the exposure time had to be lengthy. Niépce's first photograph – of the courtyard of his Provençal farmhouse – took eight hours to register, which produced the interesting effect of the sun apparently lighting up both sides of the courtyard at the same time. Although we were uncertain at that early stage exactly what chemical we would use, we did know that exposures of several hours would be needed, and as our work proceeded on a trial-and-error basis, we needed as much light as possible.

Unfortunately, the summer of 1993 was not the best on record. The many other demands of research on our time (not to mention the need to earn a living), meant that we had little time to devote to these experiments. In the end, as autumn approached and the days shortened, we reluctantly decided that we would have to use artificial means of lighting the object: we invested in some industrial ultraviolet lamps (Osram Ultra Vitalux, which are used in industry for testing materials under tropical conditions). In the main, it is the UV part of the spectrum that the substances we were using reacted to.

As the experiments intensified, the car was banished from Clive's garage at his house in Reading – coincidentally a few streets from where Fox Talbot made his photographic discoveries – as we turned it into a makeshift studio.

Early on we had to decide what to use as the model, and how far to try to take the replication. Because of the trial-and-error nature of our work, we realised that it would be implausible to try for a full-length image, as on the Shroud, for several practical reasons. One was simply lack of space. Using a camera obscura to project a life-sized image follows a simple rule: the object must be the same distance from the hole as the screen is from the hole on the other side. Apart from the difficulty in finding a life-sized model, to get the full image on the right scale you would need a room-sized camera obscura and at least twenty feet of floor space. Without full-time access to a large studio or workshop it just was not possible to get the desired effect. Once again Leonardo had the advantage over us.

So we decided to concentrate on producing an image of just

a head. Since we knew that this would have been created separately in any case, it was quite legitimate to do so, and producing a life-sized head would require much less floor space. Once we had the method right we could then extend it to a full body image.

The fact that the image is a composite – Leonardo's head added to two separate images of the body of a crucified man, on the front from the neck down only – would have presented no difficulty at all, either as a concept or in its execution. Leonardo would simply have needed to mask off the relevant parts of the Shroud, or even more simply, avoid applying any of the light sensitive chemicals to the head area until after the body image had been captured.

For the majority of our experiments we used as a subject a plaster gargoyle head, dubbed 'Bok' after a similar character in a *Dr Who* story, which is about 8 inches (20cm) high from his chin to the tip of his horns. This was for our convenience, since the exact exposure time was unknown, and it would be no fun sitting motionless for hours at a time. This, of course, did raise questions about what precisely Leonardo had used. If he used himself as the model for the head then, even given his well-recorded capacity for standing motionless staring into space, it seemed unlikely that he would have been able to sit still for hours – perhaps days. Of course, with meticulous positioning and the use of a frame that would hold his head in exactly the same position, it would be possible to carry out several sittings, but if the exposure time were more than, say, four or five hours, it would be more practical for him to have used a sculpted or plaster-cast life-mask of himself. (Leonardo was adept at taking death-masks and would have had no problem with this.) Although it would be more pleasing to think the Shroud image was one of the Maestro's own person, it is more likely that we are looking at a photograph of a model or mask of his face.

The problems involved in keeping still for so long would

hardly have affected the model for the body, as the man was very likely dead, but problems of a different nature arise. Unless very skilfully embalmed, the body would have begun to decompose rapidly, especially if it were constantly exposed to the full heat of the sun, causing tell-tale signs on the resulting image. However, it is possible that the exposure time was just short enough to avoid that eventuality. Even so, a sculpted or, more likely, a cast model could easily have been used for the body image as well – taking casts from bodies was, after all, one of the skills Leonardo had learned from his apprenticeship under Verrocchio. However, we believe that he had access to chemicals that would react in a day or, at the most, two.

The model, whether human or artificial, would have needed to be as reflective as possible. In our case we managed this by painting Bok with white gloss paint, and Leonardo would have applied something similar to his model. If he used his own face and another body he would have painted both of them with white make-up: he was an old hand at everything connected with theatricals as he had been the producer of several spectac-ulars for the court of Ludovico Sforza, the Duke of Milan and Leonardo's patron between 1482 and 1499.

We had to decide on a method of focusing. The first camera obscuras used only an aperture. The problem here is that there is a trade-off between the brightness and clarity of the image: the larger the hole the more light gets through, so the image is brighter, but less distinct. Although the first recorded use of a lens in a camera obscura was not until 1568, there is no reason why Leonardo could not have anticipated it – indeed, given his fascination with lenses it would be surprising if he had not tried it. There was nothing special about the 1568 lens – it was simply taken from a pair of spectacles. However, there remained the question of its quality, which was impossible to guess at this stage. Early lenses, we knew, had been dogged by problems of chro-matic aberration – the fragmenting of light at the edges in much the same way as in a prism. There were also problems with the 'depth of field', familiar to photographers today, where only parts of the image are in sharp focus. (Pin-hole cameras do not have this problem, as everything in the field of view is equally sharp, no matter how near or how distant.) However, Leonardo ground his own lenses, and given his expertise in so many areas his could easily have been of good quality. At that stage, though, we could not be sure of this.

Another possibility was the use of a concave mirror, or perhaps a series of mirrors. Before lenses were generally good enough, focusing was often done by such mirrors. Giovanni Battista della Porta used a concave mirror placed opposite the aperture of his camera obscura to project the image onto a paper screen above the hole, which allowed him to use a bigger aperture and create a brighter image without losing clarity. Leonardo is known to have employed a great number of parabolic mirrors in a mysterious series of experiments in Rome in the early 1500s, the object of which has been the subject of keen speculation ever since.[20] Whatever he was doing was instrumental in getting him accused of sorcery and making his stay in Rome more than a little uncomfortable. For us, though, such mirrors were almost impossible to find, since they have very little relevance now that high quality lenses can be easily manufactured.

Quest for the Key Chemicals

The problems of lighting and focusing were small compared to discovering which light-sensitive substance Leonardo might have used. It would not have been too hard for him to have overcome the first two problems – ironically, it was probably easier for him than for us. But somewhere there had to be a relatively simple substance that could fit the bill. The pioneer photographers tried out a great many. But as they have all been superseded and have only curiosity value now, it was difficult to find any information on them. We hunted through old textbooks and other sources on early photography looking for clues about the materials that were discarded as more complex and faster-reacting industrial chemicals became available.

The earliest experiments, as we have seen, used either naturally occurring substances or chemicals that could be manufactured using the tools of the alchemical trade – which were quite comprehensive, and, with the exception of electrical power, up to the standard of a modern school's chemistry department. They had the apparatus for heating, distilling, combining chemicals, extracting them from metal ore, and so on.

Niépce's first photograph, for example, had been taken using simple bitumen or asphalt. Specifically, he used Bitumen of Judea, which comes from the Dead Sea. All bitumen is light-sensitive to some extent, but the chemical make-up differs according to the area where it is found – Bitumen of Judea has a particularly good reaction to light. Niépce coated a metal plate in it and exposed it in the camera. Wherever light fell, the bitumen hardened. The unhardened parts (i.e. those which had remained in the dark) were then washed away using lavender oil or alcohol. A negative image remains, which can be used to produce positive prints on paper.

Here was a naturally occurring substance that could have been used by Leonardo. However, it could not have been responsible for the Shroud image, as the bitumen would have flaked off with the folding and rolling of the cloth over the years.

We had always been struck by a possibility that has been overlooked by Shroud researchers, one that would account for the scorch-like appearance of the image. The easiest way of producing a picture that looks similar is to use invisible ink: lemon juice is the classic example, or the readily available source employed by spies during the First and Second World Wars – urine. Invisible when applied, messages written in it appear when the paper is heated. This is because the 'ink' burns at a lower temperature than the paper, and as it does so it reduces the carbon in the paper beneath. The result is exactly as seen with the Shroud: the image is visible, not because of anything added to the cloth, but because the cloth has been oxidised and dehydrated – degraded in a way suggestive of accelerated ageing. (Heating, ageing and attack by acid all result in the same changes to the structure of the fabric.) Early on we made some simple paintings in lemon juice just to see what would happen, and found that one of the Shroud's most puzzling characteristics could easily be reproduced – providing the material was not overheated. As we have seen, the image does not penetrate the cloth, and we could produce this effect by scorching only the top fibres of one side of the cloth.

Of course, the Shroud image was far too big and detailed to have been painted in invisible ink, but it could have been block printed using the same substance. However, even prints would hardly produce the Shroud's photographic accuracy. But then Keith realised that Niépce's method had raised another intriguing possibility – that the image was photographed onto another cloth that had been coated in bitumen. The unexposed areas – the shadows on the subject – could then be washed out, leaving a hardened and slightly raised image, which could then be used as the printing 'block'.

Ingeniously simple though it was, unfortunately we were unable to try it out, as it is no longer possible to find Bitumen of Judea, the only variety we knew to be suitable, in the UK. We did try out the general method using a modern photo-stencil chemical that is used in silk-screen printing, and found it was possible to get good images. The basic method was feasible, but we needed to know just how quickly it reacted in the set-up we had constructed. Niépce's eight-hour exposure used lenses to focus a small, bright image, whereas we were trying to create a life-sized image, preferably without a lens. The photo-stencil emulsion obviously reacts much faster than bitumen, but we had no way of telling how much faster, so the experiment was invalid.

At this stage we were looking for workable techniques rather than specific chemicals, as it seemed more likely that Leonardo's process had not been the equivalent of simple snapshot photographs, with the cloth impregnated with a light-sensitive chemical, whether or not it needed subsequent developing and fixing. If the image was merely created by daubing on chemicals they would long since have been detected. Time and time again we came back to silver salts, since they had been known about in Leonardo's day, but they would be easily detectable, and in any case, the image would have disappeared long ago, just as Wedgwood's did.

It was then that, ploughing through an early twentieth-century dictionary of photography, we came across a process – or rather a series of processes – which had been used in the early days of photography, but had long since been superseded by more convenient methods. These processes did not depend on the film changing colour at all, but instead used a property of certain chemicals which, when mixed with an organic substance (derived from plants or animals), would react to light in such a way as to make the organic parts insoluble in water.[21] (Oddly enough, the exact chemical reactions involved in this process are still not fully understood.) The sensitising chemicals most often employed are chromium salts, chiefly potassium bichromate or ammonia bichromate. Many common substances were used as the organic component: gelatin (made from boiling the skin and bones of animals), gum arabic (extracted from the acacia plant) and albumen (egg-white), collectively known as colloids.

What caught our interest at first was the fact that each of the organic substances named was in common use by artists from medieval times onwards. Egg-white was a staple ingredient of paints, and gelatin[22] and gum arabic had widespread uses; so we tracked down exactly how they were employed by the early photographers.

The main shortcoming of these substances was that, although they produced the required reaction, the image was not very distinct. A simple way of overcoming this was to mix in some powdered pigment: the mixture reacts by becoming insoluble where light hits it. In a similar way to Niépce's bitumen process, the unexposed parts, where the shadows fall, can then be washed away, this time using water rather than oil. The photographer is left with an image of the exposed parts – but now, because of the added pigment, it is clearly visible. An alternative was to add ink after washing, which would stick to the exposed areas. This method was much favoured at one time because it produced highly detailed and graded images, but because it is the light areas that have trapped the pigment, it can only produce a negative image. For this reason, the process came to be chiefly used to produce prints from photographic negatives taken by other methods.

This process was extremely simple. Provided the right sensitiser could be found, it was within the reach of Leonardo's technology. However, there was one drawback: it uses pigments to make the image visible, and we were already convinced that there was no pigment in the Shroud image. Could Walter McCrone have been right after all – had he really discovered pigment on the cloth? One of the pigments favoured by nineteenth-century advocates of the method was Venetian red – the one McCrone claimed he had found. But all the arguments that we have already given against pigment being responsible for the image were still valid. Also, although pictures produced in this way do not need to be fixed in the same way as other photographs, there is still some unwanted chemical reaction when they are displayed, so they have to be treated to stop the image changing. There would have been a definite 'sheen' and the image would have cracked over time.

At this point we thought again about the 'invisible ink' idea that seemed to be telling us something significant about the final form of the Shroud image. And then we realised that the two concepts could easily be put together, because the organic parts of the colloid mixture would act as an invisible ink if the cloth were heated. No pigment was necessary. Heating the cloth, so that the colloid mixture scorched it, was a simple but effective way of fixing the image. Moreover, after scorching, the mixture could be washed out using some form of cleaning agent that would remove every trace of the original mixture while leaving the scorch marks. (Or perhaps not every last trace: albumen was detected on the Shroud image by STURP. However, not much can be said about this, since it is a common substance and fits neatly into other theories – it is a common ingredient in paint, and is present in the bodily fluids of a badly injured man.) The basic reaction between sensitiser and organic material would also take place with the cellulose in the linen itself.

Keith and Clive set out to try out this idea. After all, although it worked in theory, it may show an entirely un-Shroud-like image in practice. We obtained some ammonium bichromate solution for use as the sensitiser which out of solution is an orange-red crystal. Egg-white was the easiest source for the organic part of the mixture (although gum arabic was also tried with similar results). There was still an irritating amount of trial-and-error, since we were using the technique in a way that had not been tried before, and there were many questions still to be answered. We needed to find the correct strength of mixture, how long it would take to react in the camera (with and without a lens) and so on.

We must say straight away that there is no evidence that this particular solution was used in Leonardo's day, still less by the Maestro himself. It is, however, not impossible that it was. We were more concerned to find a method that worked, chiefly because there are so many possible substances that might fit the bill that finding and testing them all would take far more time than we had available. Finding just one method of producing a Shroud image would prove our case. We suspected that there were several ways – and, indeed subsequently we discovered we were right.

There are numerous natural substances that are light-sensitive but that have no value in modern photography. The classic study was carried out at the turn of the nineteenth century by Jean Senebier, who catalogued a huge number of such materials: various extracts of woods, many resins, alcoholic tinctures made from the petals of plants, solutions of cochineal, henna root, the juice of aloe leaves, and many others. In the inorganic world, iron salts, copper salts and mercury salts are all light-sensitive – and all were known to the alchemists. Chlorophyll from plants and mustard oil can be used as sensitisers, as can various acids and some dyes derived from sodium salts.

Several chromium salts, but chiefly ammonia and potassium bichromate, were used in the processes we were interested in, and are the best for the kind of method we were exploring. These were not officially discovered until the close of the eighteenth century, but there is no reason why Leonardo would not have been able to produce them.

The salts we worked with are derived from ferrochromite ores, in which chromium (which is never found in its pure form in nature) is combined with iron and other impurities. Chromium is the twentieth most abundant element on Earth. As far as science acknowledges, the production of chromium from the ore did not happen until 1798, when it was discovered by the French chemist Nicolas-Louis Vauqueline in red lead ore from Siberia. The material did not achieve commercial viability until the discovery of vast reserves of the ore in Siberia and South Africa. However, it is by no means rare in Europe, being found in reasonable quantities in Scandinavia, the Balkans, France and, in smaller deposits, in Italy.

The production of chromium salts from the raw ore is very easy, needing no more sophisticated equipment than a kiln. Sodium bichromate is produced by roasting the ore with soda ash and lime, the potassium salt by using potash in place of soda ash. Simple chemical reactions of the residue with common acids result in the production of ammonium bichromate, the chemical we were using.[23] Apart from the ore itself, all of the other materials and the necessary equipment were in common use (but not especially advanced) in Leonardo's day. It is not impossible that alchemists had discovered and experimented with chromium salts, although they would never have been in plentiful supply. The fact that there is no record of it having been discovered before 1798 is not too much of a problem – remember that history dates the discovery of the light-sensitivity of silver salts from 1727, whereas we have shown that alchemists knew of this at least 300 years earlier.

It is likely that there are other substances that would do the job just as well, although this has not been explored by post-nineteenth-century science. For example, within a couple of years of their discovery, the bichromate salts were being used in the tanning industry, since it makes use of exactly the same property as the one in which we were interested. The salt solution reacts with the organic material of the hide to make it water-proof, which is essentially what we were hoping to do. It is reasonable to assume that whatever materials were supplanted in the industry by the advent of bichromate salts – chiefly chemicals extracted from the barks of various trees – acted in the same way.

Leonardo's skill as a chemist should not be underestimated. Apart from his alchemical pursuits, chemistry was part of the day-to-day business of all Renaissance artists. They needed to know their chemistry in order to prepare paints, varnishes and so on, and they searched for new chemicals with which to produce more effective materials. Leonardo, particularly, excelled in this field. He even invented a kind of plastic (which he called 'vetre parrichulato' – plastic glass), a synthetic resin that he hoped to market for manufacturing chess pieces and ornaments. He kept the recipe secret, even in his notebooks.[24] (This may not have been unconnected with his photographic work. The mixtures we worked with, when left in a bowl or jar and exposed to daylight for several days, invariably hardened into a plastic-like lump, which could easily have been shaped in moulds.)

Proof Positive!

Having assembled all our equipment and chemicals, we followed this method. We made the mixture with egg-white and sensitiser. For some reason fresh eggs work best, and the reaction is also speeded up if the egg-white is beaten before the bichromate is added. We tried various strengths, but we achieved the best results with around 10ml of solution per egg (if you add too much sensitiser the reaction is inhibited). We then left the mixture in warm conditions for two hours for the sensitiser and egg to bind together properly. (Some attempts failed because it was left in the cold.) After this, the mixture, which is a vivid yellow colour, can be painted onto the screen and left to dry. Initially, we used cotton, as this was cheaper during the trial-and-error phase, but we subsequently used linen, with the same results. When dry, the screen was stretched over a wooden frame that we then put inside the camera obscura.

For the camera we used our original wooden box, with the addition of a hood of light-proof photographer's cloth over the screen end. Our one concession to modern methods was to add an aperture mechanism taken from an antique camera, which allowed us to vary the size of the hole easily. Both outdoors in the sun and indoors using the ultraviolet lamps we used arrangements of mirrors to reflect as much light on to the subject as possible.

Our first experiments were carried out using sunlight and no lens in the camera. Although a coated cloth left in the sun reacted within minutes, it did not register in the camera after being left there for a day, even with a series of mirrors reflecting more light onto Bok. We tried different combinations, but days passed with nothing to show for it.

We convinced ourselves that we were on the right track by using a different technique. To show that it was possible to create an image by light using this mixture, Keith painted, in black paint, a copy of the Shroud face on a sheet of glass. By placing this between the sun and a square of treated cloth, we did get a satisfying negative image. When the areas that had not hardened – i.e. where the black paint had masked the sun's rays – were washed out in cold water and the cloth heated, as expected, the egg-white then browned, scorching the fabric (and filling the house with a sulphurous smell!). Hot water, with a little detergent, removed the rest of the mixture, leaving a negative, scorched image of the original painting. It was scorched on one side only, just like the Shroud.[25]

Although this experiment did not confirm our whole theory, we felt we had achieved a small triumph, at least by finding a quick and easy way of making Shroud replicas. For example, if John Weston had used such a technique for *The Silent Witness* replica, painting a black negative version of the Shroud image on a large sheet of glass (or even using a full-sized transparency of the real thing) and laying it over a cloth coated in the way described, he could have completed his replica in a fraction of the time.

On one occasion, after a full day's exposure in the camera obscura, traces of an image began to appear, but the mixture had not reacted enough to survive the washing. We realised that we would need at least some advice from an expert photographer. Lynn got in touch with Amanda Nevill at the Royal Photographic Society in Bath, and on 13 October 1993 – the fifth anniversary of the release of the carbon dating results – we travelled down there to meet Amanda and Michael Austin, a professor of holography and a past president of the RPS. In a sense, we were returning to where our story had started.

When we outlined the basis of our method we were relieved to find that Michael was not as sceptical as we had feared. Surprisingly, it was not the chemical side he objected to – he readily accepted that it was possible that some such sensitising chemical might have been available in Leonardo's day. He even offered the suggestion that, since the chromate salt we were using is primarily employed in the tanning industry, the method could have arisen from there, since both parts of the mixture – the sensitiser and the animal by-products such as gelatin – would have been available together. His objection concerned the optics involved. Using an unlensed camera obscura, he acknowledged, the amount of light hitting the screen would be so reduced that exposure times of weeks would be needed, especially for the full body image, since much of the light reflecting from the body would fall off over the gap between the body and the camera. He would not say categorically that such a thing was impossible, mainly because nobody had ever worked on such a scale. (From the earliest days photographers worked in miniature, life-sized photographs being hopelessly impractical.)

Michael also made some interesting observations about the Shroud image. He was particularly intrigued by the fact that the hair and beard are more or less the same colour and tone as the rest of the face and body which, he pointed out, violates the negative effect. Shroud researchers had noted this before, but we had not given it much thought. If the man on the Shroud were anything other than white-haired the hair ought to be darker on the negative photographs. But if anything it is lighter, especially the moustache and beard. Yet after all, the hair of the man used for the full back image may have been white, and as for the front, Leonardo was known to have gone white quite suddenly and fairly early, although whether this was around the age of forty when we believe he faked the Shroud is not recorded. In any case Leonardo, realising that dark hair would be less reflective and might not show up at all, would have powdered the hair. Of course, if he were using sculpted or cast models the problem would not have arisen in the first place.

Michael also pointed out that although the face itself is realistic, the hair of the front image looks very much as though it were painted on. We looked – and realized that he was on to something. We have already discussed the bizarre foreshortening of the forehead and the unreality of the hairline: the hair here appears to be hanging straight down, which is inconsistent with a figure laid on its back.

We came away from Bath with a lot to think about. We realised that we were going to have to use lenses in our camera obscura, and we also puzzled over just what the enigma of the hair was telling us. Obviously the hair had not come out on the photographic image. We only realised why this should be so, and its significance much later. At the time we surmised that, because the hair was darker – either on the human model or because it had been painted – it had not shown up. If you take a picture of a dark-haired person against a black background – as in the Shroud image – the hair is difficult to make out. On the faint Shroud image it would have been completely invisible, and the same would apply to the beard and moustache. They would have had to be added later.

The chemical mixture, as well as being applied as a coat of emulsion to the linen, could just as well be applied by brush for 'retouching' and then treated in the same way as the rest of the image: exposed to the sun and then heated to scorch the underlying cloth before being completely washed out. This would explain why the hair looks unnatural and painted, and why the beard is much lighter in the negative pictures than it should be: as the painted-on parts would have been exposed directly to the sun rather than being projected through the camera, it would have been easy to over-expose these areas. We were, however, to discover that this reasoning was only partly correct.

In our next series of experiments with the camera obscura after returning from Bath, we used lenses. An assortment were taken from a slide projector and bits of old cameras and tried out. Modern mechanisms in cameras and projectors have a complex series of lenses to shrink or magnify the image and to correct chromatic aberration, but we still wanted to keep the system as simple as possible.

All this was eating into our time: it meant yet more trial and error to find the right lens or lenses through which to project the image. But at least we knew that using a lens removed the restriction of the lenseless camera: that the model always had to be the same distance from the aperture as the screen on the opposite side. We tried all sorts of combinations: different lenses caused different problems with the depth of field – sometimes the tip of Bok's nose would be sharp and detailed and his face a blur, but correcting the face would make the nose a blur. Again, we were handicapped by the limited resources we had to work with.

Eventually we found a lens that projected a good, life-sized image of Bok onto the screen. Although it was much brighter than the non-lens image, it still was not absolutely sharp – but neither is the Shroud image. Also, in order to get the correct-sized image Bok had to be less than a foot away from the lens, and there was a 'fish-eye' effect that we were less than happy about, but it was the best we could manage. With our new set-up we had another try at capturing the image. This time after an eight-hour exposure we were able to see that an image had been caught. It was slightly distorted but at long, long last, it was also quite distinct!

After carefully washing out the unexposed areas, we were left with a picture of Bok in the chemical mixture. Now we had to see how it would appear when scorched. We held the cloth in front of a fire, making sure that it was evenly heated. The chemicals charred before the cloth began to show any signs at all of exposure to heat. After heating it for as long as we dared, we washed the cloth in boiling water. All traces of the salt/egg-white substance were removed, and we were left with an image of Bok – life-sized (in fact, rather smaller, as we had miscalculated on the first attempt), in negative, and scorched lightly onto the top fibres of the cloth only! We photographed it and found that not only is the contrast enhanced by the emulsion in the positive print (as happens with the Shroud) but also the negative showed a much more detailed, recognisable image of the gargoyle. Over the next few weeks we produced several more versions, correcting various errors – although, to our annoyance, it was impossible to eliminate the fish-eye distortion completely.

We found that the scorching of the cloth was not completely satisfactory using just egg-white or gum arabic in the mixture, as it required a high temperature to burn, which sometimes affected the untreated cloth. However, we realised that a simple improvement – on much the same lines as the early photographers who added pigment to the mixture – was to mix in some other substance that scorched more readily at a lower temperature. Lemon juice produced some pleasing results, although there was a tendency for it to curdle with the rest of the mixture. Indelicate though it may seem, we got the most Shroud-like results with urine. (Which, both human and animal, was a staple ingredient for many Renaissance painters, including Leonardo.)

It was all very exciting, but it was only a starting point. Although Bok had done us sterling service, we still had to produce a larger image of a human head to make our point. Bok himself was only roughly half the size of the average head, and being a caricature of a human face exaggerated the distortion at the centre of the lens.

Neither of us relished the idea of remaining motionless for

hours under those ultraviolet lamps – at close range they were stronger than a sun-ray lamp and guaranteed to bestow a deep tan in half an hour – so we acquired a life-sized bust of a girl. As it was silver-grey, we painted the face white, but left the hair untouched, as this would give it a natural-looking contrast. We set up the experiment and left it for around ten hours to ensure a good exposure. As this length of time actually produces a bolder image than the Shroud, and the lamps produce less ultraviolet than comes from the sun, a shorter exposure time is possible. However, since some of our attempts with Bok had failed because we had not left it long enough – wasting most of a valuable day – we wanted to be sure of getting a result. The two lamps we used, allowing for the distance between subject and treated cloth and the reflectivity of the former, produced at most 20 per cent of the power of sunlight at the height of a British summer.[26]

As this was the first time we had used a human figure, we immediately noticed two features of the image that had not shown up with Bok (a smaller and more distorted figure to start with). The fish-eye effect was still there, which slightly widens the centre of the face, but not to the point that it looks in any way unnatural or unrecognisable. What was more striking was the effect using a human head had on the outlines of the face. First, the forehead was much foreshortened, making the distance from the eyes to the top of the head absurdly small. Secondly, the distortion had the effect of making the sides of the face much too straight and square, the edges fading into the background. The ears, although prominent on the model, did not show up at all on the image projected onto the screen. The man on the Shroud does not, apparently, have ears; his face is squared off, with blank strips on both sides, and his forehead is foreshortened. No theory, whether based on real contact with a body or on artistic forgery, has ever been able to account for these bizarre characteristics. We think ours has.

These features were noticeable when viewing the image from the back of the cloth when we started the experiment. Was there anything else that would be revealed when the final image appeared? There was. Ironically, it caused us some irritation at first until its full significance finally dawned. When the image was 'developed' by the washing and heating, it left us – as with Bok – with a perfectly graded, if faint, scorched image, visible on one side of the cloth only. However, prolonged exposure had resulted in a circle appearing in the centre of the cloth, an image of the lens itself, which was surrounded by a darker 'corona'. In our experience, although varying in intensity, this feature – a phenomenon known as 'burn-out' caused by using a simple lens over such a long exposure time – was always present.

At first we were annoyed, and concerned that it might not be possible to eradicate it even by using different lenses. However, there was a chance that Leonardo had experienced the same problem, so we looked at one of our many pictures of the face of the man on the Shroud (Lynn's living room was decorated from floor to ceiling with these images). To our absolute astonishment – and utter delight – there, over the bridge of the nose, the exact geometric centre of the face, was *precisely this same feature*: a distinct circle of light, surrounded on two sides by a dark corona where the lens had stopped the light from falling.

Mindful of the many things – coins over the eyes and so on – which have allegedly been seen on the Shroud over the years, we checked other pictures, taken at different times, from Secondo Pia's to STURP's, in both negative and positive. In all of them this circle is undeniably there, distinct even on positive photographs. We checked with other people, and they could see it too. It was unmistakable. It was precisely in the place where a lens would have been focused: the exact centre of the face.

Originally we thought that this feature had gone completely unnoticed by the Shroudies. We were wrong. They had noticed it, but with their usual inventiveness managed to ascribe the

effect of distortion to a broken nose. In fact, they had only noticed
the two points of the circumference that crossed the nose – giving
the illusion of some kind of injury – but because they already had
what they wanted, failed to notice that those points were actually
part of a circle that extended beyond the nose.

Taken together with the foreshortening – the reduction of the
forehead and the straightening of the sides of the face, making
the ears disappear – we saw that at long last we had proof positive that the face of the man on the Shroud had been created
using a lens. Nothing else explains these features. It also supplies
a reason for the 'retouching' of the hair, which was done, we
realised, only partly because of its dark colour. In our version,
the hair on the top of the head has all but vanished with the foreshortening and, although our model has her hair pulled back,
and not hanging down the sides of her face, the fact that her ears
had disappeared shows that the same thing had happened with
the Shroud image. Leonardo would therefore have had to add
hair artificially, using the same substance as in the camera, but
being forced to follow an unnatural hairline. The 'retouching' of
the hair and beard – using the same chemical mixture, which was
then exposed to the lamps, scorched, then washed out – proved
to be relatively easy and blends in well with the photographic
image. The best effect, we found, was obtained by applying the
mixture with our fingers – a brush tended to overload the cloth
with mixture which then soaked through.

Our deduction was to receive unexpected but impressive
confirmation nearly a decade later. During her examination of
the Shroud in June–July 2002, Mechthild Flury-Lemberg
completely removed the old backing cloth and examined and
photographed the underside. As in previous examinations, she
found that the body image does not penetrate the cloth, while
the bloodstains do. But she discovered something else, which
nobody had known before: that the image of the hair – especially
framing the sides of the face – *does* seep through to the back.

Taken with the fact that the hair – although with the same colour and general characteristics of the face and body image – does not conform with the negative effect, the only logical conclusion is that, like the blood, it was created separately. Although Ian Wilson speculates that the fact that the hair image has soaked through the cloth is due in some way to Jesus' hair being oiled,[27] we think that our explanation, worked out many years before Flury-Lemberg's discovery, is the more plausible.

Then we turned our attention to adding the 'bloodflows': because of their anatomical accuracy on the Shroud it has always been thought they would be difficult to fake. In fact, they were surprisingly easy. The trick is to make them *backwards*. Place a drop of 'blood' on the cloth (we used theatrical blood) then use a cocktail stick to trace out a thin line to the point where the 'wound' welled up.

Although there are still many questions to be answered – the two greatest being the exact substances Leonardo used and the problems he encountered in creating a composite image – to us these discoveries are enough to prove our thesis. Obviously we do not have the resources to double-check our work against STURP data. We cannot discover what spectrographic analysis of our image would reveal, for example. STURP noted spectrographic differences between the image and the scorching caused by the Chambéry fire: these could be explained by the substance being scorched to create the original image, as in our experiments. Do traces of the original chemicals used by Leonardo remain on the cloth and were they detected without their significance being realised? For example, we remember that STURP detected a level of iron on the cloth in both image and non-image areas, which might be significant as some iron salts can be used in the same way as chromium salts. There is no way in which we can address these points.

We must stress that our experiments have been extremely limited, both where time and materials are concerned – in fact,

professional photographers would no doubt laugh at our ama-
teurishness. But we have provided enough persuasive evidence to
show that Giovanni's information was correct, and that many of
the most cherished beliefs of the pro-authenticity lobby are not.
Our mystery man's clues have proved more than useful in this
work, which implies that he was, at least in this, telling the truth.
Perhaps it really is the case that not only did Leonardo create the
Shroud, but also that he did so using this technique. But the
point is that before 1993 nobody had succeeded in creating an
image bearing so many of the characteristics of the Shroud,
including its puzzling anomalies. But now we have.

9

Leonardo's Last Testament

'Many are those who trade in tricks and simulated miracles, duping the foolish multitude; and if nobody unmasked their subterfuges, they would impose them on everyone.'

Leonardo da Vinci[1]

Exactly a week after the first edition of this book was published in September 1994, reports appeared in the British press saying that a South African professor, Nicholas Allen, had declared that the Turin Shroud was a photograph, which he had successfully replicated.[2] We contacted him through the Port Elizabeth Technikon (of which he is now Dean of the Faculty of Art and Design) and struck up a cordial and constructive correspondence with him.

Finally, in the summer of 1995, we were able to meet, when he was flown over to Heathrow Airport by the BBC, where we were filmed greeting him. This was part of an *Everyman* programme about the Turin Shroud – based on this book – entitled 'Double Exposure', made for the BBC by Sir David Frost's independent production company, David Paradine Productions.[3] We were delighted to meet Nicholas and discuss our Shroud-replication technique with him – long into the night in his hotel room in Bloomsbury, memorably on one of the hottest nights of the year.

(We were thrilled to be able to share our work with a much

wider audience through the television programme, which also featured Elmar Gruber and Holger Kersten, besides American members of the pro-authenticity camp. Apart from anything else, we were taken to Vinci, where we were interviewed in an olive grove overlooking Leonardo's birthplace, and spent some hours in a villa in the Chianti region where tradition has it that he painted the *Mona Lisa* – and where we were able to produce our best replication to date using the brilliant Tuscan sunlight. Our subject, a bust of Marcus Aurelius, together with a flat-packed camera obscura, had caused us a few headaches getting through customs at Florence Airport, particularly as our Italian is virtually non-existent and the officers' English was not much better. However, the *Everyman* programme was to open many doors for us and we look back on it with great nostalgia.)

Nicholas had been drawn into his research by pure logic – the Shroud looks like a photograph, so is that what it really is? Like us, he was inspired by the carbon dating to delve deeper into its secret, embarking on a journey of discovery that was to lead him to write his book, *The Turin Shroud and the Crystal Lens* (1998), besides publishing several academic papers on the subject.[4] And like us, he took up the challenge of testing the photography hypothesis by using the chemicals and equipment that would have been available in the years covered by the carbon dating results. But unlike us, Nicholas had access to the sort of virtually unlimited resources that we, in our cramped garage in Reading, could only dream of. He converted a large barn on his property in Port Elizabeth into one big camera obscura and had a lens ground to his own specification – not to mention having the advantage of the brilliantly strong South African sunlight. The pervasive gloom of Reading was not quite the same thing.

With all these resources at his fingertips Nicholas was able to achieve results that were totally beyond our capabilities. He produced full-size images, whereas of course we were limited to just faces (floor space is all-important). He used a different technique –

in fact, much simpler than ours – but of course all we had set out to do was to prove it was possible to produce a photographic image at all using a camera obscura. From the first we acknowledged that there may be several different ways of doing so, and indeed Nicholas proved us right.

He begins his version of the process by coating a piece of linen in silver nitrate or silver sulphate – two chemicals definitely known to have been used in the Middle Ages – and hangs it up in his barn. Outside, the model of a man is suspended before a hole in the barn wall – the lens of the camera obscura – while the South African sun beats down on the figure. After a few days – usually about three – the image is imprinted on the cloth in the barn. The photograph has been taken, resulting in a purple-brown negative image which is then 'fixed' by immersing the cloth in ammonia or urine (which contains ammonia). This changes the image to the same colour as that of the Shroud.

However, the major difference between our methods was that he used a specially ground quartz lens, whereas we used glass lenses taken out of cameras and slide projectors. Quartz has certain major advantages over glass: not only is it much easier to grind, but it also allows ultraviolet light through, whereas glass cuts it down significantly. The chemicals that both we and Nicholas used react with UV light – although, of course, the Shroud faker would not have to have known that. The result was the important thing (although he may also have found the theory interesting). Using a quartz lens means that exposure time is considerably less than with glass. If we had had the benefit of quartz, we could have produced images much more quickly.

Like us, Nicholas thinks that a life cast was used – in his case a whole body cast – although he considers it would be possible to use a corpse for up to three days, after which the process of decomposition would make further work untenable (not to say extremely unpleasant).

Although we made the claim in the first edition of this book that we were the first people to reproduce the Shroud image photographically, in fact Nicholas had beaten us to it. However, despite claims to the contrary, we did not base our work on Nicholas' experiments – simply because we had never heard of them until after this book was published. It was one of those scientific flukes (which seem to happen so often) that we were working on essentially the same ideas at the same time but thousands of miles apart.

Nicholas' research added another, much needed dimension to our work. Not only was it independent corroboration of the photographic theory of the Shroud, but as an academic he could provide the theoretical and technical back-up that we needed. Contrary to the opinion of some, we have no problem with admitting that we are amateurs – in fact, we feel strongly that is one of the strengths of our argument. If *we* can produce an image through a very basic photographic method that has all the so-called 'miraculous' characteristics of the Turin Shroud, then – frankly – almost anyone can. And thankfully we no longer have to worry about proving that we could have scaled up our work to produce a full-length image, because Nicholas has proved it can be done.

However, while we are in full agreement that a photographic method is by far the most plausible explanation for the Shroud image, we do disagree on one major point. Nicholas does not agree that the man responsible was Leonardo, ascribing it to some unknown Arab faker of the thirteenth century. (The Arabs' scientific expertise at that time was far in advance of European knowledge.) Standing by the core dates of the carbon dating, he accepts that the Lirey and Turin Shrouds are one and the same – and so were far too early to be faked by Leonardo.

Some critics of our work have asked why, if Leonardo had invented this technique, we only have one example of it. As we explained in Chapter 8, experiments with optics were deemed to be the Devil's work to the extent that only those with a death

wish would have gone public with their results. But as this pro-
hibition would hardly have applied in the Arab world – in fact,
the Muslim rulers actually encouraged scientific research – surely
the same criticism can be levelled, with considerably more justi-
fication, at Nicholas' theory. More important, however, is the
problem with the head.

As we have seen, it is too small, ridiculously foreshortened –
and completely separate from the body. Nicholas explains the
foreshortening as a sort of fisheye effect created by photograph-
ing the whole body, but as we have demonstrated beyond doubt,
the head is *literally* separate, and in any case, his argument does
not explain the image of the lens in the centre of the face on the
nose. Besides, the image of the face is clearer and darker than the
body, suggesting strongly that it was created at a different time
and with rather more care. Whoever faked it was trying to draw
our attention to something significant about the face.

However, the important thing is that, from the perspective of
pure Shroud research, who did it is somewhat less significant
than how it was done. The photographic theory – whether ours
or Nicholas Allen's – explains *everything*. It is the only proven
technique that works. As far as most objective people are concerned, it is now a matter simply of QED. But there are those
who by no stretch of the imagination can be categorised as
objective.

Thrown out by The Shroud Crowd

So how have the Shroudies reacted to both our work and that of
Nicholas Allen? Perhaps they could hardly be expected to fall
upon our results with exclamations of joy, but one could reasonably have expected them to welcome some kind of public
debate or at least attempt an objective analysis. In fact, even
before our book came out, we had already become *personae non*

gratae to the Shroudies, particularly the leadership of the BSTS. We were amazed to discover that, according to Ian Wilson's 1998 book *The Blood and the Shroud*: '. . . despite [the BSTS] being an inoffensive, genuinely non-partisan society that makes no attempt to promote itself, even it has had its problems, in the 1990s suffering an extraordinary "infiltrate, discredit and destroy" attack from the "Leonardo da Vinci theory" authors Picknett and Prince.'[5] If true, we had obviously behaved not only despicably but also in ways completely out of proportion to the importance of the society. Why bother to go to such lengths with the BSTS? But it is instructive to look at the facts about that 'inoffensive' bunch, which may shed some light on the way that the Shroudie world as a whole operates.

What had that terrible twosome, Picknett and Prince – the infiltrators, discreditors and destroyers – actually done? When we first began to be interested in the Shroud, we did the logical thing – we joined the BSTS (of which Rodney Hoare was then Chairman and Ian Wilson Vice Chairman) with the apparently reasonable hope that we could enter into a useful debate on the subject with other enthusiasts (from both sides of the fence). While it is true that there were members who, though completely against our theory, were quite willing to enter into friendly discussion with us – particularly Ian Dickinson – the leadership from the very beginning wanted us to keep our ideas to ourselves, like all other anti-authenticity researchers. (Who, as it can be imagined, are noticeably thin on the ground in the 'non-aligned' BSTS.)

In 1991 Clive wrote an account of our theory as it then stood for the BSTS *Newsletter*, edited by Ian Wilson, and suggested that the society might be interested in a talk. But although the article was published, readers would have been in no doubt where 'Your Editor' stood about our theory. It was accompanied by the reprint of an article by Isabel Piczek on how Leonardo could not have *painted* the Shroud (an argument with which we were both totally in agreement). More seriously, however, Wilson appended some of his own comments informing readers that our work was based upon mediumistic communication with the spirit of Leonardo himself!

This was a deliberately garbled version of a conversation Wilson and Lynn had had in happier times, which took place on Sunday, 22 April 1990, at her north London home. As a then parapsychologist, Lynn had for many years taken part in all manner of paranormal experiments (for example, as a volunteer in a major experiment into telepathy at Cambridge University in the early 1980s). Always intrigued by the extraordinary powers of the mind – like Ian Wilson himself, whose book on the subject, *Superminds*, came out shortly after their relationship ended – she began a personal experiment with 'automatic writing'. Used extensively as a therapeutic tool by orthodox psychologists, automatic writing is almost always the product of the unconscious mind. You simply hold a pen or pencil lightly against a piece of paper, distract yourself, and wait for the squiggles to appear. The result is usually a mixture of repeated single letters, artistic flourishes, names and – if one is lucky – a few coherent sentences that most often reflect current preoccupations and thoughts. So it came as no surprise that, when Lynn was first immersed in Leonardo research, the squiggles in question eventually took the form of the name 'Leonardo'. Lynn added that she had also – quite separately – come into some information that hinted that Leonardo had indeed created the Shroud image, specifically in 1492. Wilson's response was very interesting, particularly in retrospect: he said, 'Yes, the Shroud did disappear around then . . .' (We later took this to be an indication that he was hinting that today's Turin Shroud could have been a substitute for the earlier one. These days he denies that this part of the conversation ever took place, even writing in the *Fortean Times* that: 'This was one of Lynn Picknett's many inventions.'[6])

Lynn's memory of these events is that this brief conversation was the only possible basis for his later accusations of mediumship. He could have been in no doubt at the time that she regarded automatic writing as a function of the unconscious mind and that her scribbles were to be seen as a novelty only. Lynn also impressed upon him that the conversation was in total confidence and he promised not to tell a soul. There was nothing sinister in this request for secrecy: unsurprisingly, she was a little embarrassed at demonstrating her 'automatic scribbles', but felt at the time that he should know about them. Being in no doubt about her feelings on this point, it was an extraordinary act of betrayal to go public with his inflated insinuations – which could only have been intended to discredit us – especially after giving his word not to do so.

The allegations of mediumship were used as a reason for rejecting the offered lecture, as were the grounds that the BSTS only deals in 'hard, checkable' research.[7] However, it rapidly became clear that this was not a criterion that they hastened to apply to the more welcome type of speaker – those who claimed to have evidence that the Shroud is genuine. One particular event left us not knowing whether to laugh or cry on behalf of the BSTS.

This was their Spring lecture in May 1992, by – in a manner of speaking – a researcher named Norma Weller. Advertised as 'New Discoveries On The Turin Shroud', Weller's talk promised revelations from a new image enhancement technique that would reveal some hitherto unseen detail on the Shroud image. But when an enlarged picture of Shroudman was proudly displayed, and we could see just what this incredibly innovative technique of hers was, hysteria began to well up. She had coloured the image in. There was more to come.

Norma Weller herself remained invisible, as she had sent her talk to be read *in absentia* by Ian Wilson. This opened with the declaration that the 'speaker' was unwilling to go into details about the enhancement process and did not wish to enter into any debate about it either. When questioned from the floor about the speaker's absence, the audience was told that Weller was 'too reticent' to give her talk. Any sympathy we might have had for a mouse-like lady racked with nerves at the very thought of public speaking disappeared immediately after the revelation that she was, by profession, a *lecturer* . . . (at Brighton Polytechnic). At this point we bit our lips and daren't catch each other's eye. The tiny audience also learned that it was lucky even to have the picture to look at that evening as it had only been delivered by car just before the meeting. Without that they would have been treated to a talk by someone who wasn't there refusing to tell them about something they couldn't see!

Despite her 'reticence', Norma Weller was persuaded to write an article on her method for the next *Newsletter.* It remains a source of complete bafflement, its only real information being that the enhancement was the result of 'the application of three-dimensional colour'. But one thing was more than clear: the secret of Weller's mysterious success at the BSTS is revealed in her declaration: 'My only wish is to authenticate the Shroud'.[8]

Also, to our amazement, Weller linked her 'discoveries' on the Shroud to the burial practices of the Middle Eastern sect of the Mandaeans. As part of her 'application of three-dimensional colour' she had coloured a patch around Shroudman's head green and declared that this was a myrtle leaf, pointing out that the Mandaeans placed them on the forehead of their dead. But while it is true that the modern Mandaeans can be traced back to Palestine, she has overlooked the central fact about that sect: *they loathe and despise Jesus*, as they believe that he usurped their beloved priest, John the Baptist. (In fact, the use of the myrtle leaf was not unique to the Mandaeans — several other Middle Eastern sects also favoured it in their burial rites.)[9]

While our absurdist streak was delighted with Ms Weller's Pythonesque 'presentation' (surely something of a classic — even the memory can still induce hysteria) we were also annoyed and astonished at the grotesquely blatant double standards employed by the BSTS leadership. Having rejected our Leonardo talk out of hand, they then welcomed this 'Dead Parrot Sketch' with open arms, and even after the disastrous evening of the non-talk, actually proceeded to give Ms Weller column inches without a word of criticism. Obviously they had not subjected her 'talk' in advance to the stringent criteria they insisted on applying to us, simply because her nonsense was pro-authenticity.

When, after the fiction about our 'mediumistic' sources, the *Newsletter* gave approving space to an Egyptian medium who channels Jesus (and yes, he confirms the Shroud is genuine) it really became a bit too much to take. Clive wrote a letter for publication in the *Newsletter* expressing concern about the direction in which the society was heading. Although it was not published, it was answered by the Secretary, Dr Michael Clift, in stridently hostile tones, which tagged both of us (in one of its less offensive remarks) as belonging to 'the more scatty side of the so-called occult'[10] (whatever that may mean). Over the next few months a number of letters were exchanged with the Chairman, Vice Chairman and Secretary. Our complaints against the pro-authenticity and pro-Christian bias of the society – which declares itself in its Constitution as 'entirely non-denominational and non-aligned' – and requests for an explanation about the unequal treatment of those opposed to authenticity were studiously ignored by all three.

In March 1993 the writer A. N. Wilson became interested in our Leonardo theory and his friend the reputable Anglican writer Ysenda Maxtone Graham interviewed us for an article for the London *Evening Standard*. (Interestingly, her personal view was that the Shroud must be some kind of fake because 'God does not behave like that'.) She also interviewed Michael Clift and BSTS member Ian Dickinson. The article, entitled 'The Turmoil That Is Tearing Apart The Shroud Crowd' appeared on 25 March 1993 – and as a direct result, Lynn was expelled from the society. (However, a much happier – and considerably more important – consequence was that the article led directly to the commissioning of this book, and, effectively, a whole new career for both of us.)

Rodney Hoare wrote to Lynn remonstrating with her bizarrely about 'an article in the *Evening Standard* which I have been told about, bringing the society into disrepute and mentioning the date of our next meeting. I am sure you realise such behaviour is not acceptable.'[11] He added that Lynn was no longer welcome at BSTS meetings.

That meeting took place in April 1993 at St John's Church Hall in Paddington, west London. We arrived and sought to get a proper explanation for Lynn's expulsion from Rodney Hoare. Instead he seized her by the arms and physically ejected her from the hall, saying, 'We do not have to give a reason.' We had been told that Lynn's expulsion was the result of 'unanimous vote' of the committee. In fact, at least one committee member, Ian Dickinson, had voted against it. Unsurprisingly, shortly afterwards, he was also threatened with expulsion. (Earlier, Dickinson's criticism of one of the BSTS officers led to his receiving, from that individual's wife, a thinly veiled accusation of having used 'occult means' to cause her father-in-law to commit suicide. Nasty, and profoundly disturbing stuff.)

After Lynn's banishment Clive was told that, by special dispensation of the Chairman, he could stay in the society provided that he behave 'like a normal member', and with the hope that he would stay 'as you might learn something about the Shroud'.[12] Shortly afterwards, Clive was proposed as Treasurer of the society after some members had raised serious questions about the way the society's finances were being handled. Almost immediately, he, too, was expelled. The Chairman's letter gave as the ludicrous reason 'You have written to me and the other officers and have stood for office'.[13] When quizzed about this at the 1993 AGM, Hoare's logic was impeccable: 'normal members don't write letters of complaint therefore he is not a normal member'.

That is the sad story of our alleged attempt to 'infiltrate, discredit and destroy' the BSTS, which apart from its sheer entertainment value, sheds some rather bleak light on the lengths to which the Shroudies are prepared to go in order to keep objective researchers from intruding into their pro-authenticity paradise. But widening the picture, let us now consider the reactions of other members of the 'Shroud Crowd' to our work and that of Nicholas Allen.

Negative and Positive

In general, they either ignored it or took refuge in extraordinary pettiness. There was and never has been any debate. The Shroud world has simply refused – in Ian Wilson's words – to give us 'the oxygen of publicity', which may sound lofty, but is in fact merely an excuse not to enter into any kind of dialogue with us. From the outset, it was BSTS policy to refuse to engage in public debate – either on the same platform or studio, although they had ample opportunity to do so. In fact, during the rather extensive publicity for the exhibition at the National Museum of Photography, Film and Television, repeated attempts were made to persuade Ian Wilson – who, although he now lives in Australia, was in Britain at the time, promoting *The Blood and the Shroud* – to appear on several television and radio programmes with us. Not only did the Museum's publicity department try to get him on various shows, but also his own publishers attempted to persuade him to avail himself of all this free publicity. But even though he was publicising his book at the time, he refused even to take part in a 'down the line' (telephone) debate on the radio. Yet despite his blanket refusal to do so, his remarks about us and our work in *The Blood and the Shroud* are so extreme as to verge on the libellous. Although we make no apology for criticising his work, at least we would positively welcome a chance to do so to his face.

Some of the objections to our theory are simply absurd. For example, Isabel Piczek listed inventions or artistic techniques of Leonardo's that failed to work, concluding that he couldn't have invented a photographic technique that *did* work.[14] She is oblivious to the fact that she seems to be saying that, because our technique works, Leonardo could not have invented it . . . Ian Wilson dismisses our replication on the grounds that the blood flows that we added bear no comparison to those on the Shroud.[15] This is more of a testimony to our lack of artistic expertise than a counter-argument to our theory – in fact, the blood flows are the least problematic aspect of the Shroud image. *They were painted on.* Ian Wilson is forced to admit that Nicholas Allen's full body image is the best replication of the Shroud image yet produced, but objects to the theory because he fails to see how the blood got across the distance from lens to linen.[16] But as Allen spells out in his account – though it should be so obvious he shouldn't have to – the blood flows were added later by hand. The anomalies with the blood flows on the Shroud, noted in Chapter 3 (but which Wilson and other critics studiously ignore) prove that the faker did the same.

Most bizarre of all, is that several critics from the *pro*-authenticity camp – again, including Ian Wilson[17] – use the results of the carbon dating against us, pointing out that, as the core dates were 1260–1390 and Leonardo wasn't born until 1452, we had made an elementary blunder. Since they are trying to claim an error of 1300 years, coming from them this is somewhat ludicrous.[18]

(Such surreally scrambled logic has always been a feature of the pro-authenticity camp. For example, Ian Wilson, referring to the D'Arcis Memorandum of 1389 – the earliest documentary reference to what is apparently today's Shroud and which, as we saw in Chapter 2, refers to it being exposed as a painted forgery some thirty years before – writes:

> . . . not a single surviving document actually from the 1350s even mentions a shroud of Lirey, let alone reports any diocesan investigation into its authenticity. Nor is there any guarantee that this Lirey shroud was the Shroud now preserved in Turin. Yet the 'reliable' fact of the Shroud being 'only traceable back to the 1350s' is all too often quoted among the 'hard' evidence corroborating its fraudulence.[19]

Here the *lack* of evidence for the existence of the Shroud in the 1350s has been curiously transmuted into evidence *against* it being a fake. But doesn't Wilson base his whole argument for the Shroud being authentic on the 'fact' that it first appeared in Lirey in the 1350s and trying to reconstruct how it got there – the Mandylion and so on? We confess to being totally at a loss with this kind of bizarre double-think.)

However, the same criticism concerning the carbon dating coming from non-Shroudies is another matter entirely. This objection was also raised by none other than Professor Harry Gove, who invented the specific radiocarbon dating technique used to date the Shroud. But when we responded that an old piece of cloth could have been used, he had the good grace to apologise. (In any case, Teddy Hall has said he would accept a date of up to 1500.)

Apart from this, the other major objection that is consistently raised (although we covered it in the first edition of this book), is that the Shroud has a documented existence from at least 1389, and by implication from the 1350s. As we explain in Chapter 6, this was the first thing we thought of. However, when we delved further we found that:

- There is no direct proof that the Lirey Shroud and today's Turin Shroud are one and the same. Admittedly, they are supposed to be the same, but there is no written or artistic evidence to confirm it. There are no depictions of the Shroud before 1516. The single – possible – exception is the pilgrim's badge found in the Seine, but this has not been definitively dated. It is only assigned to the fourteenth century by inference from the presence of the de Charny and de Vergy coats of arms.

    Even Ian Wilson, in his 1998 book, admits 'Nor is there any guarantee that this Lirey shroud was the Shroud now preserved in Turin'.

- The Shroud kept a remarkably low public profile for nearly forty years after being acquired by the Savoy family. In the first edition of this book we made the claim that the Shroud effectively 'disappeared' for this period, only re-emerging into the public gaze when it was displayed at Vercelli – close to Milan where Leonardo was working at the time – in 1494. There may be documentary references to its continued existence, but the important thing is that it was never actually taken out of its box. For the 1994 edition we went through the whole of the Shroud literature and could find no record of it being displayed between 1452 and 1494. We therefore concluded that the Shroud that was exhibited in 1494 was not the Lirey Shroud but a new version, which is of course consistent with the idea that today's Turin Shroud was created by Leonardo.

    Before the publication of our book, Ian Wilson admitted that the possibility of a substitution around this time could not be discounted, although he has since changed his mind. We have seen that he told Lynn that 'the Shroud did disappear around then' (1492), which he now emphatically denies. Ironically, it was this that originally prompted us to check the records and discover evidence of the 'missing years'.

However, in his 1998 book, Wilson lists two expositions during that period: the first was on Good Friday 1478 at Pinerolo and the second on Easter Sunday, 1488 at Savigliano – although he gives no sources for this new information.[20] But even if this were so, it does not change our basic premise; after all, there could still have been a substitution at any point during that time. All a substitution requires is that the people who see it afterwards are different from the people who saw it before. Although Giovanni told us that Leonardo had faked the Shroud in 1492, that is one of the few pieces of his information that we have never been able to prove. Besides, the 1478 and 1488 expositions were remarkably low-key events compared to the later displays.

(In the same conversation in which Wilson said that the Shroud disappeared around 1492, he also reacted strongly against the idea of Leonardo's involvement, later admitting in a letter to Lynn: 'When you try to persuade me . . . that Leonardo created the Shroud there is one part in me that feels fundamentally threatened.'[21] Certainly at the time, Lynn felt that this showed he was by no means as certain in his championship of the authenticity of the Shroud as he makes out – and upon which his entire reputation depends – nor was he truly convinced that Leonardo had *not* been involved. Having been converted to Catholicism, to which he is passionately devoted, by the miraculous nature of the Shroud, what would he do if it were proved beyond any debate or doubt to be a fake?)

• Reactions to the post-1494 Shroud were entirely different from those accorded the previous relic. The Lirey Shroud was repeatedly declared to be a blatant forgery, a painting, and other investigations reached the same conclusions, suggesting strongly that a substitution had been made.

Other objections put forward to counter our theory tend to be somewhat specious. One is that there is no record of Leonardo having any dealings with the House of Savoy, to which the only answer is 'So what?' Another is that there is no mention of the Shroud, or indeed his work on photography, in any of Leonardo's notebooks. But as we have seen, one particular notebook was mysteriously tracked down by the Savoys who promptly 'lost' it, but although we have no way of knowing what was in it, we can speculate that it may have had some connection with the emphatic and blunt statement by Maria José, Umberto II's estranged wife, that the Shroud is a fake. Perhaps it should also be pointed out that there is no evidence in Leonardo's surviving notebooks that he painted the *Mona Lisa*, either!

Not all reactions have been negative, however. In particular, scientists and photographers have been very warm in their praise for our research, which was most welcome after the treatment we received from the Shroud world. Despite Rodney Hoare's scathing indictment of our photographic knowledge, many professional photographers have come forward to congratulate us, generously offering advice and encouragement for our continuing research. The prestigious magazine *Amateur Photographer* carried an enthusiastic cover article about Leonardo as the first photographer – citing his known experiments with optics and light and the fact that he had built his own camera obscura – based on an interview with us during the time of the Bradford exhibition. Somehow it seemed particularly poignant to see Leonardo's portrait on the cover of a photography magazine, where – if we are right – it surely belongs. For the same reason, we were excited and moved to see the full-length transparency on display at the National Museum of Photography, Film and Television, particularly because of the thoughtful and visitor-friendly way it was exhibited. In our view, the 'Shroud' was more at home there than in any cathedral.

There have been other accolades. In 1995 after our talk to the august Society for Psychical Research, the Chairman, the late Ralph Noyes, asked the packed hall for a show of hands of those who believed the Shroud was a photograph. All but two put up their hands – and one of those was BSTS member Ian Dickinson and the other a notorious diehard, anti-mystery 'skeptic'.

Then there is Japan. Surprisingly perhaps, for a theory about a Christian relic, the Japanese have taken to our work with huge enthusiasm. Thanks partly to the BBC *Everyman* programme and partly to the translation of this book now available there, we are told that most well-educated Japanese now associate the Turin Shroud with Leonardo – indeed, it is his involvement that really excites them. Certainly we have had several keen film crews from Tokyo on our doorstep, with very well-prepared interviewers asking dozens of detailed questions about our work. Keith Prince also produced an excellent replication for a Japanese television programme in 1999 under less than perfect conditions, being warmly hailed as something of a genius for doing so. It was particularly interesting to note that our Japanese friends see no difficulty whatsoever in the proposition that Leonardo was the first photographer – and instantly recognise the likeness between Shroudman and the artist. In fact, they love the whole Leonardo affair, seeing what they perceive as typically dark da Vinci humour in the making of the relic, especially in the idea that he used his own face as that of Jesus.

Yet in a way, we have had an even more impressive accolade, if something of a back-handed compliment. On 5 September 1995, Cardinal Saldarini announced on television that the Shroud would be exhibited for the first time in twenty years in 1998, and again in the Holy Year of 2000. After announcing the dates and arrangements for the exposition – and declaring that 'the image on the Shroud is that of Christ and no-one else' – Saldarini went on to caution the faithful against claims about DNA and 'silly notions' such as that Jesus did not die on the cross – and the idea that the Shroud was a photograph by Leonardo da Vinci . . . As our book had not been published in Italy, this must have been rather puzzling to the Italian audience, but it amused us because in trying to warn his flock off our idea the cardinal had unwittingly only succeeded in drawing attention to it. Even more remarkable was the fact that – as he kept stressing – Cardinal Saldarini was actually speaking on the direct orders of the Pope.[22]

In the Name of the Knights

Another theory about the Shroud that has been propounded since the first edition of this book is that of Christopher Knight and Robert Lomas, which first appeared in their *The Hiram Key* in 1996, later developed in *The Second Messiah* (1997). They claim that the image on the Shroud was produced by contact with a real human body – not that of Jesus, but of Jacques de Molay, the last Grand Master of the medieval Knights Templar who was martyred in Paris in 1314 (after seven years in prison). Knight and Lomas believe that when he was captured by the Inquisition, as a heretic he was mocked by being tortured in the same way as Jesus. While still alive, he was wrapped in a shroud – and at this point the body and blood image were formed on the cloth. De Molay then recovered, only to be slowly roasted alive, and the cloth ended up in the possession of the family of his fellow prisoner, the Templar Geoffrey de Charny.

Although we have since struck up a cordial relationship with Bob Lomas, we have to admit that we find nothing convincing in this argument. It is based on just three facts: the first is that the date fits the carbon dating, the second is that there are references to de Molay being tortured – although nobody knows in what manner – and third is the connection with the Templar Lirey and de Charnys. Everything else is speculation. Not only is there no evidence at all that de Molay was tortured by crucifixion (or that the Inquisition ever tortured anybody in this way) but their argument also becomes extremely circular: he must have been tortured in this way because it is his image on the Shroud, and it is his image on the Shroud because he was tortured in this way. (Incidentally nobody knows what de Molay looked like – the only known depictions came from a much later date.)

Although Knight and Lomas claim to have finally – and quite by accident – solved the mystery of the Shroud, they have in fact missed the point. The abiding mystery of the Shroud was never whose image it was, but how that image got there. To explain it, they adopt the theory of Dr Allan Mills who, as we have seen, argues that a process involving the interaction of free radicals rising from the body with the cloth was responsible. But as we pointed out in Chapter 3, this theory simply cannot account for the image of the *back* on the cloth. And all the other reasons that led us to conclude that the Shroud is a forgery remain: the ridiculous height of the man, the disproportionately small and awkwardly positioned head – not to mention the fact that it is completely separate from the body – the problems with the blood flows (particularly in the hair), and the fact that the lack of distortion means that the cloth *had to be flat*. Another weak point in the process hypothesised by Allan Mills is that it is entirely theoretical: a fundamental part being that once the initial reaction has taken place it takes several decades for a visible image to start to appear, therefore it can never be demonstrated experimentally in a laboratory. Besides, if the image was that of a wounded de Molay, he would have had to have kept extremely still.

So what do Knight and Lomas have to say about the photographic theory – ours and Nicholas Allen's? In their initial reconstruction, based on the idea that the cloth was in direct contact with the body, they concluded that when the image was formed the man must have been lying on a soft surface, which made his body crumple up: they think this because the cloth would not otherwise have been in contact with the whole of the back. So, they say, if the man had been photographed in this position, he would have appeared crumpled up, not lying stretched out.[23] What they have done, however, is take the position of the body required by *their* theory and relate it to the position of the cloth required by *ours*. In our theory (and Nicholas Allen's) the body would be in a different position to start with, and, of course, nowhere near the cloth. In any case, by now it should be apparent that the image *is* a photograph.

They dismiss Leonardo's involvement first by citing the usual line about the Shroud being around before he was born, and secondly arguing rather curiously that he could never have created the whip marks fraudulently.[24] This is rather puzzling, seeing as we have made it clear that he crucified a real human body – not his own – in the way described in the New Testament, which includes flagellation. Then he took a photograph of it. We are at a loss to understand how this is at odds with the anatomical perfection of the whip marks – quite the reverse, in fact.

Inspired by Heresy

Another theory of the Shroud's origin that centres on the Templars – and which agrees that it is a photographic image – was put forward in 2000 by British writer and documentary film-maker Keith Laidler, in his book *The Divine Deception*. Laidler builds on the central theory of his earlier work, *The Head of God* (1998): the secret of the Templars was that they owned the embalmed head of Jesus, which today is sealed beneath the enigmatic Rosslyn Chapel in Scotland.

Beginning with the puzzle of the Templars' documented reverence for a disembodied head or heads, he argues that the Nazarite (Nasorean) sect to which Jesus belonged incorporated a secret tradition, stretching back ultimately to the Egypt of the 'heretic pharaoh' Akhenaten, in which the heads of its holiest figures were severed after death, then embalmed and preserved. Laidler argues that this is what happened to Jesus: his embalmed head eventually came under the protection of the Templars, the heirs of the Nazarite tradition, and the head was transported to Scotland when the Order was suppressed.

The weakness in Laidler's overall argument is that there is a complete lack of independent historical evidence for the existence of such a head cult either within the Aten religion championed by Akhenaten, or in the early Jewish religion founded by Moses – which was, many have suggested, and Laidler accepts, a continuation of Aten-worship. (Laidler argues that the head rituals were a closely guarded inner secret of both religions, detectable only by oblique references in their texts.) And, according to Laidler, as all Nazarite holy men were treated in this way, and there was nothing intrinsically special about Jesus compared to the sect's other leaders, why should his head have been singled out for preservation through the following centuries?

In any case, we believe that the documented existence of an alternative 'Church' of those who believed John the Baptist to be the true Christ provides a much more convincing explanation for the Templars' 'head cult' (especially given the knights' acknowledged reverence for the Baptist). After all, of the two 'Christs', it was John, not Jesus, whose beheading is recorded in the Gospels, so if anyone's head is buried under Rosslyn Chapel, obviously John would be the better candidate – although in our view no such relic languishes there.

Be that as it may, in *The Divine Deception* Laidler proposes that the Templars' ownership of Jesus' head provides the solution to the mystery of the Shroud. He agrees with us that the image is a photograph. However, as he accepts that the Turin and Lirey Shrouds were one and the same, he rejects what he terms the 'Leonardo Conspiracy' theory, declaring us to be dupes of a misinformation exercise by the Priory of Sion who were trying to *prevent* the Shroud's true message being discovered – overlooking the fact that Giovanni's tip-offs were only ever guidelines for our subsequent, much more thorough research, and were *never* simply swallowed hook and all.[25])

His other main argument against our conclusions is that the core dates of the carbon dating place the cloth before Leonardo's birth; like many of our critics, he fails to consider that Leonardo would naturally use old cloth to fake a supposedly ancient relic – a point that is addressed in this book. Laidler also agrees that the image of the head of the man on the Shroud was produced separately, citing the head's incorrect proportions and positioning, and the definite demarcation between head and body images. (He claims to have discovered these things but as far as we know, we were the first to do so in the 1994 edition of this book.)

Laidler believes that the Shroud was the work of the Templars, who in the thirteenth century produced the image employing a photographic process learned from the Arabs, and using the real, embalmed head of Jesus and a dead body. The Shroud is therefore at once genuine *and* fake: the face really is Jesus', but the Shroud itself is the product of the Middle Ages – which is nothing if not ingenious! However, like Knight and Lomas', his argument is ultimately circular, depending entirely on the existence of Jesus' severed head in the first place, whether or not it was a cult relic. Other aspects of Laidler's reconstruction are unclear: if they venerated Christ's head, why would the Templars have wanted to create a full-length image on a fake burial shroud? Laider rejects the idea that it was for financial gain. According to him, having faked the Shroud, the Templars then kept it secret. Although theoretically possible, in our view Laidler fails to build a convincing case.

The Hymn to Heresy

If the prospect of female DNA on the Shroud was to raise the hackles of the male-dominated clergy, the performance of British artist Caroline Rye has also sent shudders throughout the Shroudie world. Inspired by our book, her 'Turin Machine' sets out to highlight the artistic elements of fake Shroud-making, celebrating its almost mystical concept of freezing a moment in time by taking a photograph with a camera obscura. Never intended to be a scientific experiment (she uses modern photographic chemicals) nevertheless her performance – in which she stands naked and covered in white body paint for hours, while the audience, one at a time, takes turns to look through a peephole at the unfolding process of the image taking shape on the 'Shroud' – results in sheets of cloth imprinted with her negative image, each of which is hung up with the others at the end of every session. It makes a point, capturing the sort of exciting, transcendental feeling that Leonardo must have experienced as he experimented behind closed doors with the slow emergence of terribly realistic images, unlike anything else in his time. We have become so used to photography that we take it for granted, but in his day it must have been truly fantastic – the science fiction of the era – and of course, had the added frisson of being *forbidden*.

We were very grateful to Caroline – with whom we spent a delightful evening in Bristol – for reminding us that there was another aspect to Shroud-making. We had become so bogged down with the details of chemicals and lenses, and with historical minutiae that it was refreshing to be able to see the process through the eyes of an artist. For a brief moment, we could begin to understand why Leonardo, at least as an artist, was involved.

But why would he have risked his life by faking the ultimate *Christian* relic if he was, as we believe, so opposed to Christianity?

The way we approached the problem of Leonardo and the Shroud was to set out to establish whether or not he had the means, motive and opportunity to do it – just as if we were detectives investigating a crime. We believe that, after gathering all the evidence, we have set out a convincing case. His work on optics and his alchemical pursuits provided him with the means, and he certainly had the opportunity. Finally, Leonardo's heretical and unorthodox beliefs – particularly his Johannite persuasion – gave him the necessary motive. One might add to this that his own strength of character and rebellious streak gave him the sheer audacity needed to effect this, the greatest fraud of all.

We now know that the Shroud was not the winding sheet of Jesus, but an astonishingly ingenious piece of work even by Leonardo's standards. The risks were astronomical, the consequences of being found out would have been unthinkable. If the laity had discovered Leonardo in the process of forging the Holy Shroud there would have been outcry enough, but what if the Church, who possibly connived in this, or even actually commissioned it, found that he was using such a technique? Just one generation after Leonardo, Giovanni Battista della Porta was accused of sorcery simply for experimenting with projected images. Given the immense trouble involved, why did Leonardo do it?

One reason may be simple: Giovanni said that Leonardo had been commissioned by the Pope himself to provide another, better 'Holy Shroud' with which to pull in the crowds. We have found no direct evidence for this, but tales of Church corruption were commonplace in those days. Other artists may well have rejected the work of faking the Shroud for reasons of superstition. Even in the cynical world of the Renaissance, creating the image of the crucified Jesus would have given one pause for thought, but clearly Leonardo had no such qualms. If anything, he had good reasons for committing this act of what would have been to many a grave sacrilege.

Make no mistake, only a heretic would have dared fake the Turin Shroud. Many believers have said that if it turns out to be a fake then it is still a work of profound Christian piety. For example, Maria Consolata Corti – who also believes it is a self-portrait by Leonardo, albeit created artistically, not photographically – sees it as a sign of Leonardo's own deep Christian spirituality and his identification with Jesus' Passion. But to create a faked Holy Shroud of Jesus complete with what is believed to be his redemptive blood, and to pass it off as *real*, cannot have been undertaken by a devout Christian.

It seems likely that the idea of putting the image of his face on the cloth was his own. There would not have been the danger that such a confidence trick would carry with it today, when celebrities are so instantly recognisable: in those days, even in his native land, few people knew what the Maestro Leonardo looked like. Besides, the technique itself ensured anonymity, for the likeness is not apparent to the naked eye, only leaping into focus when seen in photographic negative.

Leonardo worked with optics, lenses and projected images. Serge Bramly wrote of him: '. . . the deductions in his notebooks are dazzling. Whereas men of his age thought that vision was created by particles (*spezie*) projected by the eye, Leonardo understood that the eye did not transmit anything but received rays of light . . . he also perceived that the eye registered a reversed image . . . and envisaged a sort of contact lens . . . He was the first to note the principle of stereoscopic vision – that is, the perception of three-dimensional relief . . . He seems to have invented some kind of telescope a century before Galileo. He writes: "Make glasses to see the Moon enlarged." He assembled lenses . . .'[26]

He also worked on a secret 'machine made of mirrors' in the 1490s, the purpose of which is unknown, but of course mirrors concentrate light and heat – and both are required to produce an image like that on the Shroud, by the method we have shown.

He was, in all probability, a practising alchemist with a wide range of chemicals at his disposal. He was also in the right place at the right time and had the opportunity and the means. But if, as seems likely, he did not accept the commission to fake the Shroud simply for the money, what were his true motives for committing this act of high sacrilege?

In our view, a major clue lies in the fact that Shroudman's head is – apparently – severed. As we have seen, there is no doubt about this. We hope we have shown that there were practical reasons for this apparent anomaly, for Leonardo used his own face and some-one else's body, inevitably leaving a demarcation line between the two separately created images. Yet this obvious dislocation can also be seen as symbolic: is Leonardo's visual pun saying to us across the centuries that the one who was beheaded is 'over' one who was crucified? As a Johannite, Leonardo venerated John the Baptist, who was of course beheaded, while reserving utter contempt for the crucified Jesus. This interpretation of what amounts to just one line on the Turin Shroud may seem rather fanciful, but fur-ther investigation reveals that this fits not only the Johannite view but also Leonardo's own mindset perfectly.

Relic of the Other Christ

The original edition of this book set us on a path that went well beyond the Shroud itself, leading us into a complex and com-prehensive investigation into European heresy and the very origins of Christianity itself, finally finding expression in *The Templar Revelation: Secret Guardians of the True Identity of Christ* – which partly inspired *The Da Vinci Code.* Although the full story belongs to that book we will attempt to summarise the relevant points here.

We found that the modern Priory of Sion is part of a network of secret societies that align themselves firmly with the Johannite heresy. They also trace their descent back to the medieval Knights Templar, whose founding fathers and inner circle we discovered to be resolutely Johannite. As we have seen from the research of Noel Currer-Briggs, the families that were connected with the origins of the Templars and with those who escaped the suppression, subsequently played a role in the history of the Shroud. Those connections and the evidence of our own research strongly suggest they were also Johannite.

The Johannite tradition itself has it that the original Knights Templar learned their doctrines from 'the Johannites of the East', whom they encountered during the Crusades. It is possible now to identify this mysterious group as a sect known as the Mandaeans (whose burial practices were so mysteriously cited by Norma Weller), who until the end of the first Gulf war in 1991 were confined to Iraq and parts of Iran, but many are now refugees all over the globe from Holland to Australia. The essential points about the Mandaean religion are that they are Gnostic, venerate John the Baptist – and pour complete contempt on Jesus, whom they anathematise as 'the lying Messiah'. They claim he usurped John's following and 'perverted all the cults'. It is possible to go back even further, tracing the Mandaeans to John the Baptist's following.[27]

It came as something of a shock to us to discover that Biblical scholars have known for some time that John the Baptist and Jesus were, in fact, *rivals* – some even believe that their rivalry was bitter indeed. The concept of John as Jesus' forerunner, as the inferior who fell at his feet, is extremely unlikely to be true. The story seems to have been deliberately created by the propagandists of the Jesus faction in order to seriously misrepresent John the Baptist's status and to explain why Jesus began his career as the Baptist's subordinate. The story was also designed to explain why Jesus had to be baptised by John – the same problem covered by the legend depicted, albeit with some hidden extras, in Leonardo's *Virgin of the Rocks*.

However, the more dyed-in-the-wool Johannites seem to reserve a personal loathing for Jesus that appears to be out of all proportion to the idea that he may have stolen a few of the Baptist's followers, and a very long time ago at that – as the Mandaeans believe. But further research reveals that they claim to have good reason for this astonishingly passionate and long-lived hatred. They believe that Jesus committed a grave crime against John, one that they are unwilling to forgive, even across the space of many centuries. Although the Johannites believe that John was the Chosen One and that Jesus deliberately usurped his role, this alleged crime – as we discovered in our research for *The Templar Revelation* – eclipses even that, and prompts some serious heart-searching about the true origins of Christianity.

This is just a brief summary of a much more complex story, although it is necessary to establish that there was such a thing as the Johannite tradition. Our research also uncovered connections between Mary Magdalene, the cult of the Black Madonna and the Egyptian goddess Isis – but with apologies, that, as they say, is another story, which is also discussed in Lynn's *Mary Magdalene: Christianity's Hidden Goddess* (2003).[28]

It is also interesting that the key places in this story are dedicated to John the Baptist: Leonardo's own city of Florence itself, and the cathedral at Turin wherein the Shroud is kept. The only surviving sculpture that involved Leonardo in its making is the statue of John the Baptist above the entrance to the Baptistry in Florence. Leonardo's last painting was *St John the Baptist*, showing him with the same half smile as the *Mona Lisa*, and pointing straight upwards with the index finger of his right hand – the ubiquitous 'John gesture'. In the *Adoration of the Magi* a person stands by the elevated roots of a carob tree – John's tree – while making this gesture. In his famous Cartoon St Anne also does this with great deliberation, apparently warning an oblivious Virgin. Make of it what you will, the disciple whose face is perhaps accusingly close to Jesus' in *The Last Supper* is also making this gesture. In every case, the message is the same: 'Remember John . . .'

In October 1993 Lynn was invited by the American art historian Professor Bill Homer and his wife Christine to a dinner at the National Portrait Gallery in London. As the conversation flowed, she was asked by others at the table – international art collectors and curators of galleries – to expand on our research for this book. Not unnaturally, it caused something of a stir, but there were considerably fewer hostile or even critical comments than one might imagine. Interest was great, perhaps because, as one collector said: 'If you are right, then that piece of cloth is not only the world's first photograph, but it's also a self-portrait of da Vinci . . . My God, it is literally the world's most priceless artefact . . .'

We think it is, and for that reason we urge the Church authorities to look after it well, although they are unlikely to heed our words. But it is not just a hitherto undiscovered Leonardo; it is not just the world's first known photograph; it is considerably more even than that.

Believers have said that the Shroud is a 'time bomb', that it carries a profound spiritual message through the centuries, which will explode upon a dissolute and irreligious world when its moment has truly come. In that, we are in agreement. But the message is not what they will want to hear, even if thousands of others are already keen to do so. Leonardo regarded the Shroud as a magical talisman, an object imbued with the seeds of his own life, thrown like a message in a bottle upon the seas of the future.

With one of history's more extreme ironies, Leonardo's Shroud challenges the very religion it is supposed to personify so uniquely – not as a focus for Christian piety, but instead a savage Johannite indictment of Jesus himself. The Turin Shroud is the last object in the world to be a true Christian relic: in fact, it is a hymn to heresy. Not only do we have the subliminal message of the severed head being 'over' the crucified body, but Leonardo has gone further, carefully giving the man still-flowing blood to indicate that, as blood does not flow on a corpse, Jesus was still alive when taken down from the cross. And as he is supposed to have given his blood in a sacrificial death to save us all, a failed martyrdom effectively undermines the whole of the Christian religion. If he did not die on the cross, he was not the son of God, and the Church has been feeding its flock lies. Yes, in quite a different way, the Turin Shroud *is* a time bomb.

Nothing about Leonardo's Shroud is an accident. Every detail tells a story – his way – and it was intended to reach the widest possible audience. So it was entirely in keeping with his characteristically dark humour that he ensured that this, his most daring and innovative work, was preserved for posterity – perhaps until it was recognised for what it was – *by the very priests of the Church he so despised*. By using his photographic technique to create the ultimate Christian relic, he gave it the best chance of surviving through the centuries. If that is a good joke, there is a better one (although there are millions who would consider it rather sick). Because the image of the face is not that of Jesus, but of the artist himself, Leonardo no doubt guessed – correctly, as it turned out – that generations of pilgrims would reverently cross themselves over *his own image*. Not only has Leonardo, as the *Mona Lisa*, been hailed as 'the most beautiful woman in the world' but for centuries he has been worshipped as the Son of God . . . perhaps, some might think, an excessive achievement for just one, long-dead man. His genius in other fields almost pales in comparison. Leonardo the hoaxer and Leonardo the heretic may be new concepts to the world, but perhaps he would prefer us to recognise them rather than pore over his engineering sketches or doodles of dragons.

If as we believe, the Church originally commissioned Leonardo to fake the Shroud, then certain cabals within the Vatican must still know its real nature. In the first edition of this book, we said

'For that reason, perhaps we will find very soon that the Turin
Shroud is "stolen", or that it "disintegrates" with convenient
speed'. As events proved, this was almost prophetic, for the fire
in Turin Cathedral in April 1997 nearly destroyed the cloth.
Although reported at the time as the result of an accident,
probably due to an electrical fault in the building equipment in
the Royal Chapel, it is now virtually certain that it was arson. In
fact, the police received a warning about it earlier that evening
(in which case, one wonders why the arsonist almost succeeded
in burning the place down, especially as the cathedral was playing host to 130 distinguished guests, including the Secretary
General of the United Nations, that evening).[29] There was also,
mysteriously, an apparent delay of an hour before the fire brigade
was summoned.[30] Of course there could be many reasons – from
mindless vandalism to a political statement by Italian anarchist
groups (*autonomi*), which had been demonstrating outside the
cathedral that same day – but nobody has ever claimed responsi-
bility and no culprit has ever been found. No-one knows who
did it or why.

Even if the Turin Shroud were to be utterly destroyed – or
mysteriously vanish – tomorrow, that would not be the end of
Leonardo's story. As a grimly determined spiritual revolutionary,
he was part of a vast heretical movement spanning the centuries.
He was not working alone, and even 500 years later his ambitions are shared by new generations of Johannites – as Giovanni's
background suggests. However, the important thing about
Giovanni's information, which initially sounded so totally outrageous, was that it *actually checked out* in almost every detail. Clearly,
the Johannite secret societies of which he was a member want this
to come out. And now – as researchers having investigated this
matter for some years – so do we.

Epilogue

In His Own Image

Many critics have dismissed our theory because there is no *concrete* and unassailable evidence to link Leonardo with the Shroud – no documented connection between him and either the relic itself or its owners, the Savoys. We have presented certain thought-provoking, but unfortunately circumstantial, evidence to link the Florentine Maestro with the alleged winding sheet of Jesus, but as he and his fellow conspirators were playing a desperately dangerous game in seeking to fake the holiest relic in Christendom – the punishment for being discovered being too grim to contemplate – they would have had to work under the strictest secrecy. They would have ensured there would be no possibility of letters or other documents lying around as incriminating evidence. But of course the lack of tangible proof was ultimately enormously frustrating for us, even as fate chose us to pick up Leonardo's 'message in a bottle' for posterity.

However, just before the revised and updated edition of this book went into production, we found ourselves shaken by yet another almost magical 'eureka!' moment which answered the critics. In fact, thanks to one of those quirks of fate that seem to follow us around, we realised that evidence – if not proof – of a connection between Leonardo and the Shroud had been literally staring us in the face all along . . .

This came in the form of Leonardo's painting the *Salvator Mundi* (*Saviour of the World*). A popular theme in Christian art

and iconography from the Middle Ages it was – ironically under
the circumstances – inspired by artistic depictions of the
Mandylion, the holy cloth of Edessa, and other *acheiropoieta* ('not
made by human hands') images.[1] Of the many different versions,
Leonardo's contribution to the genre is characteristically eye-
catching and somewhat disturbing. Showing Jesus facing the
viewer, with his right hand raised in blessing and a globe held in
his left, to modern viewers it is an unappealing depiction of Jesus:
his eyes are cold, almost glacial – or perhaps utterly dead. This is
not a welcoming, and certainly not a cuddly Christ.

Not only are there contemporary references to Leonardo's
Salvator Mundi, but it was one of his most copied works – about
a dozen copies survive. His pupils even began making copies
before their Master had finished his. Leonardo's original is
known to have survived until the mid-seventeenth century, but
until recently it was believed lost.

However, in the 1970s Joanne Snow-Smith of the University
of Washington in Seattle built a strong case (set out in her 1982
book, *The Salvator Mundi of Leonardo da Vinci*) that one of the
'copies', painted on a wood panel and then in the collection of
the Marquis Jean-Louis de Ganay in Paris, was in fact Leonardo's
'lost' original. Snow-Smith's argument – which convinced many
eminent art experts and historians – was based on several lines of
enquiry, including style, use of colour, materials and technique,
as well as examination under X-rays, ultraviolet and infrared
light conducted by the Louvre laboratory. It was noted that the
technique of the *Salvator Mundi* was very similar to Leonardo's
St John the Baptist – for example the complete absence of detectable brushstrokes, a characteristic of his later work. Snow-Smith
concluded that Leonardo's *Salvator Mundi* was the result of a
commission from Louis XII of France, completed in 1513 after
Leonardo had worked on it for perhaps as long as five or six
years, at the same time as he was also painting his beloved *St John
the Baptist*.[2]

The *Salvator Mundi* had crossed our paths before. As this was Leonardo's only full-face depiction of Christ, originally we considered comparing it with the face of the man on the Shroud in case it had some secrets to divulge. However, we dropped the idea because in the early 1990s we would have had to make the comparison by hand – a complicated and laborious process of measuring and scaling up. And in any case, superficially at least, beyond showing Jesus in a similar pose, the two images are not strikingly alike: the Christ of the *Salvator Mundi* is much younger, with smooth unlined features (particularly the forehead) – perhaps a somewhat more feminine appearance than the apparently rugged Shroudman. But shortly after finishing the revisions in 2005 for this latest edition, it occurred to us that computer software readily available today would make the process of comparison much easier. So finally we did it – and suddenly our Leonardo theory had more than a glimmer of the elusive proof. Perhaps the Holy Grail of Shroud research was within our grasp at last . . .

First, we scanned photographs of Shroudman and the *Salvator Mundi*, then adjusted the digital images until they were the same scale. Then, using a standard photo-editing package (PhotoImpression 4 by ArcSoft), we simply overlaid the two images and adjusted their relative transparency so that one gradually showed more strongly through the other, enabling us at a glance to see how the two matched.

Frankly, we nearly fell off our chairs. It was immediately apparent that the faces of Leonardo's *Salvator Mundi* and the man on the Shroud – which of course we believe to be a photographic image not only by, but also of, Leonardo himself – matched *absolutely perfectly*.

All the features corresponded, as did the shape of the face, the hairline, and even the neck, which on the painting – tellingly – ends *exactly* where the 'demarcation line' is on the Shroud. And slowly increasing the transparency of the Shroud image so that the *Salvator Mundi* showed through more and more boldly gave the spooky impression that the man on the Shroud was opening his eyes and coming to life. Perhaps in a sense, he was.

Unfortunately, frozen at the moment of printing, images in a book can never reproduce the compelling drama of the evidence gradually emerging as we saw it on our computer screen, but the 'split screen' comparison between the two images in the illustration section more than makes the point.

The Moment of Truth

Having scanned images from photographs of the two works and adjusted them to the same relative size, we checked the actual size of the originals. The precise dimensions of the *Salvator Mundi* are given in Snow-Smith's book, so it was easy to work out the size of Jesus' face – 7.15 inches (18.2 cm) from hairline to chin. As we know, measuring the face of the man on the Shroud precisely is difficult because the image's outline is too faint. However, even allowing for the greatest possible leeway, we found the two images differ *at most* by just three-quarters of an inch! In other words, not only do they match each other in shape and form, but they are also the same size. Although, as Leonardo painted his Jesus life-size we would expect the two to be approximately the same size – as we noted earlier, the face of Shroudman is in the correct scale for a human being, although out of proportion against the giant's body – the closeness of the match is simply staggering.

However, we realised we had to tread carefully. Even given the impressive match, because of the faintness and fuzziness of the Shroud image we wanted to find some way of double-checking that we were not seeing what is simply not there – as in the case of those who perceive similarities between the Shroud and the tiniest of coins, or Greek letters, brooms and sponges. It occurred to us that there was a way of doing this – by comparing Leonardo's *Salvator Mundi* to Ariel Aggemian's portrait painted from a photograph of the man on the Shroud in 1935.

When we applied the same technique of overlaying the two images, once again our breath was taken away. The results were equally impressive and exciting. Yet again the two matched precisely. As the images merge into one another on the computer screen, all the features remain unchanged, with the exception of the eyes, which on the *Salvator Mundi* are larger and set slightly wider apart. Of course, as Shroudman's eyes are closed, Aggemian had to guess how they would look when open. However, although the two sets of eyes are different in size and shape, the eye sockets are identical. (The eyebrows also differ, but again Aggemian had to use his imagination.) The rest of the features, and the overall shape and size of the face, simply do not change at all. Overlaying the *Salvator Mundi* and the Aggemian portraits reveals the fact that the two faces match precisely. Despite the superficial differences at first glance, essentially *we are looking at the same man*.

The extraordinarily far-reaching implications of the discovery still took a while to sink in. Here we had two paintings, painted over 400 years apart, which matched each other perfectly. Normally, this would be explained by the fact that the later work had been copied from the earlier one. However, in this case we know that Aggemian's portrait was copied from the Turin Shroud. The only logical conclusion is that Leonardo's *Salvator Mundi* was also copied from the Shroud . . .

Of course it could be argued that we might have found such a match using other *Salvator Mundi*s, so we checked. We scanned as many other variations on the theme as we could find (obviously avoiding those based on Leonardo's), as well as other full-face depictions of Jesus dating back centuries. No other image matched that of the Shroud or Aggemian's portrait with such stunning precision as Leonardo's *Salvator Mundi*.

At the very least, it proves beyond any reasonable doubt that there *was* a connection between Leonardo and the Shroud which has been so glibly dismissed by most Shroudies. The correspondence between the two images is far too precise to be coincidental. (Despite the wealth of evidence amassed by Snow-Smith, her identification of the Marquis de Ganay's *Salvator Mundi* as Leonardo's original is not accepted by all art experts. However, even those who believe it to be a pupil's copy acknowledge that, of all the existing versions, it is by far the most faithful to Leonardo's technique and style – and therefore a true reproduction of the original.)

Of course our discovery does not prove that the rest of our hypothesis is correct: that Leonardo created the Shroud image photographically, or even necessarily that he used his own face as the model. But it proves an otherwise unrecorded and undocumented link between Leonardo and the Shroud – and that he did have a personal interest in the relic.

There are only two possible explanations for the perfect match of the two images. The most obvious is that Leonardo deliberately based his *Salvator Mundi* on the Turin Shroud. (The similarity is too great for the *Salvator Mundi* to have been painted from memory – at least he must have sketched directly from the image on the Shroud.) But *why* did he want his Christ to be identical to the Shroud? Given what we discovered about his heretical mindset – his anti-Jesus Johannitism – he of all people was unlikely to paint from the Shroud because he wanted to convey its holiness. Was the *Salvator Mundi* actually another of the real 'da Vinci codes' passed on for us in the future – a tangible clue that he was the real creator of the Shroud?

If Snow-Smith is correct, the *Salvator Mundi* was painted during the last years of Leonardo's life, in the early 1510s, when he was in Milan and the Shroud was in Chambéry. (As we believe Leonardo's substitute 'Holy Shroud' to have been on display from 1494, the *Salvator Mundi* was painted over a decade later.) If Leonardo went to see the Shroud, it is odd that no record exists of such a momentous visit – after all, he was a celebrity in his lifetime – or the fact that his painting of Christ was based on the relic. Therefore the visit must have been kept secret, for some very good reason.

There is yet another possibility. Perhaps the match can be explained if Leonardo did not paint his *Salvator Mundi* from the Shroud, but based it on *his own image* – painting himself as Christ (as had Albrecht Dürer some ten years earlier). In that case, the match between the two would prove our contention that the man on the Shroud is Leonardo. In our view, this alternative is less likely because the artist had aged so rapidly during the intervening years (the famous self-portrait in the Royal Library in Turin is usually dated to 1514, about the same time as the *Salvator Mundi*).

If we are right that the Shroud image is a photograph of Leonardo himself, then it is possible that both explanations could be correct. Tantalisingly, when painting himself as a younger man for the *Salvator Mundi*, perhaps – like many other artists since, but not before – Leonardo da Vinci simply referred to a photograph of himself for the self-portrait, hundreds of years prior to the acknowledged birth of photography. Perhaps that photograph was his greatest, if least-known work: the Shroud of Turin.

Notes and References

Introduction: Irony and Inspiration

1 'How a Nun upstaged Tom Hanks over Da Vinci Film', *Daily Mail*, 16 August 2005.

Chapter One: More Questions than Answers

1 Walsh, p. ix.

2 During the 1978 STURP examination, scientists found traces of pitch around the edges of the holes, consistent with accidental drips from a torch. See Schwalbe and Rogers.

3 Pia wrote his own account of the discovery in 'Memoria sulla riproduzione fotografia della santissima Sindone' (1907), which was reprinted in the April 1960 edition of *Sindon*. The full story is also given in Chapter Two of John Walsh's *The Shroud*.

4 *Sindon*, April 1991.

5 See for example the attempts made shortly after Pia's discovery by two Italian artists, Carlo Cussetti and Enrico Raffi, reproduced in Wilcox.

6 Enrie wrote his own account, *La Santa Sindone rivelata dalla fotografia* (Turin, 1938). Again, John Walsh gives a full account in Chapter Ten of *The Shroud*.

7 The commission's report was published in *Rivista Diocesa Torinese*, January 1976. A detailed account of their work and findings is given in Part 2 of Ian Wilson's *The Turin Shroud*.

8 Produced and directed by David Rolfe. There was also an accompanying book, written by Peter Brent and David Rolfe.

9 Brent and Rolfe, p. 9.

10 STURP's findings were published in a variety of scientific and technical journals. Summaries can be found in Ian Wilson's *The Evidence of the Shroud* and John Heller's *Report on the Shroud of Turin*. Wilson's book contains a full bibliography of STURP's papers.

11 Sox, pp. 21–2.

12 Wilson, *The Blood and the Shroud*, pp. 105–6.

13 The laboratories' full findings were published in *Nature*, on 16

February 1989 in a paper signed by all the scientists involved. For a full account of the carbon dating, see the book by Professor Gove.

14 Quoted in the *Independent*, 14 October 1988.

15 Quoted in *Fortean Times*, no. 51, p. 4.

16 Wilson, *The Turin Shroud*, p. 95.

17 Wilson, *The Evidence of the Shroud*, p. 136.

18 Wilson, *Holy Faces, Secret Places*, p. 255. In the *BSTS Newsletter* (no. 31, May 1992) Wilson, the newsletter Editor, likened the squabbling among Shroudies following the carbon dating to the fight to divide Jesus' clothes at the foot of the cross.

19 Hoare, *A Piece of Cloth*, p. 19.

20 Letter from Rodney Hoare to Clive Prince, 12 April 1993.

21 *La Contre-reforme Catholique au XXe siècle*, No. 238, April 1991.

22 Quoted in Kersten and Gruber, p. 321.

23 *BSTS Newsletter*, no. 47 (May/July 1998). Ballestrero's comments were first published in a Carmelite review, then picked up by the Italian and German media.

24 *BSTS Newsletter*, no. 35 (September 1993), pp. 18–20.

25 Wilcox, pp. 59–73.

26 Marino and Benford.

27 Rogers, 'Studies on the Radiocarbon Sample from the Shroud of Turin'. In his *Thermochimica Acta* paper, Rogers claimed not only that the 1988 dating was wrong, but that he had found another way of dating the Shroud – which showed that it could be genuine after all. This was based on measurements of vanillin, a carbohydrate produced when the lignin in linen breaks down; over time the amount of vanillin declines and eventually disappears altogether. Rogers found that samples from the Shroud did not contain any vanillin, whereas those from its backing cloth (added in 1534), and from other medieval linen cloths, do. Rogers argued that this indicates that the Shroud is much older than the other cloths – he calculated at least 1300 years old but probably more.

These conclusions have been criticised on several grounds (see, for example, Nickell, 'Claims of Invalid "Shroud" Radiocarbon Date Cut from Whole Cloth'). Again, the samples he used were simply far too small for such far-reaching conclusions. It is possible that something in the Shroud's history – the way it was stored, or the 1532 fire – affected its vanillin content. (Rogers acknowledged that heating reduces the vanillin content, but argued that the fire was not intense enough to remove so much vanillin – which as neither he nor any other modern researcher was present, is something of a specious argument.) Other critics point out that the method Rogers used to determine the amount of vanillin – in which a chemical is added that changes colour when it reacts with vanillin – is not particularly accurate, and that he ignored other more precise methods.

Finally, vanillin measurements have never been used this way before, as a way of determining the age of a cloth – so Rogers was effectively creating a whole new science. Critics say that a great many more samples, of known ages, would need to be tested before such a technique could be accepted. (For a balanced discussion of Rogers' claims, presenting both sides of the argument, see the Religious Tolerance website, www.religioustolerance.org/chr_shro7.htm.)

28 Jumper et al., pp. 454–6.
29 An examination of the underside in 2002 found that the image of the hair *does* penetrate the cloth – a very significant discovery in the light of our conclusions, as explained in Chapter 8.
30 Quoted in Sox, p. 45.
31 Vignon, *The Shroud of Christ*, p. 137.
32 Heller and Adler.
33 For example, Raymond Rogers in a talk to the BSTS in June 1980.
34 *BSTS Newsletter*, no. 42 (January 1996), pp. 6–8 (reproduced from *Avenire*, 7 October 1995).
35 Barbet, Chapter 5.
36 Quoted in ibid., p. 112.
37 ibid., Chapter 3.
38 Hoare, *A Piece of Cloth*, Chapter 6.
39 Barbet, p. 21.
40 Willis' findings are summarised in Wilson, *The Turin Shroud*, pp. 42–3.
41 Currer-Briggs, *Shroud Mafia*, pp. 27–8.
42 Hoare, *A Piece of Cloth*, p. 96.
43 Sox, pp. 26–7.
44 Foley, p. 15.
45 Alan Whanger.
46 Guscin, pp. 7–8.
47 Schonfield, p. 278.

Chapter Two: The Verdict of History

1 Thurston, 'The Turin Shroud and the Verdict of History', p. 29.
2 The letter is preserved in the Bibliothèque Nationale, Paris (Champagne Collection, vol. 154, folio 138). A translation of the full text of d'Arcis' letter by Rev. Herbert Thurston appeared in *The Month* in 1903, and is reproduced in Wilson's *The Turin Shroud* and Sox's *The Image on the Shroud*.
3 Wilson, *The Turin Shroud*, p. 100.

4 The Latin text is as follows: *Et tandem, solerti diligencia precedente et infor-macione super hoc facta, finaliter reperit fraudem et quomodo pannus ille artificialiter depictus fuerat, et probatum fuit ecian per artificem qui illum depinx-erat, ipsum humano ope factum, non miraculose confectum vel concessum.*

5 Nickell, *Inquest on the Shroud of Turin*, p. 15.

6 In the archives of the Département of the Aube.

7 Even a year later, in 1357, there was no mention of the Shroud in a list of Lirey's relics.

8 Despite this, some believers insist that the earliest date that the Shroud is known to have existed was 1353, since that is when the Lirey church was founded. To them, four or five years is seen as critical.

9 Wilson, *The Turin Shroud*, p. 241.

10 Quoted in Cope, p. 157.

11 Quoted in Nickell, *Inquest on the Shroud of Turin*, p. 23.

12 Cope, p. 157.

13 The earliest such theory was advanced by Hippolyte Chopin in 1900. A more recent version was put forward by Geoffrey Crawley in the *British Journal of Photography* in March 1967.

14 John Tyrer, *BSTS Newsletter*, December 1988. Tyrer was remarkably quick off the mark as his letter is dated 20 October 1988 – just a week after the carbon dating results were released.

15 For example, John A. T. Robinson, 'The Shroud and the New Testament' in Jennings.

16 Although generally believed to be the last of the four gospels to be written, John is the only one that claims to be derived from an eye-witness (the disciple himself). Many scholars have concluded that, because of its attention to detail and intimate knowledge of the layout and customs of the Jerusalem of Jesus' day, this gospel is indeed drawn from an eyewitness account, among other sources. See our *The Templar Revelation*, pp. 312–13 and 414–16.

17 The most thorough study is that of Maurus Green.

18 Ian Wilson, *The Blood and the Shroud*, p. 164.

19 Shaw, p. 92. (Shaw's *Chronicles of the Crusades* contains Geoffrey de Villehardouin's full account of the Fourth Crusade.)

20 Translated in vol. III of Roberts and Donaldson.

21 Cameron's inaugural lecture, 'The Sceptic and the Shroud', given in April 1980, was published as a booklet by King's College, London. Our thanks to the late Alan Wills for supplying us with a copy.

22 Currer-Briggs, *Shroud Mafia*, p. 42.

23 Ian Wilson, *The Blood and the Shroud*, pp. 175–6.

24 Ian Wilson, *Holy Faces, Secret Places*, p. 213.

25 Ian Wilson, *The Turin Shroud*, pp. 189–90.

26 ibid., p. 169.

27 Philip M. J. McNair, 'The Shroud and History: Fantasy, Fake or Fact?' in Jennings.

28 Brent and Rolfe, p. 67.

29 This great publishing debacle came to a head in 1983 when *Stern* magazine bought the alleged diaries of Adolf Hitler for $4 million, after having been assured by three handwriting experts, including Frei, that they were genuine. However, almost immediately after extracts were published in *Stern* and the *Sunday Times*, forensic tests proved that the diaries were in fact crude fakes. Frei had made the mistake of using for his comparison forged handwriting samples supplied to him from the same source as the diaries, despite the ready availability of genuine samples of the Führer's handwriting. See Robert Harris, pp. 181–2 and 195–6.

30 Schwalbe and Rogers, p. 47.

31 Ian Wilson, *The Blood and the Shroud*, p. 121.

32 Nickell, 'Pollens on the "Shroud"', p. 382.

33 Ian Wilson, *The Blood and the Shroud*, pp. 119–21.

34 ibid., p. 121.

35 Nickell, 'Pollens on the "Shroud"', p 384.

36 ibid.

37 See Ian Wilson, *The Turin Shroud*, pp. 215–6, and Currer-Briggs, *The Shroud and the Grail*, pp. 105–6.

38 Currer-Briggs, *The Shroud and the Grail*, Chapters 5 and 6.

39 See Ian Wilson, *The Evidence of the Shroud*, pp. 107–10.

40 For summaries of Whanger's claims, see Danin, 'Pressed Flowers' and Iannone, 'Floral Images and Pollen Grains on the Shroud of Turin'.

41 See, for example, Ian Wilson's Editorial in *BSTS Newsletter* no. 46 (Nov/Dec 1997).

42 Danin and Baruch.

43 See Bryant's review of the book by Danin, Baruch and the Whangers in *Palynos: Newsletter of the International Federation of Palynological Studies*, vol. 23, no. 1, June 2000, pp. 10–14

44 ibid., p. 14.

45 Ian Wilson, *Holy Faces, Secret Places*, Chapter 12.

46 Cope, Plate VII.

47 Ian Wilson, *The Blood and the Shroud*, pp. 168–71.

Chapter Three: Theories

1 Schwalbe and Rogers, p. 45.

2 Hoare, *A Piece of Cloth*, p. 139.

3 On thoughtography, see Picknett *Encyclopaedia of the Paranormal*, pp. 79–80.

4 See Ian Wilson, *The Turin Shroud*, Chapter 24. The theory was postulated as long ago as 1931 by P. W. O'Gorman.

5 For example, Ian Wilson, *The Turin Shroud*, pp. 280–1.

6 Rogers, 'The Shroud of Turin: Radiation Effects, Aging and Image Formation'.

7 Hoare argued that the Shroud proves that the Resurrection was simply a recovery from coma, which shows that Jesus was purely human and not divine. Oddly, Hoare did not see this as an obstacle to his Anglicanism, and moreover believed that the Shroud has been divinely protected to bring this 'message' to the present day, when it will be the instrument that will bring about the reconciliation of Christians, Jews and Muslims. (Hoare, *The Testimony of the Shroud*, p. 122.)

8 Ian Wilson, 'Riddle of the Dead Man's Hand'. See also *Fortean Times*, no. 51, p. 7.

9 McCrone, 'Authenticity of Medieval Document tested by Small-Particle Analysis'.

10 Cahill *et al*. For an account of the controversy see Shoemaker.

11 Quoted in Shoemaker, p. 24.

12 Sox, p. 22.

13 McCrone published his results in a series of three articles in *The Microscope* and in his book *Judgment Day for the Shroud of Turin*. The full text of McCrone's second report to STURP (rejected by them) is given in Sox, Appendix B.

14 Ian Wilson, *The Evidence of the Shroud*, p. 63.

15 Details of this highly technical debate – much of which went on only in private correspondence and the pages of STURP's internal newsletter – are given in Sox.

16 Morris, Schwalbe and London.

17 Heller and Adler, 'A Chemical Investigation of the Shroud of Turin'.

18 Heller and Adler, 'Blood on the Shroud of Turin'.

19 See Sox, p. 35.

20 Published in the first of *The Microscope* articles.

21 Sox, p. 39.

22 Ian Wilson, *The Evidence of the Shroud*, pp. 87–8.

23 Nickell, *Inquest on the Shroud of Turin*, Chapter 9.

24 See Sox, p. 88, and César Tort's letter in the *Journal of the Society for Psychical Research*, vol. 56, no. 820 (July 1990).

25 For example, Ian Wilson, *The Turin Shroud*, pp. 277–8.

26 Hoare, *A Piece of Cloth*, p. 72.

27 Freeland's work remains unpublished but is quoted extensively in Sox.

28 Nickell, *Inquest on the Shroud of Turin*, p. 60.
29 Anthony Harris, p. 77.
30 Ian Wilson, *The Blood and the Shroud*, p. 59.
31 ibid., pp. 59–62.
32 Schwalbe and Rogers, p. 10.

Chapter Four: Correspondents

1 Quoted in Ian Wilson, *Holy Faces, Secret Places*, p. 33.
 2 Baigent, Leigh and Lincoln, *The Messianic Legacy*, p. 284.
 3 *Leonardo – The Man Behind the Shroud*, produced by Stefilm and
    HIT Wildlife for the National Geographic Channel, directed by
    Susan Gray, 2001.
 4 For a fuller account of the Rennes-le-Château mystery see
    Chapters 7 and 8 of our *The Templar Revelation*. On its connection
    with the Priory of Sion, see Chapters 3 and 4 of our *The Sion
    Revelation*.
 5 It is frequently stated that Saunière suffered the heart attack or
    stroke that was to kill him on 17 January, a date of special signifi-
    cance to the Priory of Sion. However, while the priest was struck
    down a few days before his death, contemporary records do not
    specify the precise date. Fixing it as 17 January seems to have been
    part of the later mythmaking to which the Saunière affair has been
    subjected.
 6 'The Lost Treasure of Jerusalem?' (1972), 'The Priest, the Painter
    and the Devil' (1974) and 'The Shadow of the Templars' (1979).
    All three were part of the BBC's *Chronicle* series.
 7 A complete list of the alleged Grand Masters is given in Appendix
    One of *The Sion Revelation*.
 8 There is evidence, unknown to us at the time of writing the first
    edition of this book, that the Priory of Sion was indeed going
    through a period of internal upheaval at that time – see *The Sion
    Revelation*, pp. 36–8.
 9 Robert Anton Wilson.
10 This is discussed more fully in *The Sion Revelation*, Chapter 6.
11 Letter from Ian Wilson to Clive Prince, 5 June 1991.
12 Phone conversation between Lynn Picknett and Ian Dickinson,
    January 1994.
13 Kersten and Gruber, p. 64.

Chapter Five: 'Faust's Italian Brother'

1 Quoted in Rinaldi, p. 37.
 2 Brent and Rolfe, p. 78.
 3 Ian Wilson, *The Evidence of the Shroud*, p. 82.

Notes and References

4 Currer-Briggs, *The Shroud and the Grail,* p. 31.

5 Kersten and Gruber, p. 15.

6 See Ian Wilson, *The Evidence of the Shroud*, Chapter 5.

7 Anthony Harris, Chapter 3.

8 Augusto Marinoni, 'The Bicycle', Appendix to Reti, vol. II.

9 Quigley, p. 32.

10 Bramly, p. 443.

11 Baigent, Leigh and Lincoln, *The Holy Blood and the Holy Grail*, p. 126.

12 The story of the Rosicrucian Manifestos, and the subsequent growth of the movement is told in Yates's *The Rosicrucian Enlightenment*, which includes translations of the full texts of the Manifestos.

13 The man generally accepted as the author of the Rosicrucian Manifestos, Johann Valentin Andreae, was also responsible for setting up the Christian Unions, a network of secret societies devoted to preserving knowledge threatened by the Counter-Reformation. Some believe that these groups either became, or at least influenced, the lodge system of Freemasonry. Andreae is claimed by the Priory of Sion as its seventeenth Grand Master. See Baigent, Leigh and Lincoln, *The Holy Blood and the Holy Grail*, pp. 144–8.

14 See Thompson, Chapter XXII.

15 The Priory of Sion, in its *Dossiers secrets*, claims that the Rosicrucians emerged from its higher degrees.

16 This diagram is reproduced in several books on the Rosicrucians and the Cabala – see, for example, Spence, p. 341 – but appeared originally in a work by B. Arius Montanus entitled *Antiquitatum Judacarum Libri IX*. The British Library copy of this work is reported as having been stolen. We are indebted to Gareth Medway for this information.

17 Yates, *Giordano Bruno and the Hermetic Tradition*, p. 435.

18 Yates, *The Art of Memory*, p. 224.

19 Yates, *The Occult Philosophy in the Elizabethan Age*, pp. 40–1.

20 See Chapter 17 of Yates' *The Art of Memory* for a discussion of the influence of occult thought on the growth of the scientific method.

21 Yates, *The Art of Memory*, pp. 153 and 309–11.

22 Yates, *The Occult Philosophy in the Elizabethan Age*, pp. 14–15.

23 Yates, *Giordano Bruno and the Hermetic Tradition*, pp. 76–7.

24 Yates, *The Occult Philosophy in the Elizabethan Age*, p. 187.

25 See Yates, *Giordano Bruno and the Hermetic Tradition*, Chapters IV and V.

26 Hook, p. 11.

27 ibid., p 12.
28 Leonardo wrote that he would not let his body become 'a tomb for other animals, an inn of the dead . . . a container of corruption' (*Codex Atlanticus*, 76, quoted in Bramly, p. 240).
29 Bramly, p. 13.
30 ibid., p. 357. Besides his collaboration with Rustici, Leonardo had a long association with the occultist Tomaso Masini (who used the name 'Zoroastro de Peretola'), with whom he travelled from Florence to the court of Milan in 1482. In 1493, Masini joined Leonardo's household and was still recorded as an assistant during his return to Florence in 1503. Leonardo's protector and patron in Rome during the period 1513–1515 was Giuliano de Medici (the son of Lorenzo and brother of Pope Leo X), who was an alchemist.
31 ibid., p. 387.
32 The French historian Jules Michelet, quoted in ibid., p. 12.
33 ibid.
34 The Cathar heresy did in fact survive in northern Italy long after it had been suppressed in France. See Birks and Gilbert, pp. 73–6.
35 Rowden, p. 28.
36 Vasari, pp. 208–13.
37 ibid., p. 270.
38 Baigent, Leigh and Lincoln, *The Holy Blood and the Holy Grail*, pp. 448–9.
39 *Codex Atlanticus* (Ambrosiana, Milan), 159, quoted in Bramly, p. 384.
40 On the previously unseen side of sheets in the *Codex Atlanticus*, until 1965 glued on to pages of the *Codex*.
41 Bramly, p. 121.
42 Schwartz.
43 Reported in *The Times*, 14 December 1992.
44 See Holroyd and Powell, p. 239.
45 ibid., p. 144.
46 ibid., p. 143.
47 'Witch using a Magic Mirror' is the title by which the French scholar Grillot de Givry – who acknowledges (p. 306) a possible 'alchemistic meaning' – refers to the sketch. However, Christ College, Oxford, the owners of the drawing, officially list it as 'Allegory alluding to the political state of Milan'.
48 De Givry, p. 350.
49 Quoted in Leonardo da Vinci, *The Notebooks of Leonardo da Vinci*, p. 10.
50 Holroyd and Powell, p. 162.
51 De Givry, p. 384.
52 Bramly, p. 25.

53 Manuscript 19054v in the Royal Collection at Windsor.

Chapter Six: The Shroud Conspiracy

1 Cocteau, *Journal d'un inconnu*, p. 143. (Authors' translation.)
2 In his Foreword to Jennings.
3 Some believers – for example, Mgr. Arthur Stapylton Barnes writing in the 1930s – have attempted to argue that the Shroud was actually kept in Besançon Cathedral before being acquired by the de Charnys, and that the Besançon copy was made at this time. There is not a shred of evidence to support this theory, which is simply a conjecture based on the desire to give the Shroud a pre-Lirey provenance. The Besançon Shroud was a sixteenth-century copy – see Ian Wilson, *The Turin Shroud*, p. 342.
4 Ian Wilson, *The Blood and the Shroud*, p. 147.
5 For example, Nickell, *Inquest on the Shroud of Turin*, p. 12.
6 Quoted in Humber, p. 120.
7 Ian Wilson, 'Mystery of the Missing Mandylion'.
8 Ian Wilson, *The Evidence of the Shroud*, p. 70.
9 See pages 273–4.
10 The document is included in Chevalier. Sixtus' account refers only to the Shroud being 'preserved with great devotion' by the Savoys with no details of where or how it was kept.
11 Quoted in de Rosa, p. 141.
12 Colin Wilson, p. 345.
13 *Codex* of the Earl of Leicester (kept at Holkham Hall, Norfolk), 10v, and the *Codex Atlanticus*, 87v. See Leonardo da Vinci, *The Notebooks of Leonardo da Vinci*, p. 333.
14 Reti, p. 59.
15 Sox, p. 31.
16 Ian Wilson, *The Evidence of the Shroud*, p. 70.
17 Smyth, pp. 288–9.
18 By convention, the Templar Geoffrey's family name is spelt 'Charnay'. For consistency, we have used the 'Charny' spelling throughout this chapter. There is no significance in the different versions as there was no standard spelling in the fourteenth century and the name appears in many other variations in documents of the period.
19 Ian Wilson, *The Turin Shroud*, pp. 222–3.
20 ibid., pp. 200–15.
21 See Barber and Chapters 3 and 4 of Partner.
22 Currer-Briggs, *The Shroud and the Grail*, pp. 90–1.
23 Kersten and Gruber, p. 203.
24 Ian Wilson, *The Turin Shroud*, pp. 208–9.

25 Currer-Briggs, *The Shroud and the Grail*, Chapter 1.
26 It is even possible that Jacques de Molay himself (whose ancestry is a matter of dispute among historians) may have been related to the de Charny and de Vergy families, being the son of Henri de Vergy, the great-grandfather of the Lirey Geoffrey de Charny's wife. See ibid., p. 111.
27 ibid., p. 114.
28 ibid., p. 150.
29 See Shaw, Introduction.
30 The standard historical account of the early days of the Templars is entirely based on William of Tyre's *A History of Deeds Done Beyond the Sea*, written between 1175 and 1185.
31 Hancock, Chapter 5.
32 See Baigent, Leigh and Lincoln, *The Holy Blood and the Holy Grail*, pp. 85–6.
33 ibid., p. 88.
34 ibid.
35 Currer-Briggs, *The Shroud and the Grail*, p. 135.
36 ibid., p. 152.
37 ibid., p. 176.
38 ibid., p. 34.
39 Baigent, Leigh and Lincoln, *The Holy Blood and the Holy Grail*, p. 316.
40 John, p. 302.
41 Archives Nationales, JJ77, No. 395.

Chapter Seven: Getting the Measure of Shroudman

1 We discussed the possibility of computer matching the images with Lillian Schwartz herself when she visited London in the summer of 1993. Over dinner with Lillian, her husband Jack and our colleague Tony Pritchett (who used to work with Lillian at the Bell Laboratories in America), we outlined our theory and showed her pictures of the Shroud and portraits of Leonardo. Although captivated by the idea – she is a Leonardophile – she, too, pointed out the near-impossibility of proving the connection using the available portraits.
2 Bramly, p. 17.
3 ibid., p. 422.
4 Letter from Ian Wilson to Clive Prince, 12 April 1991.
5 During questions at Lynn Picknett's talk 'Did Leonardo da Vinci Fake the Turin Shroud?' at the London Earth Mysteries Circle, 9 April 1991.
6 Quoted in Wilcox, pp. 30–1.

7 Nickell, *Inquest on the Shroud of Turin*, p. 109.
8 Ian Wilson, *The Blood and the Shroud*, p. 30.
9 Hoare, *A Piece of Cloth*, p. 75.
10 De Rosa, p. 3.
11 Nickell, *Inquest on the Shroud of Turin*, p. 86.
12 Don Devan, John Jackson and Eric Jumper, 'Computer Related Investigations of the Holy Shroud' and John Jackson, Eric Jumper, William Mottern and Kenneth Stevenson, 'The Three Dimensional Image on Jesus' Burial Cloth', both in Stevenson.
13 Kersten and Gruber, p. 297.
14 This and the following quotes are from Nickell, *Inquest on the Shroud of Turin*, pp. 88–92.
15 Ian Wilson, *The Turin Shroud,* p. 258.
16 Ian Wilson, *The Evidence of the Shroud*, pp. 47–9.
17 Quoted in Sox, pp. 106–7.
18 Vala's work was first published in *Amateur Photographer* in March 1967. His sculpture – pictured for example in Wilcox's *Shroud* – vividly illustrates the unnaturalness of the hairline and the foreshortening of the forehead.

Chapter Eight: Positive Developments

1 Manuscript A in the Library of the Institut de France, quoted in Reti, vol II, p. 135.
2 *Codex* of the Earl of Leicester, 22, quoted in Bramly, p. 313.
3 See Leonardo da Vinci, *The Notebooks of Leonardo da Vinci*, pp. 107–17.
4 Manuscript C of the Library of the Institut de France, cited in Bramly, p. 263.
5 Leonardo's method is described in Eder's *History of Photography*, pp. 33–40.
6 'The Spirit of the Shroud', *The Times*, 14 October 1988.
7 Brent and Rolfe, pp. 130–4.
8 In a treatise entitled *Perspectiva communis*.
9 *Codex Atlanticus*, vol. D, folio 8. See Leonardo da Vinci, *The Notebooks of Leonardo da Vinci*, p. 113.
10 Manuscript D of the Library of the Institut de France, cited in ibid., p. 115.
11 See Eder, pp. 40–2.
12 Rowden, p. 117.
13 Letter from Rodney Hoare to Clive Prince, 10 October 1991.
14 Pliny, *Natural History*, xxxiii, 55.
15 Eder, p. 15.
16 Neblette, p. 1.

17 Stroebel and Zaka, p. 709
18 Eder, p. 77.
19 *Forster Codex I*, 44v, Victoria and Albert Museum.
20 Bramly, pp. 386–7.
21 The first patented process exploiting this principle was that of Scot Mungo Ponton in 1839. There were many variations of the basic process, for example the gum-bichromate process, Artigues process and the carbon process. The method led to the development of photo-mechanical printing processes, allowing the reproduction of photographs in print, as it could be used to create printing blocks from photographs.
22 Gelatin reacts to ultraviolet light on its own, without the addition of chemical sensitisers. However (although we have not tried it experimentally) the reaction would certainly be much slower when unsensitised, to the point that exposure times become impractical.
23 Gragson, p. 277.
24 *Codex Atlanticus*, 313v. See Bramly, p. 372. Leonardo gives part of the recipe, which consists, significantly, of egg white, glue and several vegetable dyes.
25 A similar technique was proposed as that used by the Shroud's forger by Nathan Wilson, a Fellow of Literature at St Andrews College in Idaho, who announced his discovery in the magazine *Book and Culture* in March 2005. Wilson painted an image on a sheet of glass and placed this over a cloth, then simply left it out in the sun for several days. The sun bleached the cloth, creating a negative image.
26 Based on the manufacturer's technical data. Exact calculations are difficult because of the many variables involved, such as the number of lamps used, the distances between lamp and subject and between subject and camera, and the reflectivity of the subject.
27 Ian Wilson, 'The New, Restored Turin Shroud'.

Chapter Nine: Leonardo's Last Testament

1 Manuscript F of the Institut de France, 5v, quoted in Bramly, p. 274.
2 A one-paragraph item appeared in the on-line section of the *Guardian* (15 September 1994), with a longer article in *The Times* the following day.
3 Produced by Trevor Poots and directed by Nikki Stockley.
4 Allen's papers can be found on his website, www.petech.ac.za/ shroud. His critique of our Leonardo theory is in 'How Leonardo did *not* fake the Shroud of Turin'.
5 Ian Wilson, *The Blood and the Shroud*, pp. 274–5.
6 *Fortean Times*, no. 71 (November 1993), p. 65.
7 Letter from Ian Wilson to Clive Prince, 18 April 1991.

8 Weller, 'Concerning the Meeting on May 27 1992'.
9 Gündüz, p. 78.
10 Letter from Michael Clift to Clive Prince, 21 February 1993.
11 Letter from Rodney Hoare to Lynn Picknett, 12 April 1993.
12 Letter from Rodney Hoare to Clive Prince, 29 May 1993.
13 Letter from Rodney Hoare to Clive Prince, 28 June 1993.
14 Piczek.
15 Ian Wilson, *The Blood and the Shroud*, p. 245.
16 ibid., p. 250.
17 ibid., p. 232.
18 See Sorensen for a typical example of the believers' response to our hypothesis. Sorensen lists a number of objections, but fails to mention that we have addressed, and supplied counter-arguments to, *every one* of them. While he personally might disagree with those counter-arguments, ignoring the fact that we have even made them suggests a zeal to dismiss our work once and for all.
19 Ian Wilson, *The Blood and the Shroud*, p. 129.
20 ibid., pp. 338–9.
21 Letter from Ian Wilson to Lynn Picknett, 11 June 1990.
22 Translation of the report of Saldarini's press conference from, *Il Tempo*, (6 September 1995), in *Shroud News*, no. 90 (1995).
23 Knight and Lomas, *The Second Messiah*, pp. 154–5.
24 ibid., pp. 155–6.
25 Laidler, *The Divine Deception*, pp. 201–6.
26 Bramly, pp. 262–3.
27 On the Mandaeans, see our *The Templar Revelation*, Chapter 15.
28 See ibid., Chapter 3, and Lynn's *Mary Magdalene*, Chapter 6.
29 Ian Wilson, *The Blood and the Shroud*, p. 2.
30 *Fortean Times*, no. 100 (July 1997), p. 11. This account of the event is drawn from a variety of newspaper reports.

Epilogue: In His Own Image

1 Snow-Smith, Chapter 5.
2 ibid., pp. 18–25.

Bibliography

Main entries are for the editions cited in the text. Where this is not the first edition, details of the original publication (where known) follow in brackets.

Allen, Nicholas P. L., 'Is the Shroud of Turin the First Recorded Photograph?', Port Elizabeth Technikon website, ww.petech.ac.za/shroud/isthe.htm, 1993
—— 'Verification of the Nature and Causes of the Photo-negative Images on the Shroud of Lirey-Chambéry-Turin', Port Elizabeth Technikon website, www.petech.ac.za/shroud/nature.htm, 1995
—— 'How Leonardo did *not* fake the Shroud of Turin', Port Elizabeth Technikon website, www.petech.ac.za/shroud/leonard, 1995
—— *The Turin Shroud and the Crystal Lens: Testament to a Lost Technology*, Empowerment Technologies Pty, Port Elizabeth, 1998

Baigent, Michael, and Richard Leigh, *The Temple and the Lodge*, Jonathan Cape, London, 1989
Baigent, Michael, Richard Leigh and Henry Lincoln, *The Holy Blood and the Holy Grail*, revised edition, Arrow, London, 1996 (Jonathan Cape, London, 1982)
—— *The Messianic Legacy*, Jonathan Cape, London, 1986
Barber, Malcolm, *The Trial of the Templars*, Cambridge University Press, Cambridge, 1978
Barbet, Pierre, *A Doctor at Calvary: The Passion of Our Lord Jesus Christ as Described by a Surgeon*, Image Books, New York, 1963 (*Le passion de N-S Jésus Christ selon le chirurgien*, Dillen & Cie, Paris, 1950)
Birks, Walter, and R. A. Gilbert, *The Treasure of Montségur: A Study of the Cathar Heresy and the Nature of the Cathar Secret*, Crucible, Wellingborough, 1987
Boussel, Patrice, *Leonardo da Vinci*, Tiger Books, London, 1992
Bramly, Serge, *Leonardo: The Artist and the Man*, Michael Joseph, London, 1992 (*Léonard de Vinci*, Éditions Jean-Claude Lattés, Paris, 1988)
Brent, Peter, and David Rolfe, *The Silent Witness*, Futura, London, 1978

Brucker, Gene A., *Renaissance Florence*, John Wiley & Sons, London, 1969

Burman, Edward, *The Templars: Knights of God*, Crucible, London, 1986

Cahill, T. A., *et al.*, 'The Vinland Map Revisited: New Compositional Evidence on its Inks and Parchment,' *Analytical Chemistry*, no. 59, 1987

Cameron, Averil, *The Sceptic and the Shroud*, King's College, London, 1980

Cavendish, Richard, *A History of Magic*, Weidenfeld & Nicolson, London, 1977

Chevalier, Ulysses, *Étude critique sur l'origine de Sainte Suaire de Lirey-Chambéry-Turin*, A. Picard, Paris, 1900

Clark, Kenneth, *Leonardo da Vinci: An Account of his Development as an Artist*, Cambridge University Press, Cambridge, 1940

Coe, Brian, and Mark Haworth-Booth, *A Guide to Early Photographic Processes*, Victoria and Albert Museum, London, 1983

Cope, Christopher, *Phoenix Frustrated: The Lost Kingdom of Burgundy*, Constable, London, 1986

Currer-Briggs, Noel, *The Shroud and the Grail: A Modern Quest for the True Grail*, Weidenfeld & Nicolson, London, 1987

—— *Shroud Mafia: The Creation of a Relic?*, The Book Guild, Lewes, 1995

Danin, Avinoam, 'Pressed Flowers: Where did the Shroud of Turin Originate? A Botanical Quest', *Eretz*, Nov/Dec 1997

Danin, Avinoam, and Uri Baruch, 'Floristic Indicators for the Origin of the Shroud of Turin', Shroud of Turin website, www.shroud.com/pdfs/daninx.pdf (paper originally presented at the International Congress on the Shroud of Turin, Turin, 6 June 1998)

Danin, Avinoam, Alan D. Whanger, Uri Baruch and Mary Whanger, *Flora of the Shroud of Turin*, Missouri Botanical Garden Press, St Louis, 1999

de Givry, Grillot, *Witchcraft, Magic and Alchemy*, G. G. Harrap, London, 1931 (*La musée des sorciers, mages et alchimistes*, Librairie de France, Paris, 1929)

de Rosa, Peter, *Vicars of Christ: The Dark Side of the Papacy*, Bantam Press, London, 1988

Doerner, Max, *The Materials of the Artist and Their Use in Painting*, revised edition, Rupert Hart-Davis, London, 1969 (G. G. Harrap, London, 1935)

Eder, Josef Maria, *History of Photography*, Columbia University Press, New York, 1945 (*Geshichte der Photographie*, Knapp, Halle am Saale, 1932)

Eisler, Robert, *The Messiah Jesus and John the Baptist, according to Flavius Josephus' 'Capture of Jerusalem'*, Methuen & Co., London, 1931

Filas, Francis, *The Dating of the Shroud of Turin from Coins of Pontius Pilate*, Cogan Productions, Arizona, 1982

Foley, Fr Charles, 'Ablatio', *Shroud News*, no. 89, June 1995

Frei, Max, 'Nine Years of Palynological Studies on the Shroud', *Shroud Spectrum International*, no. 3, 1982

Garza-Valdès, Leoncio A., *The DNA of God?: The True Story of the Scientist who Re-established the Case for the Authenticity of the Shroud of Turin and Discovered its Incredible Secrets*, Doubleday, New York, 1999

Gove, Harry E., *Relic, Icon or Hoax?: Carbon Dating the Turin Shroud*, Institute of Physics Publishing, Philadelphia, 1996

Gragson, Martin, *The Kirk-Othmer Encyclopedia of Chemical Terminology*, John Wiley & Sons, New York, 1985

Green, Maurus, 'Enshrouded in Silence', *Ampleforth Journal*, no. 74, 1969

Gündüz, Sinasi, *The Knowledge of Life: The Origins and Early History of the Mandaeans and Their Relation to the Sabians of the Qur'an and to the Harranians*, Oxford University Press, Oxford, 1994

Guscin, Mark, 'Nice 12–13 May, 1997: Some notes on the Nice Symposium', *BSTS Newsletter*, no. 46, Nov/Dec 1997

Haeffner, Mark, *The Dictionary of Alchemy*, Aquarian Press, London, 1991

Hancock, Graham, *The Sign and the Seal: A Quest for the Lost Ark of the Covenant*, William Heinemann, London, 1992

Harris, Anthony, *The Sacred Virgin and the Holy Whore*, Sphere, London, 1988

Harris, Robert, *Selling Hitler: The Story of the Hitler Diaries*, Faber & Faber, London, 1986

Heller, John H., *Report on the Shroud of Turin*, Houghton Mifflin, Boston, 1983

Heller, J., and A. Adler, 'Blood on the Shroud of Turin', *Applied Optics*, vol. 19, no. 12, June 1980

—— 'A Chemical Investigation of the Shroud of Turin', *Canadian Society of Forensic Science Journal*, vol. 14, no. 3, 1981

Hoare, Rodney, *The Testimony of the Shroud: Deductions from the Photographic and Written Evidence of the Crucifixion and Resurrection of Jesus Christ*, Quartet, London, 1978

—— *A Piece of Cloth: The Turin Shroud Investigated*, Aquarian Press, Wellingborough, 1984

—— *The Turin Shroud is Genuine: The Irrefutable Evidence*, Souvenir Press, London, 1994

Holroyd, Stuart, and Neil Powell, *Mysteries of Magic*, Bloomsbury Books, London, 1991 (first published as separate volumes: Stuart Holroyd, *Magic, Words and Numbers*, and Neil Powell, *The Supernatural: Alchemy, the Ancient Science*, both Aldus Books, London, 1976)

Hook, Judith, *Lorenzo de Medici: An Historical Biography*, Hamish Hamilton, London, 1984

Humber, Thomas, *The Fifth Gospel*, Pocket Books, New York, 1974

Iannone, John C., *The Mystery of the Turin Shroud: New Scientific Evidence*, Alba House, New York, 1998

—— 'Floral Images and Pollen Grains on the Shroud of Turin': An Interview with Dr Alan Whanger and Dr Avinoam Danin', Shroud of Turin website, www.shroud.com/iannone.pdf, undated

Jennings, Peter (ed.), *Face to Face with the Turin Shroud*, Mayhew-McCrimmon & A. R. Mowbray, London, 1978

John, Eric (ed.), *The Popes: A Concise Biographical History*, Burns & Oates, London, 1964

Johnson, Kenneth Rayner, 'The Image of Perfection', *The Unexplained*, no. 45, 1982

Jumper, E., A. Adler, J. Jackson, S. Pellicori, J. Heller and J. Druzic, 'A Comprehensive Examination of the Various Stains and Images on the Shroud of Turin', *Advances in Chemistry*, series. 205, 1984.

Kemp, Martin, *Leonardo da Vinci: The Marvellous Works of Nature and Man*, J. M. Dent & Sons, London, 1981

Kersten, Holger, and Elmar R. Gruber, *The Jesus Conspiracy: The Turin Shroud and the Truth about the Resurrection*, Element Books, Shaftesbury, 1994 (*Das Jesus Komplott*, Langen Verlag, Munich, 1992)

Knight, Christopher, and Robert Lomas, *The Hiram Key: Pharaohs, Freemasons and the Discovery of the Secret Scrolls of Jesus*, Century, London, 1996

—— *The Second Messiah: Templars, the Turin Shroud and the Great Secret of Freemasonry*, Century, London, 1997

Kosar, Jaromir, *Light-Sensitive Systems: Chemistry and Application of Nonsilver Halide Photographic Processes*, John Wiley & Sons, New York, 1965

Laidler, Keith, *The Head of God: The Lost Secret of the Templars*, Weidenfeld & Nicolson, London, 1998

—— *The Divine Deception: The Church, the Shroud and the Creation of a Holy Fraud*, Headline, London, 2001 (first edition 2000)

Leonardo da Vinci (ed. Jean Paul Richter and Irma A. Richter), *The Literary Works of Leonardo da Vinci, Compiled and Edited from the Original Manuscripts*, Oxford University Press, Oxford, 1939 (ed. Irma A. Richter)
—— *The Notebooks of Leonardo da Vinci*, Oxford University Press, Oxford, 1952

Marino, Joseph G., and M. Sue Benford, 'Evidence for the Skewing of the C-14 Dating of the Shroud of Turin due to Repairs', Shroud of Turin website, www.shroud.com/pdfs/marben.pdf, 2000
McCrone, W. C., 'Authenticity of Medieval Document tested by Small-Particle Analysis', *Analytical Chemistry*, no. 48, 1976
—— *Judgment Day for the Turin Shroud*, Microscope Publications, Chicago, 1996
Mills, Allan A., 'Image Formation on the Shroud of Turin: The Reactive Oxidation Intermediates Hypothesis', *Interdisciplinary Science Reviews*, vol. 20, No. 4, December 1995
Morris, R. A., L. A. Schwalbe and J. R. London, 'X-Ray Fluorescence Investigation of the Shroud of Turin', *Journal of the Canadian Society of Forensic Science*, vol. 14, no. 3, 1981

Neblette, C. B., *Photography: Its Materials and Processes*, 6th edition, Van Nostrand Reinhold, New York, 1962
Nickell, Joe, *Inquest on the Shroud of Turin*, revised edition, Prometheus Books, Amherst, 1987 (first edition 1983)
—— 'Pollens on the "Shroud": A Study in Deception', *Skeptical Inquirer*, vol. 18, Summer 1994
—— 'Claims of Invalid "Shroud" Radiocarbon Date Cut from Whole Cloth', CSICOP website, www.csicop.org/specialarticles/shroud.html, 2005

Partner, Peter, *The Murdered Magicians: The Templars and their Myth*, Oxford University Press, Oxford, 1981
Picknett, Lynn, (ed.), *The Encyclopaedia of the Paranormal: A Complete Guide to the Unexplained*, Macmillan, London, 1990
—— *Mary Magdalene: Christianity's Hidden Goddess*, Robinson, 2003
—— *The Secret History of Lucifer*, Robinson, London, 2005
Picknett, Lynn, and Clive Prince, *The Templar Revelation: Secret Guardians of the True Identity of Christ*, Bantam Press, London, 1997
—— *The Sion Revelation: Inside the Shadowy World of Europe's Secret Masters*, Time Warner, London, 2006
Piczek, Isabel, 'Alice in Wonderland and the Shroud of Turin', Shroud of Turin website, www.shroud.com/piczek2.htm, 1996

Quigley Jr., Martin, *Magic Shadows: The Story of the Origin of Motion Pictures*, Georgetown University Press, Washington DC, 1948

Reti, Ladislao (ed.), *The Unknown Leonardo*, 3 vols, McGraw-Hill, New York, 1974

Rinaldi, Peter M., *The Man in the Shroud*, Futura, London, 1974

Robert de Clari (trans. and ed. Edgar H. McNeal), *The Conquest of Constantinople*, Columbia University Press, New York, 1936

Roberts, Rev. Alexander, and Sir James Donaldson, (eds), *The Ante-Nicene Christan Library: Translations of the Writings of the Fathers Down to AD 325*, 25 vols, T & T Clark, Edinburgh, 1867–97

Robinson, John J., *Born in Blood: The Lost Secrets of Freemasonry*, Century, London, 1990

Rogers, Raymond N., 'Studies on the Radiocarbon Sample from the Shroud of Turin', *Thermochimica Acta*, vol. 425, issues 1–2, January 2005

—— 'The Shroud of Turin: Radiation Effects, Aging and Image Formation', Shroud of Turin website, www.shroud.com/pdfs/rogers8. pdf, 2005

Rowden, Maurice, *Leonardo da Vinci*, Weidenfeld & Nicolson, London, 1975

Schonfield, Hugh J., *The Pentecost Revolution: The Story of the Jesus Party in Israel, AD 36–66*, Hutchinson, London, 1974

Schwalbe, L. A., and R. N. Rogers, 'Physics and Chemistry of the Shroud of Turin: A Summary of the 1978 Investigation', *Analytica Chimica Arta*, 135, 1982

Schwartz, Lillian, 'Leonardo's Mona Lisa', *Art and Antiques*, January 1987

Shaw, M. R. B. (ed. and trans.), *Chronicles of the Crusades*, Penguin, London, 1963

Shoemaker, Michael T., 'Debunking the Debunkers: The Vinland Map', *Strange Magazine*, no. 3, 1988

Siren, Osvald, *Leonardo da Vinci: The Artist and the Man*, Oxford University Press, Oxford, 1916

Smyth, Frank, 'Is this the Face of Christ?', *The Unexplained*, no. 18, 1981

Snow-Smith, Joanne, *The Salvator Mundi of Leonardo da Vinci*, University of Michigan Press, Seattle, 1982

Sorensen, Richard B., 'Answering the Savoy/Leonardo Da Vinci Hypothesis', Shroud of Turin website,www.shroud.com/pdfs/sorensen.pdf, 2005

Sox, H. David, *The Image on the Shroud: Is the Turin Shroud a Forgery?*, Unwin, London, 1981

Spence, Lewis, *An Encyclopaedia of Occultism*, G. Routledge & Sons, London, 1920

Stevenson, Kenneth E. (ed.), *Proceedings of the 1977 United States Conference of Research on the Shroud of Turin*, Holy Shroud Guild, New York, 1977

Stevenson, Kenneth E., and Gary R. Habermas, *Verdict on the Shroud: Evidence for the Death and Resurrection of Jesus Christ*, Servant, Ann Arbor, 1981

Stroebel, Leslie, and Richard Zakia (eds), *The Focal Encyclopaedia of Photography*, Third edition, Focal Press, London, 1993 (first edition 1956)

Thompson, C. J. S., *The Lure and Romance of Alchemy*, Bell Publishing, New York, 1990 (George Harrap & Co., London, 1932)

Thurston, Rev. Herbert, 'The Turin Shroud and the Verdict of History', *The Month*, CI, Jan 1903

Tort, César, 'The Turin Shroud: A Case of Retrocognitive Thoughtography?', *Journal of the Society for Psychical Research*, vol. 56, no. 818, January 1990

Vasari, Giorgio (trans. and ed. George Bull), *Lives of the Artists*, Penguin Books, London, 1965

Vignon, Paul, *The Shroud of Christ*, Archibald Constable & Co., London, 1902 (*Le linceul du Christ: Étude Scientifique*, Éditions de Paris, Paris, 1902)

—— *La Sainte Suaire de Turin devant la science, l'archéologie, l'histoire, l'iconographie, le logique*, Masson, Paris, 1939

Volckringer, Jean, *Le problème des empreintes devant le science*, Libraire du Carmel, Paris, 1942

Walsh, John, *The Shroud*, W. H. Allen, London, 1963

Weller, Norma, 'Concerning the Meeting on May 27 1992', *BSTS Newsletter*, no. 33, February 1993

Whanger, Alan D., 'A Reply to Doubts Concerning the Coins Over the Eyes', Shroud of Turin website, www.shroud.com/lombatti.htm, 1997

Whanger, Mary and Alan, *The Shroud of Turin: An Adventure of Discovery*, Providence House, Franklin, 1998

Wilcox, Robert K., *Shroud*, Corgi, London, 1977

Wilson, Colin, *A Criminal History of Mankind*, Granada, London, 1984

Wilson, Ian, *The Turin Shroud*, revised edition, Penguin, London, 1979 (Victor Gollancz, London, 1978)

—— *The Evidence of the Shroud*, Michael O'Mara, London, 1986

—— 'Riddle of the Dead Man's Hand', *Observer Magazine*, 31 January 1988

—— *Holy Faces, Secret Places: The Quest for Jesus' True Likeness*, Doubleday, London, 1991

—— 'Mystery of the Missing Mandylion', *BSTS Newsletter*, no. 36, January 1994

—— *The Blood and the Shroud: The Passionate Controversy Still Enflaming the World's Most Famous Carbon-Dating Test*, Weidenfeld & Nicolson, London, 1998

—— 'The New, Restored Turin Shroud', *BSTS Newsletter*, no. 56, December 2002

Wilson, Ian, and Barrie Schwortz, *The Turin Shroud: The Illustrated Evidence*, Michael O'Mara, London, 2000

Wilson, Robert Anton, 'The Priory of Sion', *Gnosis*, no.6, Winter 1987–8

Wuenschel, Edward A., *Self-Portrait of Christ: The Holy Shroud of Turin*, Holy Shroud Guild, New York, 1957

Yates, Frances A., *Giordano Bruno and the Hermetic Tradition*, Routledge & Kegan Paul, London, 1964

—— *The Art of Memory*, Routledge & Kegan Paul, London, 1966

—— *The Rosicrucian Enlightenment*, Routledge & Kegan Paul, London, 1972

—— *The Occult Philosophy in the Elizabethan Age*, Routledge & Kegan Paul, London, 1979

Index

THE STARGATE CONSPIRACY

Lynn Picknett and Clive Prince

The Stargate Conspiracy is the ground-breaking exposé of the most dangerous – and insidious – plot of our times. It reveals the existence of an extraordinary, long-term scheme to harness many of the most exciting and radical ideas of the late twentieth century, and centres on the belief that the ancient Egyptian gods were real extra-terrestrial beings – and that *they're about to return* to usher in a new age.

Tracing the intricate network of intelligence operatives, leading politicians, cutting-edge scientists, certain 'New Egyptologists', New Age cults and would-be Messiahs back to its roots, Lynn Picknett and Clive Prince reveal a shocking political subtext behind the conspiracy. The sugar-coating of exciting ideas about returning ancient gods is designed to conceal a bitter pill indeed – which, in all innocence, millions seem happy to swallow.

THE SION REVELATION

Lynn Picknett and Clive Prince

In their bestselling books *Turin Shroud: In Whose Image?* and *The Templar Revelation*, which Dan Brown cites as an influence for *The Da Vinci Code*, Lynn Picknett and Clive Prince uncovered age-old conspiracies surrounding secret knowledge of Jesus, Mary Magdalene and John the Baptist, much of which concentrated on the activities of individuals and groups allegedly connected with the Priory of Sion. Now, in *The Sion Revelation*, Picknett and Prince look more closely at this French-based organisation, the centre of much controversy, said to be the ancient protector of great religious and historical secrets.

Written in a similar style to *The Stargate Conspiracy*, where the authors argued that apparently bizarre belief systems actually hide real activity on behalf of intelligence agencies and of military and political movers and shakers, *The Sion Revelation* will reveal just how important the Priory of Sion really is – and why we should all care . . .

Other bestselling Time Warner Books titles available by mail: